THE STORY OF JESUS

A History and Theology of Christ

Matthew the Poor

Compiled, translated, and edited by James Helmy

ANCIENT FAITH PUBLISHING   CHESTERTON, INDIANA

The Story of Jesus: A History and Theology of Christ
Compilation and English translation copyright © 2022 James Helmy

Published by:
Ancient Faith Publishing
A Division of Ancient Faith Ministries
P.O. Box 748
Chesterton, IN 46304

Unless otherwise noted, Scripture quotations are taken from the New King James Version, © 1979, 1980, 1982 by Thomas Nelson, Inc. Used by permission.

ISBN: 978-1-955890-20-5

Library of Congress Control Number: 2022946336

To my parents
—JH

Contents

Preface   7

CHAPTER ONE: Introduction to the Person and Work
  of Christ   11
  The Meaning and Significance of Christ   11
  Our Ultimate Good Realized in Christ   12
  Christ Reveals the Holy Trinity   14
  How Are We to Understand Christ?   15

CHAPTER TWO: Events before the Nativity   17
  Heaven Prepares for the Son of Man's Descent   17
  Earth Prepares for the Son of Man's Coming: The Jews   21
  Earth Prepares for the Son of Man's Coming: The Heathen   27
  Earth Prepares for the Son of Man's Coming: The Greeks   31
  Earth Prepares for the Son of Man's Coming:
    The Roman Empire   38
  Roman and Jew   40

CHAPTER THREE: From the Nativity to the Beginning
  of the Ministry   43
  The Son Is Sent   44
  The Annunciation   46
  Mary's Song   50
  The Nativity   53
  The Angels Announce to the Shepherds   56
  The Visit of the Magi   57
  Herod Moves to Slay the Infant Christ   60
  The Flight to Egypt   61
  The Return to Israel   63
  The Childhood in Nazareth   67

CHAPTER FOUR: The Baptism and Temptation of Christ   72

   John the Baptist Prepares the Way for the Messiah   72

   The Teacher in the Wilderness   75

   John the Baptist's Work Compared to the Messiah's Work   77

   The Baptism of Christ   79

   The Temptation   81

CHAPTER FIVE: Christ Begins His Ministry in Judea   88

   Miracles in Christ's Life   88

   The First Miracle   90

   Jesus at the Passover   93

   Nicodemus   95

   The Woman at the Well   98

CHAPTER SIX: The Early Galilean Ministry   104

   Healing of the Nobleman's Son   104

   The Synagogue at Nazareth   106

   Jesus Begins to Work in Capernaum   111

   Jesus Heals the Afflicted   114

   The Election of the Twelve   120

   The Sermon on the Mount   124

   The Compassionate Jesus: Acts of Mercy   129

   The Embassy of the Baptist   131

   The Woman Who Was a Sinner   133

CHAPTER SEVEN: The Later Galilean Ministry   136

   Sabbath Controversies   136

   The First Parables   140

   Calming the Tempest   143

   Jairus's Daughter and the Bleeding Woman   145

   The Mission of the Twelve   148

   The Feeding of Five Thousand   152

   Jesus Walks on the Sea   154

Peter's Confession and Rebuke   156
The Transfiguration   160
Descent from the Mountain and Healing of
    the Epileptic Boy   162
The Dispute as to Who Would Be the Greatest and Christ's
    Warning against Sectarianism   164

CHAPTER EIGHT: The Final Judean and Perean Ministry   167
Jesus at the Feast of Tabernacles   167
The Woman Caught in Adultery   170
The Man Born Blind, Part One   173
The Man Born Blind, Part Two   176
Jesus at the Feast of Dedication   179
The Perean Ministry Begins   183
The Good Samaritan   185
The Visit to Mary and Martha   187
The Lord's Prayer   190
Parables of the Lost Sheep, the Lost Coin, and the Lost Son   193
The Raising of Lazarus   197
Zacchaeus the Chief Tax Collector   203
Mary Washes the Feet of Jesus   205

CHAPTER NINE: Holy Week   208
Hosanna Sunday (Palm Sunday)   208
The Temple Is Cleansed   211
Confrontation with the Temple Authorities   213
The Question Regarding the Roman Tax   215
The Withered Fig Tree   217
The Parable of the Wedding Banquet   219
Woes Pronounced on the Scribes and Pharisees   222
Discourse on the End Times   225
Certain Greeks Desire to See Jesus   227

CHAPTER TEN: The Betrayal, Arrest, and Trial 231

The Plot to Destroy Jesus 231

The Last Supper 234

Jesus Washes the Disciples' Feet 236

The Eucharist 240

Gethsemane 245

The Arrest 248

The Religious Trial 250

Peter's Denial 256

The Civil Trial: Pilate Encounters Jesus 258

The Civil Trial: Pilate Strives to Release Jesus 261

CHAPTER ELEVEN: The Crucifixion and Resurrection 266

The Crucifixion 266

The Death of Christ 271

The Burial 275

The Resurrection 277

Jesus Appears to Mary Magdalene 282

Jesus Appears to the Disciples 284

Jesus Appears to Thomas and to the Disciples by the Sea 287

The Great Commission and the Ascension 292

Preface

This is the story of the greatest life ever lived, as told and expounded by one of the great spiritual teachers of our time. The study of the life of Christ is surely one of the most instructive and fruitful endeavors a believer can undertake, and any Christian's bookshelf would be sadly deficient without at least one very good book about our Lord's life on earth. I would not have undertaken the translation of such a voluminous work had I not thought that it would profoundly affect my life, and I would not have offered it up for publication if I had not believed that it would be a great boon to its readers.

The works and teachings of Jesus tend to float about in the average believer's mind without any plan or method to unite them into a coherent system. When exactly did Christ meet with Nicodemus? What was the significance of the Transfiguration in relation to the unfolding events of that year? Why did our Lord visit Bethany on the night before Palm Sunday? What parables did our Lord teach during Holy Week, and how did they relate to the Cross? These are all seminal questions; and unless a Christian comes to grips with them and studiously tries to find answers to them, the logic and meaning of Jesus' life in Palestine will remain a hazy mystery to his or her mind.

It is my strong belief that a real study of Jesus' life is prerequisite to the inner life of a Christian. There is a reason Christians are cold in their faith these days. There is a reason we have lost our first love—to use the dramatic language of Revelation—and why it is so fashionable now for people to say that the Church has failed them. We have grown distant from Christ. His heart, spirit, compassion, and countercultural (sometimes shocking) views of society and the world— these are things we have too often forgotten or taken for granted. Complacency has set in among us, like a colorless and odorless gas that fills our nostrils and sedates our thinking, and has stolen from us the rich fruit of the Gospel.

Each generation thus needs to return to Christ. Each generation—just like the generation of the first century AD—must abandon its paganism and rediscover the Lord Jesus. We twenty-first-century believers must restudy and reevaluate the Gospels for ourselves. Athanasius and Augustine and Chrysostom may help us by the light of their marvelous theology, but they cannot *live* that theology for us. The Church Fathers may help us on our way to repentance by their wisdom, but they cannot repent for us. We must walk along the way with our own footsteps; and the way is begun by learning about Christ's own life.

There was an old English clergyman named Farrar who wrote a *Life of Christ* that became a wild success in the nineteenth century. As he described the cleansing of the temple, he asked a very simple question. Why was it that the temple guardians, the Jewish leaders, and all the people stood by watching in frozen bewilderment as Christ overturned the tables and threw the money-changers out of the temple court? They were many, and He was but one. The answer Farrar provides is compelling: *because sin is weakness.* Their consciences were stricken, he notes, and their moral fiber was withered to nothing. They were powerless to raise a finger against the righteous indignation pouring forth from the Prophet from Nazareth.

Reading the life of Christ should be challenging. If it feels easy, then it is not being understood. There is a real toughness to Christ's message, and it should motivate the reader to learn that *virtue is strength*. A good deal of sappy, lukewarm spirituality has been injected into the minds of Christians, and they are taught that Jesus wanted us to be docile like sheep. But to act sheepish today is to be a failure. The world is not kind to sheep, and it tends to crush them. No—Christ commanded us to *trust* Him like sheep, but to be wise as serpents in the world. Jesus is the Lamb of God, but He is also the Lion of the tribe of Judah. He sacrifices, but He fights too. He comforts, but He also roars. He was gentle as a lamb to the weak (a sinful woman, a tax collector), but fierce as a lion to the mighty (Caiaphas, Herod, Pilate). The Gospels ought not to make us weak and vain but humble and strong.

MATTHEW THE POOR'S LIFE REFLECTED this type of meek but bold Christianity envisioned by the Gospels. Born at the end of World War I as the last of seven children to a poor family, he was nursed in all the precepts of the Faith from as early as he could remember. As he grew to early manhood, he developed a keen interest in certain aspects of worldly living, such as education, career, art, and social life. But the overarching passion that quickly eclipsed all other interests was his love for the Bible, prayer, and spiritual living. In consequence, he felt irrevocably called to the monastic life. How else was he to dedicate every waking moment to the contemplation of God and His word? That was the incessant question that burned in his heart. So he sold everything he owned—his business, his villas, his automobiles—and bought a one-way ticket into the Egyptian desert.

The following six decades of his life form a saga that can rival the stories of the most interesting wonderworking saints of church history. He spent years living in some of the oldest and poorest monastic sites in the world, ever receiving the adulation of admiring disciples and ever haunted by the spite of unreasonable opponents. He would meet with penniless believers who needed a word of direction as well as with powerful presidents who sought his advice on civil affairs. It was all the same to him. To establish one of the most famous monasteries in the world, or to write some of the most famous books in the Middle East, were incidental tasks for one who saw his central vocation in life to be the study of God's word and reflection on its majestic Author.

Matthew the Poor's commentaries on the life of Christ and the Gospels stretch to eight enormous volumes. His favorite sources are the wisdom contained in the Church Fathers, as well as the ground-breaking scholarship generated by eighteenth-, nineteenth-, and twentieth-century English and continental scholars. The thoroughness and depth of his work are staggering, and the labor involved in reading, sifting, selecting, and translating all this material seemed at first a task too daunting to pursue. But the great value of the commentaries demanded that they be brought within the reach of the English-speaking Orthodox world, and I felt that the aid of divine grace would propel the project forward when mere human effort would fail. It is my prayer that the reader will find as much joy and wisdom in these pages as I have for many, many years.

James Helmy
The Holy Fifty Days of Resurrection 2019

CHAPTER ONE

Introduction to the Person and Work of Christ

The Meaning and Significance of Christ

Two fundamental truths were incarnate in the Person of Christ: the truth of God and the truth of man.

Without Christ, the truth of God would remain foreign to man's mind and distant from his emotions. God would be an entity utterly removed from man's experience; the only grounds for extolling Him would be His stark "otherness," His sheer separation from our meager, sinful state.

Without Christ, the truth of man would likewise be obscured. For man would see himself only as a creation of dust, who, by forgetting the eternal status of his soul, would fail to realize his everlasting destiny. Sin would dispossess him of his greatest attribute—spiritual freedom; and death would one day dispossess him altogether of existence. His single purpose in life consequently would be to eat, procreate, then die; and spiritual things would serve no real purpose in his vision of life.

Alternatively, if man were to realize the lofty status of his being, yet without Christ, then he would become a god without a God;

he would locate the purpose and destiny of life within himself. He would forget his lowly creatureliness, he would forget his sinfulness, and he would be ignorant of his servitude to the biological impulses that control him and drive him on to death and decay.

So, in order for us to comprehend the greatness of the mystery that is Christ—who is the perfect union between divine truth and human truth—we must begin by asking the question: What is the purpose of man's life? Or, toward what final point is humanity moving?

And we must repudiate from the outset the notion that the purpose of man's existence can be explained simply on materialistic grounds; for it would follow that he really differs in nothing from the animals. But we know deep in our hearts that man has been made lord over the visible creation, that he has been given authority over it, and that he is appointed its steward. Man is motivated by something more than just survival and self-preservation. He seeks for higher truth; he searches for transcendent meaning in the world.

And so man must find his final purpose in something (or someone) infinitely greater than himself—something *for which* he was created, *in which* his purpose is fulfilled, and *through which* his life is made complete and his happiness is realized.

Our Ultimate Good Realized in Christ

GOD CREATED MAN IN HIS own image, so that his being could be a reflection of and witness to God's being. Man's life and work and intelligence were to become a doxology to God's honor. Once man understands this role and accepts it, he becomes reconciled to God—and reconciled to himself. He finally rests in the knowledge that he is fulfilling the purpose of his life: to bear grateful witness to God by his words and works. And so man successfully concludes the "experiment" of his life with the firmly evidenced truth that he finds total happiness in converting his life into a perpetual doxology to God's glory. There is, therefore, an irrevocable link between God and man.

Now this link was obscured by the blurring effects of man's ignorance. But one day, in the deep workings of history, it was suddenly manifested and made clear again by the light of humanity's great representative, Jesus Christ. A new era in history was begun in which man recognized and understood his intimate relationship to God, because it was revealed in Christ. Man realized furthermore that it was by the light of that relationship, and by its light alone, that he could see the reason for his existence and could find the secret to his happiness.

So through Christ's life, God appears to us as divine truth in visible form. Perfect truth, sacrificial love, and spotless holiness are all offered to man in Christ. In the life of Christ, human nature also appears in its completest form. Christ's sincere humility and total obedience transfigure humanity; humanity is lifted out of the ashes and raised heavenward in order to find its place in God. In other words, through Christ, humanity's ideal relationship to God is achieved. We behold in Christ the highest glory of God and of man: God's glory is seen in His astonishing descent to take the form of a man, and man's glory is seen in his astonishing ascent to fulfill and perfect the image of God.

Christ is, therefore, the apex of the human pyramid. The key to the mystery of our creation is found in Him. He is the archetypal human being, and He is humanity's resurrection. Accordingly, Christ styles Himself our *alpha and omega*, our *beginning and end*—that is, the power that completes our life in God. He is our *first and last*—that is to say, the absolute perfection of everything we need, outside of whom there is to be found no other satisfaction: "for whom *are* all things and by whom *are* all things" (Heb. 2:10). Therefore, without an intimate knowledge of the Person of Jesus Christ, our knowledge of God remains meager, insubstantial, and joyless.

Christ Reveals the Holy Trinity

CHRIST DID NOT COME TO bring us a philosophy from God. He did not provide us with mere proverbs or good advice. He came to reveal God the Father. Through Christ, the Person of the Father becomes visible, tangible, and comprehensible. He reveals the Father's love toward the weak—not just by words, but in the act of surrendering Himself to death. He reveals the Father's mercy toward the sinful—not by words, but by the shedding of His blood. Christ is thus truly the "Word of God" to us—not just a written word, but the personified expression of God's love, mercy, and forgiveness.

Again, Christ is not a messenger from God, but He is the message itself. He is God's "Word" appearing with a body and a personality, in the form of a man. And He is not a message that begins and ends; He is not an isolated act of love or mercy that is once rendered and afterward is past. Rather, He is perpetual love, eternal and never-ending mercy. He is resurrection. He is salvation. He is our reconciliation to God.

So we now call God "Father" because Jesus has revealed Him so; and Jesus has shown us also that He is "Son" through the divine works He performed—works that no man before had ever done. And the one unified nature of the Father and Son is impossible to divide: "He who has seen Me has seen the Father." The Son's Incarnation was the preliminary to the Father's revelation. Every man on earth has the essence of fatherhood and sonship latent within his human nature; every man is potentially a father and a son at the same time. But marriage and procreation are the prerequisites for these familial natures to arise. God's familial nature, however, needed no procreative event in time to come about, for it existed from eternity past. God's fatherhood is the source of all fatherhood on earth, and His sonship is the foundation of all sonship. The divinity and equality of the divine essence is a mystery.

Now, the intimate bond or relation between Father and Son in the Godhead is itself a form of life; it is a living power, a vital force that proceeds from the Father and rests in the Son. In the human race, when a father begets, his life or spirit is transmitted to the son. This transferal is invisible, and yet it is a living reality nonetheless. The passing on of the father's spirit to the son is precisely what creates the father's fatherhood and the son's sonship. Similarly, in the Godhead, the life that eternally proceeds from the Father to the Son is the Holy Spirit. The Spirit is the "life" of God, yet is neither the Father nor the Son. He is not a contingent or bounded attribute of God, but is a free, distinct, and active agent. And as all fatherhood springs from the Father, and as all sonship springs from the Son, so does all spirit and life in the world ultimately spring from the Holy Spirit.

How Are We to Understand Christ?

WE MUST FIRST OF ALL distinguish between the two widely disparate methods of acquiring knowledge: scientific versus spiritual. Scientific or intellectual knowledge concerns itself strictly with the physical world, and it is best pursued on the principles of skepticism and doubt. Its veracity is typically gauged by comparing new theories with previously established facts.

Spiritual truth, on the other hand, can never find its way into the heart and mind of man except by man's humble readiness to receive it. This means that man's conscience must be prepared in advance to open itself up to divine knowledge without haggling or argumentation. That is, if ever divine truth begins to shine in a person's mind and to knock at the door of his heart, it must not find the door closed by doubt or the path blocked by obstinacy, so that the person may rejoice in the light revealed.

Christian truth is unique in that it does not rest on foundations that require an advanced intelligence or a clever shrewdness to understand. It rests on the living Person of Jesus Christ, who Himself possesses the ability to deposit the truth regarding Himself into the willing heart: "Behold, I stand at the door and knock. If anyone hears My voice and opens the door, I will come in to him and dine with him, and he with Me" (Rev. 3:20).

The primary key to all Christian theology is, therefore, a deep faith in Jesus Christ residing in the heart. Christ is in such a case the expositor of His own theology: "He expounded to them in all the Scriptures the things concerning Himself" (Luke 24:27). Thus, all the theological studies a person may undertake will lie under the dark shadow of human understanding unless Christ is found present in the heart to illuminate it. Darkness then is traded for light, without the slightest need for mental toil or stress: "I am the light of the world. He who follows Me shall not walk in darkness, but have the light of life" (John 8:12).

So the Son of God appeared to us in human flesh: He was thus introduced to our race after being concealed in the ineffable being of God. And His descent into human time was not sudden or unannounced, but was foretold thousands of years prior in the form of prophecy. The coming Messiah was, in the prophets' minds, the Alpha and Omega of their entire message. On the day of Christ's birth, the regular events of human history began to be penetrated by eternal events: the Incarnation, the redemption on the Cross, the Resurrection, the Ascension, and the sitting at the Father's right hand. The life of Christ, therefore, is not merely a series of miracles in which I am "required" to believe. They are events rather that directly involve me: this is the story of *my* life as a new creation.

CHAPTER TWO

Events before the Nativity

Heaven Prepares for the Son of Man's Descent

The life of Christ is the earthly unfolding of a life written by God for One who was to bear God's very name and image— Jesus Christ—who also came to do His will and complete His work. The source and essence of that life was heavenly, but its heavenliness was concealed—not because it had to be so, but because of man's inability to understand divine things or to see divinely. Life's heavenly nature was concealed from man until the day his spiritual eyes would be opened and he could perceive such things for himself. Once he could see them, he would become a partaker in them. The heavenly blessings of that life came for man's good; for they are ultimate truth, and truth always draws in and embraces every person who understands it.

Heaven and earth joined hands to prepare for the coming of Christ; each element and constituent of the cosmos played a role in the great drama. And this synthesis of all things is one of the most excellent things to contemplate, for it reveals a divine plan in the unfolding of all things, as well as God's love for man. This also furnishes to man the bright hope that life will find its happy conclusion in Christ; and this hope also consoles man and recompenses him for the pain and suffering he must endure in this age. For Christ is Himself a statement of God's love. He is the pledge of God's blessed desire to bring joy and gladness to the heart of man.

Those who in past generations came to write a "Life of Christ" attempted to harmonize the events recorded by the four evangelists: from the Nativity, to the Jordan, to the traveling ministry, all the way through the Crucifixion and Resurrection. But the Christian mind desires more; when the Christian believer increases in religious knowledge, he increases as well in his ambition to learn about transcendent realities. And so he has become deeply desirous to learn about the life of the Son of God *prior* to the Nativity. Saint John's Gospel steps in here to give us a very brief glimpse of the Son's preexistence:

In the beginning was the Word,
and the Word was with God,
and the Word was God.
He was in the beginning with God. (John 1:1, 2)

Then he introduces the Nativity with these words: "And the Word became flesh" (John 1:14).

Despite the extremely concise and shrouded nature of these words, they are the first rays of light to reach our minds respecting the Son's preexistence. They point to God's presence before the beginning of time, for time was born at Creation's inception. But even in God's eternal presence in the past, there was still a "beginning"—the beginning of the divine plan to reveal Himself to *us*.

Here we begin to take our first steps into the life of Christ, for it is in essence a revealing of the deep purposes of God; and this is important, because that life is also a revealing of the deep purposes of *our* existence and of *our* future. In other words, that life is an attempt to offer a picture of divine truth in the form of a human being. Though Christ's life appears in many ways to be just a regular human life, it is in reality so much more than that. And when we speak about the unveiling of God's truth through the life of Christ, we directly introduce the concept of *revelation*. Revelation is the uncovering or revealing of truths that transcend the everyday events of our earthly lives.

Saint John's Gospel refers to Christ as the Word that was with God, to allude to His divine status that existed before the Incarnation, and specifically to the fact that the Word created the cosmos, or alternatively, that God created the cosmos "through the Word." "All things were made through Him, and without Him nothing was made that was made. In Him was life, and the life was the light of men" (John 1:3, 4). We gather therefore that the nature of the Word must be superior to the cosmos; and this superiority must in turn apply to the Word Incarnate, that is, to Christ. So although He put on the cloak of humanity, the material of creation, He is still greater than everything in creation. The Incarnation hence takes on a beautiful and sublime meaning for us: Christ descends into His creation in order to raise it up to Himself. He does not transform into it but redeems it from within. He purposely takes His body from creation in order to unite with it, so that with that body, He may become partaker of creation's travails and death; but through the power of His divinity, He pulls it up from death by His Resurrection and makes it co-heir with Him in glory.

One may ask the question: How did Christ achieve the Incarnation? That is, how did He become man? In order for the Word of God to take flesh and dwell among us, He had of necessity to divest Himself of that divine glory that no human eye could ever have tolerated or even understood. Man's comprehension is limited to the sensory data of his external environment. For this reason, whenever

God spoke to the prophets of old, they would be thrown into a sort of trance that would release them from the physical and mental limitations of their normal lives. They could see what was beyond the sense of vision; they could hear what was beyond the sense of hearing; they could understand what was beyond the logic and categories of the mind. They were made capable therefore of receiving and relaying God's messages and commands to the people. But now God wished to communicate with His people directly. He desired to speak to them Himself; He desired to deliver to them the things of God without any intermediary. In order to accomplish this, He had to meet them at the level of their own senses and understanding. He needed to be like them in every way—in order to avoid baffling them, or indeed, to avoid provoking terror in them.

So the greatest work carried out by the Word prior to the Incarnation was the abandoning of all outward appearances of His divinity. And this abandonment of the external glories of divinity, this self-emptying, was the official beginning of God's mission to man through the Word-made-flesh. For it enabled Him to dwell in a human body with the utmost fullness of His being and nature without evincing the slightest outward trace of His divinity. This is how the Son of God, the Word, became a full and complete human being without attracting the notice of anybody at all, save those who were witnesses to the special events of the Nativity. To recapitulate: the self-emptying of the Word of God was the first step silently taken by God in heaven for the sake of man's salvation.

Two biblical citations develop this concept. The first speaks about God's intention to redeem the world by a grand act of salvation that would require everything the Father and Son could give, so that it could be given freely to man and would prove to be a sign of God's immense love for the world. The verse comes from Christ's own lips: "For God so loved the world that He gave His only begotten Son, that whoever believes in Him should not perish but have everlasting life. For God did not send His Son into the world to condemn the world, but that the world through Him might be saved" (John 3:16, 17).

The second verse speaks about the great act of self-emptying carried out by the Son of God, the Word, right before His descent into the world. The verse proceeds from the Apostle Paul's inspired pen: "Let this mind be in you which was also in Christ Jesus, who, being in the form of God, did not consider it robbery to be equal with God, but made Himself of no reputation, taking the form of a bondservant, *and* coming in the likeness of men. And being found in appearance as a man, He humbled Himself and became obedient to *the point of* death, even the death of the cross" (Phil. 2:5–8).

These verses make it clear that the Father surrendered His Incarnate Son to death, for the love of and for the sake of every individual who would willingly receive the redemption offered to his soul. And the Son too voluntarily obeyed the will of the Father and gave Himself up to the death of the Cross for His love of humanity, His love for every single person, every person who would accept Him. And this is where the role of heaven ends. The Father *willed*, the Son *obeyed* and *executed* that will; and earth from that moment begins its part in the drama of redemption.

Earth Prepares for the Son of Man's Coming: The Jews

THREE PRINCIPAL BRANCHES OF EARTH'S population played a decisive role in the preparation for the advent of the Incarnate Word: the Jews, the heathen, and the Greeks and Romans. Our aim here is to draw up a spiritual map of the world (if the expression may so be used) to determine how each section of that map contributed to the great preparation. Our focus will be placed only on the positive attributes and virtuous aspirations of each people-group, for they played a key role in making ready for the annunciation of the gospel and the birth of Christianity in the world.

Now we must begin of course with the Jews, for they laid the original religious foundation for the reception of the Messiah; as Christ classically said to the Samaritan woman, "Salvation is of the Jews" (John 4:22). The Samaritan woman stood before Christ as a representative of the heathen world that awaited the Messiah in its thirst for God. Her very words expressed this thirst, despite her disreputable condition, which was also representative of the condition of the entire heathen world. This is evident in their dialogue (John 4:22–26):

> Christ: "You worship what you do not know; we know what we worship, for salvation is of the Jews. But the hour is coming, and now is, when the true worshipers will worship the Father in spirit and truth; for the Father is seeking such to worship Him." . . .
> Samaritan Woman: "I know that Messiah is coming" (who is called Christ). "When He comes, He will tell us all things."
> Christ: "I who speak to you am *He!*"

Judaism existed amid the darkness of the heathen world like the burning bush;[1] just as that bush gave off its light without being consumed, so did Judaism shine the light of the knowledge of Yahweh without being consumed by the depraved heathen environment surrounding it. Its Mosaic Law became an object of admiration and respect throughout the entire world; it cleared the way for the coming of Christ and also gave out the first cry at His Birth.

---

1   The thorny bush Moses saw as he was walking through the wilderness. It burned but was not destroyed, and when Moses stood to gaze at it, God's word proceeded from it.

The Jewish nation finds its origin in Abraham, who is the arche-type of faith to the entire world. The childhood of the nation was spent in Egypt, and there they were educated in the finest literature of the greatest civilization of the time. All the elements needed for their development into a national people were found there. In Egypt, that is, Israel first began to forge its identity as an immigrant nation by drawing on the science, literature, and philosophy of the Egyptians and by imbibing the mysteries of their way of life.

One of the greatest figures in history was tutored there: Moses. After that giant of the race was reared and educated in Pharaoh's own household, he transferred the wisdom and philosophy of Egyptian civilization to the service of Yahweh. And when the day of Israel's departure from Egypt had finally come, Israel had reached the state of a fully fledged nation. The nation was officially born at the exodus; what followed was forty years of desert wandering, led by God's hand to ward off the defiling effects of heathen society. During this critical period of moral isolation in the wilderness, a new generation of Israelites was born. The Hebrew people at last entered Canaan, inherited the land, and raised its house on the ruins of the heathen nations that it swallowed and absorbed into its body.

Judaism finally reached the zenith of its might in the days of King David, the beloved and chosen of God, that "sweet psalmist of Israel" (2 Sam./2 Kg. 23:1). His compilation of the canticles of Israel has become the finest religious treasury in all the world; indeed, the Psalter alone was sufficient to build the soul of the whole nation— nay, even of all other nations. The Psalter is also that flowing spring that has watered Christianity from its earliest days. Its waters cannot be spoiled; it draws the thirsty soul to God's Spirit; it flows downward from God's high presence, bringing down new blessings to us every day.

For these reasons, Judaism became a school of religion to the world by its inspired literature, which was given of God by the hand of the prophets. The religion of the Jews gave off, as it were, shafts of light that penetrated the human soul. The light was passed on from generation to generation, bearing with it the blessings of Abraham and God's covenant with him: that through his seed all the nations of the earth would be blessed. The Jews existed for the world's sake; they held on to those arrows of light even through their darkest days—as, for instance, during the time of the captivity. And they preserved that light so that they might one day deliver it into the bosom of the Gentiles.

The guardians of this profound spiritual inheritance were some of the greatest men who ever lived. There was (again) Moses, the renowned leader who guided a multitude of souls in an epic journey across the desert. There was David, who erected the first-ever spiritual kingdom in history—presided over by God, who sat on an unseen throne in its midst, making it a microcosm of the Kingdom of God. There was the great prophet Isaiah, whose prophetic history was living before world history itself. His spiritual history foresaw the promised Messiah, the holy Seed, and delineated the nature of His days from the womb till the brighter future:

> And His name will be called
> Wonderful, Counselor, Mighty God,
> Everlasting Father, Prince of Peace. . . .
> Upon the throne of David and over His kingdom,
> To order it and establish it with judgment and justice
> From that time forward, even forever. (Is. 9:6, 7)

Isaiah would also describe the Messiah's days of suffering and death, and for this he is often styled the "evangelical prophet." The Jewish people also gave birth to the vigorous prophet Elijah, who although living prior to Isaiah, had his soul propelled forward into the heart and being of John the Baptist, Christ's forerunner. Now Elijah and Moses both, from behind the veil of ancient time, attended the days of the Messiah—namely at the scene of the Transfiguration on Mount Tabor. Moses as representative of the Law and Elijah as representative of the prophets were both present to surrender into the Messiah's hands the entire religious heritage and covenant of the Jewish people. Moses handed over the Torah, and Elijah handed over the prophecies: for the Messiah came to fulfill both. Thus, the greatest of Israel's guardians preserved their religious birthright by giving the arrow of light into the hands of the Holy One of Israel.

However, the long years spent by the people dwelling among pagan nations exhausted their moral strength; and consequently, spiritual disease and pestilences seeped into the people's life, which called forth the stern rebuke of the prophets. Their evil became enormous; they turned their faces away from Yahweh and stuck out their hands at Him in rejection. "All day long I have stretched out My hands / To a disobedient and contrary people" (Rom. 10:21). Their hearts grew distant from God, so God grew distant from them, till they became as a people without a God. And this was all despite the outward appearance of religiosity and piety.

Two of the historical monuments to David's legacy are Jerusalem, "the City of the Great God," a kingdom which he dedicated to God, and the temple, "the house of God," which he envisioned. Jewish pilgrims from all over the world discharged their perpetual duty to make a pilgrimage to these holy sites in order to set forth their offerings to Yahweh, their personal God, their King of kings and Lord of lords. They went to be filled with Jerusalem's blessings, to feel its sacredness, to make contact with its rocks and soil, to understand its eternal state; they would go to experience all these things every year of their lives. And a Jew could not go before God empty-handed, but needed to bring with him gifts—for which reason Jerusalem became the world's capital in wealth and glory.

Despite the great geographical expansion of the kingdom achieved by its first kings, and its extensive borders touching those of other nations, they were able to strictly preserve their isolation as a people. Everything from their language, to their narrow lines of communication, to their peculiar customs served to preserve their distinct identity as a people. And despite the captivity they endured for seventy years, along with their dispersal throughout the whole world, their Law became to them a perpetual birthright that none of the nations could abolish. So, while the pagan carried his gods in his luggage with him wherever he traveled, the Jew came from the ends of the earth to Jerusalem in order to meet with Yahweh. This centralization of their identity in one great city is what cemented their national unity and protected their distinctive character as a people, despite the multifarious locations and languages of the world amid which they lived. To take a counterexample, Babylon, the empire that dragged them into harrowing captivity, did not endure; but its glory collapsed to the ground, and its cities, temples, and riches were all buried in ruins. And the Babylonian Empire ceased to have any existence except in the pages of history. The Jewish nation, however, is continually asserting its existence; and its history, glory, and worship live on despite the passing of many centuries.

Thus Israel has preserved in itself its history and religion; and even after the passing of millennia, it remains a testimony to God's faithfulness and a keeper of God's promises—even if it has not gained from them. But even though Israel survived the hostility of foreign nations, and even raised its horn against them and defeated them, it was not permitted to retain its sovereignty in the land. For God willed that Israel should be subjugated to the might and tyranny of Rome. Thus, Pompey besieged and conquered Israel in 63 BC, the year in which Caesar Augustus was born, and appointed an Idumean king, Herod, to rule over them. Israel's subjugation was exasperated further under Herod's children and other Roman governors who came afterward. By becoming incorporated into the Roman Empire, the Jewish people were effectively brought into bondage to their mortal enemies, the heathen. Hence, they intensified their hopes and waited in earnest expectation for their one last hope—the Messiah.

Earth Prepares for the Son of Man's Coming: The Heathen

WHEN WE COME TO SPEAK about the "heathen," we must always remember that we are referring to our own human ancestors. We were as they were, whether Egyptian, Indian, English, American, or Asian. All of these heathen races were still under God's care, and they certainly received heaven's aid for the refinement of their character as well as for their spiritual progress. The heathen peoples undertook major efforts to come to a better understanding of God, even if their methods were immature and elementary. The gods of the Egyptians and the Greeks and those of other nations were merely attempts to come closer to the one true God. Though they were deprived of those divine courtesies the Jews enjoyed, such as prophets and scripture-writers, and though they often languished in the depths of ignorance, yet the heathen groped for the truth. But in the end, it was given to them to know the time of the Messiah's birth, which the Jews themselves did not realize. And this further led to the wondrous phenomenon that when the Apostle Paul went preaching Christianity through all the cities of Asia, Greece, and Rome, the heathen Gentiles were much swifter in receiving the Word than were the Jews.

This is why heathendom, through faith in the Messiah, came to equal Israel in its knowledge of the One God; and in one generation, it gained all the spiritual benefits Israel had previously enjoyed over the span of two thousand years. The best description ever given of the heathens' attempts at approaching God through their pagan worship was given by the Apostle Paul: "the One whom you worship without knowing" (Acts 17:23). And Christ spoke similarly to the Samaritan woman: "You worship what you do not know" (John 4:22). And we may notice something interesting here regarding teaching and learning. The Samaritan woman, having heard, accepted the Messiah more quickly and readily and truly than did the hesitant Nicodemus, who was a member of the Sanhedrin—and they both had the same teacher.

The fact that the heathen resorted to flogging and lacerating their bodies as a method of worshipping God is at least testimony to the seriousness and desperation of the heathen to know God, even if their methods were flawed. It was all basically an expression of their feelings of estrangement from God. They made their children pass through the fire and sacrificed them on altars, but it was all done in the darkness of ignorance. As long as man is man, he will always yearn for his Creator and for truth; but he must be shown the way. Christ saw this receptivity in them whenever He encountered Gentiles in Israel who were searching for God. The behavior of the Roman centurion induced Christ to pronounce this statement regarding him: "Assuredly, I say to you, I have not found such great faith, not even in Israel!" (Matt. 8:10). When we come to the Canaanite woman, a heathen who now serves as a model for us—who rebukes our lukewarm faith and humbles our supposed humility—we must remember how she answered our Lord's comment about not throwing the children's bread to the dogs: "Yes, Lord, yet even the little dogs eat the crumbs which fall from their masters' table" (Matt. 15:27). And her response compelled our Lord to bear witness to her faith: "Then Jesus answered and said to her, 'O woman, great *is* your faith! Let it be to you as you desire.' And her daughter was healed from that very hour" (Matt. 15:28, 29).

And I lack space to tell my readers about that towering personality known as Melchizedek, "priest of the most high God," the great prototype of the priesthood, into whose order Christ was anointed! He appears on the biblical scene as a friend and superior to Abraham; he receives from Abraham the mystical gifts of bread and wine and blesses them; he receives from Abraham a tithe of everything as God's representative. My pen hesitates to refer to him as "heathen," for he is considered to be a chief spiritual figure who existed before Abraham, and who does not die in the biblical narrative.

A similar case is that of Jethro, Moses' father-in-law and priest of Midian, because he was to Moses what Melchizedek was to Abraham. These were Gentiles to whom the Jews gave primary positions in their story of faith and salvation. We also have Ruth the Moabitess, who was honored to have the Messiah emerge from her line. We have the widow of Zarephath, who offered refuge to Elijah the Prophet in his flight. We have Hiram the King of Tyre, a dear friend of David's, without whose aid Solomon could not have erected the temple. We have the Queen of Sheba, who came from the far South to hear the wisdom of Solomon. We have Naaman, the commander-in-chief of Aram, who made the long trek from his country to Israel and stepped over enemy lines in order to seek the prayers of an Israelite prophet. We have Balaam the son of Beor, who saw God in visions and who was prohibited by God from speaking one deprecatory word against Israel. And it ought to suffice the whole heathen world to have given birth to Job the Righteous, one who by God's direct testimony has become the great standard of faith, patience, thanksgiving, and wisdom.

The presence of all these figures added a heavenly luster to the Old Testament era, and humanity should be proud to have given birth to them in a time when heathendom was without prophets and without God. And when we leave aside the religious criterion and go in search of other illustrious names who adorned pagan history with their wisdom and intellect, we will find fine specimens of humanity before whose philosophy and virtue we will feel compelled to bow. They were lacking in nothing save the seal of the Holy Spirit and initiation into the mystery of the truth. They were of the same caliber as the greatest of Israel's prophets: Socrates, Plato, Aristotle, Pindar, Sophocles, Cicero, Virgil, Seneca, and Plutarch.

Such names were the choicest specimens of humanity born before the knowledge of God. They enlightened and instructed their world; and in so doing, they helped to prepare the world's mind and heart for the coming of the divine light. These wise men and philosophers were witnesses to the Word, because their intellects were a light in a period of darkness. Their knowledge was like a ray of light emanating from the Word and touching down in minds which they in turn used to enlighten the world by their wisdom, their philosophy, their art, their aesthetics, their literature, and their poetry. It is indeed a rare and marvelous story of how their superlative gifts, which were so freely bestowed on them, arrayed the cities of Greece and Rome. They lacked only the mystery of the Holy Spirit! It was as though they prepared the way for the footsteps of the Apostle Paul, who crowned their achievements with the very mystery of Christ. When the Christian Faith finally made headway into the empire, these heathen seized it furiously and began to radiate with its light. Thus, Christianity inherited the splendid glories of heathendom and incorporated them as a part of its spiritual fabric. And in so doing, Christianity reconciled the world together: the Jews with their treasury of divine knowledge; the Greeks with their arts, language, and literature; and the Romans, with their system of law, jurisprudence, and mastery of administration.

And on the day in which Pontius Pilate raised the banner over the head of the crucified Christ in these three languages—Hebrew, Greek, and Latin—it was the declaration of the lifting of the enmity between the different branches of mankind, and of a new fellowship between them in the crucified One. This was to strike a new way forward for the world by His new vision.

Earth Prepares for the Son of Man's Coming: The Greeks

WHILE THE SECULAR WORLD WAS enriching itself with the results of the best human thinking it could produce, Israel in the same period prided itself on in its Torah, as well on the rest of its religious literature—which for the Jews guided and prescribed every detail of life. The older portion of the world, the secular, grew and progressed within the boundaries it had set for itself, while the younger portion, the religious, grew within the boundaries set by God through the hand of Moses. And it was as though these two portions of humanity had arranged a preappointed time in which they would meet and combine their secular and spiritual riches into one common storehouse of goods—in order to sweeten and elevate the human race, so that it would benefit from the gifts bestowed by God on all human beings according to their capacities.

So we may think of Greek and Roman society as having provided, by its lofty philosophy and art, as it were an exquisite human vessel into which Judaism could pour its lavish treasures—goods that reached their highest caliber in Christianity. Now if we think deeply about the long-term results of man's natural efforts and what fruit God has brought about by them in the end, we will recognize the vast contributions made by these two civilizations (Greek and Roman) to laying the foundations for the making of modern man. Judaism then steps in to grant modern man a soul by erecting a spiritual structure over that foundation. When the future man comes to contemplate his origins, he will find at the source the most pristine springs of art and language and literature, whose immeasurable value cannot be exhausted were they to be studied for a hundred years.

Christ steps into history at a relatively late period, because His will was to establish the Kingdom not upon a premature earth and among primitive man, but upon a prepared earthly scene that God had foreseen from the beginning. The philosophers and scientists and literary men of the world were thus busily engaged in their multifarious pursuits for many centuries before Christ's coming, all along laying that essential foundation upon which Christ Himself would eventually come and build in order to launch humanity's new course toward eternity.

Despite the limited population of the Greek race on earth, God had endowed them with such phenomenal natural gifts that the offerings they made to the world—offerings of an exquisite language, of science, and of literature—gradually permeated the globe to serve the multiform needs of humanity. One of the truly marvelous characteristics of Greek society was the power of their literature and poetry to rid human life of those old ghosts that haunted the East— the particular cast of mind that threw a dark gloom over Eastern life and clogged the portals of light from illuminating man, and which consequently obstructed his ability to undergo a genuine spiritual awakening. This dark feature of the Eastern mind—especially the idea that blind nature was teeming with hostile spirits—tended to sabotage people's lives. The cathartic element in Greek thought served to purge humanity of such vain conceits.

Plato is a good example: this philosopher's lofty reasoning may be worthily compared to the contemplations of Christian saints. It is an undeniable fact that Plato and his kind served Christianity by equipping mankind with the tools needed to soar to new and wondrous spiritual heights.

When we come to the arena of moral truth and conscience, we find that another of their great achievements was to sever the human mind from the cords that previously bound it, and to replace them with a natural collective conscience to which all could rationally subscribe. This conscience was based on certain premises laid down by their greatest thinkers; it was to reliably govern the conduct of individuals, as well as to guide and stabilize social life.

Thus, Christianity received systematic instruction in the various workings of the natural human conscience, particularly in what nourishes it and what damages it. This natural conscience was then sanctified by the superimposition of Christ's teaching; His influence raised the natural conscience to new levels and enabled it to rise above the burdensome feeling of sin—by virtue of the salvation that was so freely offered to every person—and to avoid the blight of sorrow that is spawned by sin, which invades the conscience and corrupts it.

We must satisfy ourselves with the brief comments made thus far on the virtues of Greek thought and society, for an exhaustive investigation of them would require numerous volumes to be written. Let us come now to the Greek language. To those who can study and appreciate Greek, it must be considered one of the marvels of the ancient world. For it has such an admirable capacity to express the exact meaning of a given thought that the thinking mind is made capable of expanding its height and depth beyond limit. The Greek verb has the flexibility to define a particular event in its minutest details: what happened, how it happened, whether it happened within a circumscribed period in the past, or whether it happened in the past but has effects lingering into the present and future. The Greek verb expresses a given action so precisely, in fact, that there is virtually no room for misunderstanding left.

The Greek language was thus pressed into the service of the Gospels and made them the greatest pieces of literature of all time. The ideas contained in the Gospels sparkle with a heavenly beauty; but the finesse of Greek adds to that beauty. The native splendor and glory of God's word are increased by the magnificence of Greek diction. Thus, God used the vocabulary and genius of the Greek language in order to preserve the richness of the Gospel—to put it in a form so refined that it seems to proceed directly from the mouth of God.[2]

This marvelous agreement between the precision of the Holy Spirit's message in the Gospel and the precision of the Greek language compels us to conclude that it was originally a part of God's great plan written before the ages. The Holy Spirit who crafted the message must have also crafted the language; and these two entities, which were so critical to the preparation for the Kingdom, were joined into a hymn that man could lift up to bring gladness to God's heart.

And just as the Greeks excelled in all aspects of language and literature, so did God grant them to excel in the art of sculpture; it was their particular gift to transform shapeless stone into images that would portray—in much the same way their language did—what was in the heart of man. Their skill allowed stones to "speak" truth without the help of a human tongue; and the fluency of that speech was nearly as eloquent as the utterings of the Spirit. The Western Church inherited this skill and has adapted it splendidly to create works of art that express the inward movements of the Spirit. And though our Orthodox doctrine prohibits the use of statues in our worship, we must say that we have been given a compensating perspicuity in spiritual things: visions and revelations that transcend the limits of sculpture.

---

2   See Philip Schaff, *History of the Christian Church*, Vol. 1 (Grand Rapids, MI: Eerdmans, 1994), 76–84.

We find a truly extraordinary fact in the role of the Romans in this whole process. God had sought a nation that could disperse this universal language throughout the entire civilized world. The Roman Empire alone possessed the resources and communication network to accomplish this; and in so doing, the empire provided a universal language for Christianity, by which the evangelists were made able to spread the gospel throughout the empire to an unparalleled extent.

What we may find more extraordinary than the role of the Romans in this preparatory program is the role of the Jews. When the diffusion of the Greek language throughout the empire practically appointed it as the official language of the world, the Jews felt the pressing need to translate their Scriptures into Greek for the sake of their brethren in the diaspora, who had completely lost the use of Hebrew and even of Aramaic. In response to this need, seventy Jewish scholars who were experts in the fields of rabbinical teaching and linguistics convened in Alexandria to produce the Greek translation of the Old Testament known as the Septuagint. It is a work that reflects deep insight into the original text and meaning of the Hebrew Scriptures, and it also reflects the lofty spiritual and literary gifts of the translators. Thus, the Word of God contained in the Old Testament Scriptures was preserved whole and unimpaired until the coming of Christianity; and the evangelists would come to rely heavily on its inspired and prophetic nature for the announcement of the Messiah.

Think, my happy reader, on this marvel: how the Greeks provided a universal language, which was dispersed everywhere by the universal sovereignty of the Romans, which the Jews in turn used to spread the universal riches of their Scriptures—and finally, how this whole process was finalized and put into the hands of the apostles for the spread of the gospel! One cannot miss the hand of God in all this, the hand that directed the process to work out quietly and patiently through the centuries to prepare for the Messiah's coming. The mind staggers at the thought! "Greek," says the Roman orator Cicero, "is read in almost all nations; Latin is confined by its own narrow boundaries."[3]

But we come now to the greatest service Greek philosophy provided to Christianity. Plato and Aristotle innovated the conventional modes of thought that would come to be typically used when speaking about the deities, or at least when speaking about those truths that were discoverable behind the forms of the deities. The conceptual and linguistic elements of this conventional thought were vital to the shaping of the Greek mind, and they guided it in its contemplation of transcendent truth. Thus these elements became foundational to the development of natural theology.

Christianity then appeared and swiftly engaged this conventional thought and speech to express Christian truth and to draft its meticulous theological vocabulary. Examples are the ideas contained in words such as [in English translation] *hypostasis, nature, essence, self, equality, likeness, absolute, temporal, omnipresence, unlimited, docetic, theologian, truth, pseudo-truth,* and *falsehood.* Of course, Christianity had no objection to adopting such conventional Greek terms to express theological truth. Thus, Christian theology was the beneficiary of all that was best in Hellenic thought. For without these conventional Greek modes of theological discourse, Christian theology would not have been able to present itself in such clearcut forms and be so luminous to man's mind and spirit. When one first comes to listen to Christian theology, one tends to imagine that such precise and elegant language must have been a new gift of the Holy Spirit; although, in reality, it proceeded from the minds of people who lived centuries before Christ.

The logic of Greek theological discourse was part and parcel of

---

3   Ibid., 77.

the orations delivered by the Greek philosophers from the Athenian podiums. The audience would hear the speeches, then go out and debate the topics among themselves, thus allowing the same logic to permeate their own minds. Greek logic was thus turned into a spiritual weapon for the defense of God and Christ. And when the Gospels came to be preached in the world, the same Greek logical forms were baptized and used on the lips of the preachers and saints who adorned the podiums of the Church, such as John Chrysostom and the Cappadocian Fathers. The ruminations of Plato and Plutarch have found their way into Christian discourse.[4] And scholars have also noted that the language of the Apostle Paul often bears a strong affinity to that of his contemporary, the Roman philosopher Seneca.[5]

Thus, many of the early Church Fathers who received instruction in Greek philosophy spoke of it as a practical device for evangelism. They compared it to an aqueduct that served as a connector between paganism and Christianity, or to a schoolmaster who led his pupils from the classroom to the temple. Foremost among such Fathers were Justin Martyr, Clement of Alexandria, Origen, and Augustine. As for the children of the Greek Church itself, it is obvious that they were thoroughly imbued with the language and spirit of the Greek philosophy that was infused into the spirit of Christianity.

It was God's sovereign will that permitted the grandeur of Greek philosophy and literature to wane with the coming of Christianity, so that the Church could inherit all that was good in Hellenism and cast aside all that was erroneous or perverse. These thoughts lead us to conclude that the fervent activity that took place in the early centuries of Greek civilization prepared the way for the colossal structure of Christianity that would one day stand in its place;

---

4   Ibid., 78.

5   Lightfoot. *Commentary on the Philippians* (London: Macmillan & Co., 1896). 270.

and when that mission was complete, the role of the heathen world came to a close, it having bequeathed to the Church the best of its achievements.

Earth Prepares for the Son of Man's Coming: The Roman Empire

WHILE GREECE WAS A LAND accomplished in the areas of art and philosophy, Rome was the land of law, order, and practical action. The twin concepts of a world government and a universal code of law were firmly rooted in the Roman psyche, and the idea of a global empire was the dream of the earliest Roman conquerors. They envisaged the frontiers of the empire as stretching eventually from the Euphrates to the Atlantic Ocean, from the deserts of Libya to the banks of the Rhine, encompassing all the lands touching the Mediterranean in Asia, Africa, and Europe.

And so it was. The ambitious dreams of the Roman monarchs quickly became a reality: as soon as their pens drew up boundary lines on maps, their armies went about conquering lands, erecting fortresses, paving roads, and placing their milestones, which can still be seen today. The saying "All roads lead to Rome" was literally true, for the milestones began their numbering in Rome and proceeded outward in all directions, so that a person could know precisely how many miles separated him from the capital. The Romans were very keen on their censuses; they estimated the total number of people under their rule to be about one hundred million, which at the time was around one-third of the world's population.[6] The geographical dimensions of the empire bore witness to its immense political and historical significance.

Whereas God allowed the Greeks to influence the world through

---

6   Schaff, 79.

their artistic and literary gifts, He allowed the Romans to change the world through their force of character. And whereas the Greeks viewed non-Greeks as a mere swarm of barbarians, the Romans looked on non-Romans as enemies—only to be conquered and reduced to servitude. War and triumph were their highest conceptions of glory; and having conquered the world by the sword, they organized it by law. Rome expected every living being to bow before its glory and to submit to its forced peace. Caesar Augustus himself turned Rome from a city of brick huts to a capital of marble palaces; he spent his life embellishing the city with victory arches and stately pillars. No expense was spared in importing the very finest handiwork and craftsmanship the ingenuity of foreign peoples could produce. And in line with this extravagant building campaign came Herod the Great, who built up the grandeur of Jerusalem's temple with polished marble.

General security and political rights were established for every citizen by right of law; and the consequent rights to life, liberty, and free speech raised the state of society. Every violator of the law met with a swift penalty regardless of his position in society. Rome thus became master of the world, and a state of relative peace and stability ensued. Roads were expanded, and transportation and trade between the farthest reaches of the empire were made possible. A merchant could travel abroad knowing that the law protected his goods; and so statues, textiles, and diamonds circulated freely throughout Greece and Rome. The world became as one city under one ruler.

Perhaps the most vivid description of Rome's glory and riches is to be found in St. John the Theologian's Revelation, where he describes her fall:

> The kings of the earth who committed fornication and lived luxuriously with her will weep and lament for her. . . . And

the merchants of the earth will weep and mourn over her, for no one buys their merchandise anymore: merchandise of gold and silver, precious stones and pearls, fine linen and purple, silk and scarlet, every kind of citron wood, every kind of object of ivory, every kind of object of most precious wood, bronze, iron, and marble; and cinnamon and incense, fragrant oil and frankincense, wine and oil, fine flour and wheat, cattle and sheep, horses and chariots, and bodies and souls of men. (Rev. 18:9–13)

Roman and Jew

ONE OF THE NOTABLE POLICIES of the Caesars—in which they were preceded by Alexander the Great—was a certain respect and toleration for ancestral religions. Every land they conquered possessed a host of gods, which they would add to their own number, and to which they would assign Latin names and offer sacrifice. The gods of Macedonia, Egypt, Syria, and Persia were all Romanized, and this process brought about a leveling of the barriers that separated the diverse religions. They eventually constructed a temple that would serve as an abode for all the gods that were absorbed by Rome—the Pantheon, or "the place of all gods." It rests atop the Capitoline Hill (the Roman senate's meeting-grounds) and is one of the most beautiful temples in Rome; indeed, it was the center of the ancient heathen world.

The Jews were the first people to execute a compact with Rome for the preservation of their particular religious creed. Since the Babylonian captivity, the Jews had been dispersed across the whole earth; and according to the testimonies of Josephus and Strabo, there could not be found a spot on earth that did not contain Jews. This fact is also attested in Acts when it mentions Jews from all over the earth meeting in Jerusalem on the Day of Pentecost. The Romans declared Judaism to be a *religio licita* (legal religion), and so the Jews enjoyed certain benefits and advantages throughout the empire. In spite of the fierce antipathy of the Gentiles, they had by their talent and industry risen to wealth and privilege.

After Pompey subjugated Palestine, he brought a sizable number of Jews from Jerusalem to the capital, settled them on the banks of the Tiber, and made them Roman citizens. By establishing this community he unwittingly laid the foundation for the Roman church. When Julius Caesar ascended the throne, he made himself the protector and benefactor of the Jewish people; and as a result, the Jews venerated him so highly that on his death, they mourned before his corpse for days until it was finally burned. He had granted them freedom of worship and thus gave them legal status as a religious society. Augustus Caesar continued this policy, and the Jews under him continued to enjoy their special rights. However, the Jews' relationship with Rome fell on rocky times during Tiberius's reign; and when he was succeeded by Claudius Caesar, they were expelled from the capital. The result of this historical process was the introduction of the idea of one supreme God into the Roman world, and the hope in a coming Messiah was found on the banks of the Tiber.

We had mentioned before that the Greek rendering of the Torah was accomplished at least two hundred years before Christ, and consequently the Jewish Scriptures were being publicly read across the whole empire. As a result, every synagogue had set apart a special quarter of its building to seat Gentiles who wanted to hear the reading of the Torah; and many of the heathen did show a great alacrity for learning about this "Yahweh." Because of this strategy, the synagogues were peacefully preparing the way for the Messiah, as well as reserving a place in their buildings for the preaching of the apostles. The reading of the prophets prepared humanity's ears for hearing the Gospel.

It is interesting to note that some of the first converts to Christianity were women and men who came from these very synagogues, such as Lydia, the Philippian seller of purple, and Timothy of Lystra. Another notable observation is the fact that the Jews of the diaspora were far more receptive to the gospel than the Jews of Palestine. Greek language and culture happened to open their minds to new ideas and truths; and the liberty of spirit that characterized the Jews living in different parts of the empire reduced the barriers to faith that barred entrance for the extremely contentious Jews of Palestine. In confirmation of this, we find that it was the Jews from the synagogues of the diaspora, such as Paul and Barnabas, who embraced Christianity and preached it to the world, who became the bridges over which the heathen would cross to receive the faith with joy inexpressible. In short, the evangelistic campaign these believers launched throughout the empire was under the protection of Roman law, facilitated by paved Roman roads, guarded by armed Roman soldiers, and unified by a single Greek language and culture. Thus, the earth's soil was plowed and made ready for the planting of the gospel.

CHAPTER THREE

From the Nativity to the Beginning of the Ministry

When the fullness of the time had come,
God sent forth His Son.
GALATIANS 4:4

He appeared in the "fullness of time," when the process of
preparation was finished, and the world's need
for redemption fully disclosed.
PHILIP SCHAFF, HISTORY OF THE CHRISTIAN CHURCH

Therefore, when He came into the world, He said:
"Sacrifice and offering You did not desire,
But a body You have prepared for Me.
In burnt offerings and sacrifices for sin
You had no pleasure.
Then I said, 'Behold, I have come—
In the volume of the book it is written of Me—
To do Your will, O God.'"
HEBREWS 10:5–7

The Son Is Sent

The verses above are some of the most important statements that speak of the grand transition from the Old Covenant to the New Covenant, from the Old Era to the New Era. Hebrews achieves this by placing the words of Psalm 40:6–8 directly into the mouth of Christ, as if He were uttering them upon His entrance into the world, as an explanation of His relation to God the Father in the Old Testament. "Instead of sacrifice and offering," says Christ, "You have given me a body." "Since You took no pleasure in burnt offering and sacrifice," He continues, "I have come to do Your will." With these mystical yet astounding statements, the apostle's inspired pen elucidates for us how and why Christ came to earth and with what sort of plan devised by God. On the basis of that plan Christ comes and releases us from the obligation of ritual offering by the supreme offering of His body.

Of course, we cannot forget the sterling verse that stands preeminent in the history of man's redemption: "For God so loved the world that He gave His only begotten Son, that whoever believes in Him should not perish but have everlasting life" (John 3:16). That *giving* of Himself supplanted all those offerings and sacrifices that exhausted humankind by their demands throughout the ages, and which had failed to fulfill man's hope or add to God's pleasure. God's will is finally done by the offering of that unique body: "Behold, I have come to do Your will, O God."

Therefore, the Nativity was not properly the beginning of the Life of Christ, but rather a bodily extension of His eternal spiritual presence. His Incarnation was only the means for His entry into the world in order to carry out the strategy designed by God from eternity past. His life on earth, in other words, had roots stretching back into eternity past and reaching forward to eternity future. This is how He was able to take everything that is the Father's and declare it to us; and after He finished His work on earth, He made us partakers of His body and of His spiritual life. That felicitous phrase, "You have prepared for Me a body," is a summary of the whole Nativity story.

But the question now presents itself to us: why must He have been born of a virgin? Human logic alone will perceive that the great Figure who took upon Himself the transformation of humanity, from an earthly, ignorant, groveling race enmeshed in sin to one that is pure, luminous, and Spirit-filled, could not possibly have taken His origin from ordinary sinful man. If we are speaking of a Savior whose principal task is to change human nature itself, to remold human character and conduct, then such a Savior must necessarily be made of the same material as we are and be subject to all our weaknesses; but, at the same time, He must be made of the same material as heaven in order to set humanity free. He Himself must be of a sinless human nature in order to obliterate sin; and He likewise must bear a divine nature in order to escape the clutches of sin and rise again with human nature justified of sin. Thus, Jesus introduced a "recreated humanity" into the world.

The birth of Christ has two critical aspects. The first is the natural aspect of a human birth. The second aspect is one that transcends nature; it has the power to create new things; it can transform the low and ordinary nature of man into one that is high and heavenly. This creative transformation is the very process to which the Gospels introduce us when they talk about the Virgin Birth by the agency of the Holy Spirit. These were historical events, witnessed by heavenly and earthly beings, proclaiming that all the circumstantial details we had come to expect surrounding the Birth of the Messiah were fulfilled. Hence, the Gospels of Matthew and Luke relate events such as the Angel Gabriel's visit to Mary, the Annunciation, the pregnancy and birth, and how the Son of Man was also the Son of God.

The Gospel of John, on the other hand, does not provide us with a picture of Christ's Birth but rather reaches back to a point far before that; and St. John affirms, based on his authority as an apostle and his extreme closeness to Christ and the Virgin Mary, that Christ existed before all ages, and that He was the creative Word that generated the world. He, coequal with God the Father and His own Son, stooped with His divine nature to take up a body and be born of a Virgin—a process John calls "becoming flesh": "The Word became flesh and dwelt among us, and we beheld His glory, the glory as of the only begotten of the Father" (John 1:14).

The Annunciation

WE COME NOW TO THE period in which Mary is betrothed to Joseph. Joseph was a carpenter and of a seasoned age. Tradition indicates that Mary's father was Joachim, who bequeathed his poverty to Mary. And so, in presenting this couple to us—a lowly carpenter and a poor girl—the Gospels present the first stumbling block to faith in Christ: "And they said, 'Is not this Jesus, the son of Joseph, whose father and mother we know?'" (John 6:42). The people never found a reason to confer honor on the holy family, a point to which Christ once alluded: "Assuredly, I say to you, no prophet is accepted in his own country" (Luke 4:24). Mary and Joseph's poverty was an earthly augmentation of that greater poverty Christ endured on leaving His celestial glory: "You know the grace of our Lord Jesus Christ, that though He was rich, yet for your sakes He became poor, that you through His poverty might become rich" (2 Cor. 8:9).

The holy family resided in Nazareth of Galilee. The acute scholar Alfred Edersheim provides us with an illuminating description of the nature of the Galilean people. They were a race distinguished by their uprightness of character; they were a hardy, rustic, and courageous people. The Galileans were intensely patriotic, and, like the rest of their fellow Jews, they faced the hard realities of life undauntedly and were proud to call God their sovereign. They were a free-spirited people, unfettered by the minutiae of rabbinic teaching, enjoying the freedom of simple living. Galilean family life was intensely pure. Betrothal was as sacred as marriage, and their wedding banquets, unlike those of other Jewish districts, were celebrated with a simple and innocent joy. A Galilean bride was never judged by the size of her fortune but by the content of her character.

In terms of the holy family's pedigree, Joseph and Mary were both of the line of David, and that commonality made them at least distant relatives. Mary was also closely related to Elizabeth, who was herself both a daughter and wife of a priest. Mary's family, therefore, always had close ties to God. They were a poor couple, a fact that is evidenced by the type of sacrifice they offered when they came to present the baby Jesus to the temple. Wealthy families typically offered a bull; the middle-class offered lambs; but the poor would offer "two young pigeons" (Luke 2:24). And so their betrothal ceremony was not likely accompanied by any sort of banquet or lavish dinner but was simply performed in the presence of the required witnesses. The betrothal covenant was sealed by the Jewish rite of thanksgiving, then by the passing around of a wine cup, from which the betrothed couple were the first to drink. Thus was Mary engaged to Joseph in a holy bond, the strength of which could only be broken by the official pronouncement of a Jewish court.

And here the angel makes his sudden appearance to the betrothed virgin in her home in Nazareth. He presents himself to a dwelling of the humblest appearance in order to deliver the tidings of the most momentous event ever to happen—the birth of the Deliverer of men and the Savior of the world. The young virgin (a teenager, according to tradition) is at first startled by the radiant apparition; but the angel immediately offers words of comfort: "Rejoice, highly favored one, the Lord *is* with you; blessed *are* you among women!" (Luke 1:28). The apparition was, indeed, overwhelming to one so humble and unassuming. But the angel's gracious salute brought peace to her unsettled mind, and his expression of "grace" introduced an inner joy to her wondering heart. As she pondered what such a greeting could possibly mean, the angel offered further words of comfort:

> "Do not be afraid, Mary, for you have found favor with God. And behold, you will conceive in your womb and bring forth a Son, and shall call His name JESUS. He will be great, and will be called the Son of the Highest; and the Lord God will give Him the throne of His father David. And He will reign over the house of Jacob forever, and of His kingdom there will be no end." (Luke 1:30–33)

The angel had nothing to offer of himself, but only the news of what was about to happen to her and inside her. As he was speaking the very words, grace immediately began its secret work within her. Fear naturally entered her heart at the outset; but the angel's words, "Do not be afraid," dissolved all such fear. Grace appeared to comfort her, like the sweet avian songs that accompany the morning. Of course, her reasoning mind entered at this point to present a difficulty: "How can this be, since I do not know a man?" Had she not betrothed herself to God before being betrothed to Joseph? And so how could she conceive in her consecrated state? Is not a consecrated body like a flame of fire comparable to the burning bush? The virgin here is not protesting the angel's news, but only defending her chastity, to which God Himself was witness.

Since God had claimed her for Himself, she had likewise dedicated herself to Him; and so how could her hallowed womb bring forth any fruit? Her completely innocent and sincere question prompts the angel to reveal the mystery: "*The* Holy Spirit will come upon you, and the power of the Highest will overshadow you; therefore, also, that Holy One who is to be born will be called the Son of God" (Luke 1:35). Upon hearing these words, she understood them and accepted them; and instantly she felt the mysterious work taking place inside her. For God's *word* is *deed*. She responds, "Behold the maidservant of the Lord! Let it be to me according to your word" (Luke 1:38). This is famously called the *Fiat* in the Latin, and by it Mary meant to say, "May God do whatever is according to His will." The overshadowing of the Holy Spirit here is the first time we hear of God's descent into a human being to plant the seed of divine life.

The angel continues expressing the mystery: "The Holy One who is to be born will be called the Son of God." "Holy One" here is not a title of the one to be born but is rather a description of His divinity: "I and *My* Father are one" (John 10:30). And even though the Son came down from the Father's bosom, He is still embraced by that bosom: "The only begotten Son, who is in the bosom of the Father" (John 1:18). "No one has ascended to heaven but He who came down from heaven, *that is*, the Son of Man who is in heaven" (John 3:13). When Christ took flesh, His Incarnation included His unity with the Father; and since we are united with Christ, we are therefore united with the Father: "I *am* in My Father, and you in Me, and I in you" (John 14:20).

Since Christ has united with us, if we abide in the union, we are accepted by God. This union was begun by Christ in humility and is completed by us in faith. And the right to this union cannot be denied to anyone: "The one who comes to Me I will by no means cast out" (John 6:37). The Virgin believed this truth: "Behold the maidservant of the Lord!" How great is Mary, the daughter of Abraham! For as Abraham had faith—"he believed in the LORD, and He accounted it to him for righteousness" (Gen. 15:6)—so did Mary have the same faith, and in her womb was conceived One whom all peoples of the world would bless. Mary perfected the faith of Abraham and thereby fulfilled the promise made to him. The dialogue between the Virgin and the angel brought the story of Abraham to a marvelous conclusion.

As if providing Mary with a tangible token of the veracity of the news, the angel informs her that her aged relative Elizabeth has been pregnant now for six months. For if such a thing could be possible with God, then all things must be possible! The angel intends the young Virgin to go and pay a visit to her elder kinswoman, that she might witness the promise of God and rejoice in it. Mary accepts the angel's invitation and goes straightway to her aged relative. The journey from Nazareth to Hebron consisted of three days of arduous travel. But she took to her feet and flew over the Judean hills like a gazelle racing through the wind; her enthusiasm was perpetually replenished by the Spirit, and her panting breath renewed by grace. Elizabeth greets Mary and extols her great faith: "Blessed *is* she who believed, for there will be a fulfillment of those things which were told her from the Lord" (Luke 1:45).

Mary's Song

ELIZABETH RECEIVES MARY IN HER home and offers her a kiss, and in that holy greeting is reflected the greeting of the Baptist with Christ—a kiss of peace exchanged between the two Testaments. The Spirit that filled Mary also filled Elizabeth; and so the Baptist received the filling of the Spirit from the womb and rejoiced in it. Elizabeth utters a prophecy: "Why *is* this *granted* to me, that the mother of my Lord should come to me?" (Luke 1:43). She had felt the homage of the baby inside her upon hearing the greeting of

Mary. This occurrence increased Mary's awareness of the evangelical mystery that was now inside her, and she proceeded to utter her prophetic canticle, which would be echoed by all future generations: "Behold, henceforth all generations will call me blessed" (Luke 1:48).

And so Mary, a girl of teenage years from the village of Nazareth, believed all that was told her; and in believing so, she became the first believer in Jesus and a mother to Israel and the Church. Christ sits as King on David's throne, and she sits beside Him as the King's mother, distributing blessings and receiving honors. After all, it was from her very flesh and bones that the Son of God took His body; and it is from His flesh and bones that we are all born to new life through the resurrection. By her greatness she lifts David's fallen tabernacle; and the young girl of Nazareth lifts her voice in the Hebrew tongue to sing the following words:

"My soul magnifies the Lord,
And my spirit has rejoiced in God my Savior.
For He has regarded the lowly state of His maidservant;
For behold, henceforth all generations will call me blessed.
For He who is mighty has done great things for me,
And holy is His name.
And His mercy is on those who fear Him
From generation to generation.
He has shown strength with His arm;
He has scattered the proud in the imagination of their hearts.
He has put down the mighty from their thrones,
And exalted the lowly.
He has filled the hungry with good things,
And the rich He has sent away empty.
He has helped His servant Israel,
In remembrance of His mercy,

As He spoke to our fathers,
To Abraham and to his seed forever." (Luke 1:46–55)

It is a lyrical poem composed of four main stanzas, each stanza being punctuated by three rests. The poem reflects the longings of the Old Testament while breathing the Spirit of the New Testament. In it, the Virgin proclaims the rising of the Sun of Righteousness after a prolonged and sorrowful night, as though Israel would now wake from a dreadful centuries-old dream to open its eyes on a new dawn. God was inaugurating this new era by the advent of the Messiah. Those who seized authority in the world would now be brought low, and the lowly would be lifted up. Those who hungered for righteousness would now be fed, and those who were sated with their self-righteousness would go hungry. God would now glorify Israel and renew His mercy along with the covenant that He made with the patriarchs.

It was not for nothing that the Virgin magnified the Lord. For the Holy One was now settling into the temple of her body; and the Spirit resting in her was like a coal of fire whose burning essence ignited these bursting expressions of praise. Zechariah the Prophet foresaw this event many centuries prior and sang, "Rejoice greatly, O daughter of Zion! / Shout, O daughter of Jerusalem! / Behold, your King is coming to you" (Zech. 9:9). He saw from afar how God would do great things yet to come by the strength of His arm: by the breath of His lungs He would scatter the proud; by His death He would depose the haughty; by His Resurrection He would raise the poor. He would break the bread of His own body in order to feed the hungry, but the stubborn and defiant would go away empty. Israel's head would be lifted up and the promise to Abraham thus fulfilled. Hence Mary's song is a hymn belonging to both Testaments.

The Nativity

ONCE MARY'S THREE-MONTH VISIT TO her relative Elizabeth was completed, she returned to Nazareth; and upon finding her to be three months pregnant, Joseph began to have deep misgivings about her. But since he desired to hide her from the public eye and to conceal their divorce from the Sanhedrin, he planned to put her away secretly out of feelings of compassion. And St. Matthew's Gospel here informs us of the following: "While he thought about these things, behold, an angel of the Lord appeared to him in a dream, saying, 'Joseph, son of David, do not be afraid to take to you Mary your wife, for that which is conceived in her is of the Holy Spirit'" (Matt. 1:20, 21).

Now at that time Caesar Augustus promulgated a decree mandating a census of the Roman world. The Caesars made it one of their highest administrative priorities to keep statistics on the populations that fell under their dominion. Such numbers were critical for the right calculation of the poll-taxes they expected to collect, which were used for the maintenance of the empire's infrastructure. The laying of roads, securing of transportation routes, erection of public buildings, and all such imperial activities were necessary for the stimulation of trade and the promotion of the general welfare. Using the resulting public records and legal archives that have come down to us, scholars are able to estimate the year of our Lord's birth with relative accuracy. It is generally put down at about 4 or 5 BC.

The single historical event that brings us closest to the date of Christ's birth is the death of Herod the Great, which occurred in 4 BC, because we know that Christ was born just a short while before Herod died. In addition, there were two censuses that occurred while Quirinius was governor of Syria: one in 8 BC (see Acts 5:37) and the second in 6 BC. The archives in Rome indicate that a census took place in the Roman year 746, which corresponds to 8 BC; and the archives in Alexandria indicate that a census took place in

Egypt in the year 6 BC. We also know that the census in Palestine took place one year after that in Egypt; and so we are brought down to the year 5 BC. We are also told by Josephus that Herod's death took place after an eclipse of the moon. This lunar event astronomers calculate to have occurred in March of 750 on the Roman calendar,[7] which corresponds to a period right before 4 BC on the modern Gregorian calendar. Furthermore, Luke tells us that John the Baptist began his ministry (at the age of thirty) in the fifteenth year of Tiberius Caesar's reign, which places John's birth early in year 749 of the Roman calendar, thus placing Christ's birth toward the end of 5 BC.[8]

As it was Jewish custom to return to the city of one's birth to be registered for the census, Joseph accordingly took his betrothed with him to Bethlehem, the City of David, where that prophet of old used to shepherd his sheep and compose his psalms. Joseph took her there as his wife, according to the angel's decree, as she was in her ninth month of pregnancy. She must give birth in Bethlehem of Judea, according to the word of the prophets; for it was God's will that Jesus' name would be enrolled as a son of David in His father's city. "For there is born to you this day in the city of David a Savior, who is Christ the Lord" (Luke 2:11).

The journey to Bethlehem was difficult in every way. There was the biting cold of a Palestinian winter; it was a full three-day

---

7   Josephus, *Antiquities*, 17.6.4.

8   The Copts in Egypt have always celebrated Christmas on the 29th day of the Coptic month Khiahk. For the first fifteen centuries after Christ, Khiahk 29 coincided with what was December 25 on the Julian calendar. But in the year AD 1582, European astronomers discovered that a given number of minutes were unaccounted for during each solar year that passed. The missing minutes were added since the birth of Christ and were found to total ten days. The error was rectified by the adoption of the new Gregorian Calendar. So Europeans went to bed on October 4, 1582, and woke up the next morning on October 15. As a result, Khiahk 29 corresponded that year with January 4. From AD 1700, Khiahk 29 corresponded with January 5, then in 1800 with January 6, then in 1900 with January 7.

journey, and the Virgin had to endure it while in her ninth month of pregnancy. As they pass the outskirts of the city, she begins to feel her first birthpangs; but there is not a single vacancy for them in the lodges. They finally happen on an inn that is full but agrees to accommodate them in a special way: they are led to a grotto adjoined to the inn in which the owners' animals are kept. And when the divinely appointed moment arrives, Mary gives birth to her firstborn son, wraps him in swaddling blankets, and lays him to rest in an ox's manger.

It was a scene of utter poverty. But the manger did not enter our Lord's life by mere happenstance; it was not the chance result of an unfavorable combination of time and place. Heaven had decreed all this beforehand. "He . . . has determined their preappointed times and the boundaries of their dwellings" (Acts 17:26). For the circumstances of our Lord's birth must be commensurate with His mission and message; and how could that mission be better launched among the human race? The manger and the Cross, from a theological standpoint, possess a depth of meaning beyond the mind's ability to comprehend; they push man's faith to the very limits of what is possible. The One who said, "Look at the birds of the air, for they neither sow nor reap. . . . Consider the lilies of the field, how they grow: they neither toil nor spin" (Matt. 6:26, 28), purposely submitted to such a meager birthplace. Simplicity was the adornment of His birth, and meekness was its beauty. He who divested Himself of heaven's grandeur was also free to divest Himself of earth's pomp. And the very dearth of spectacle prohibited the evangelists from providing much detail regarding the Lord's Nativity. Aside from the simple image of the gentle mother's hands placing her babe in a manger, a veil is drawn over the mystery of this most sacred birth.[9]

---

9   An early testimony to the scene of the Nativity being in a cave comes to us from Justin Martyr. This saint and apologist was born in Shechem of

The Angels Announce to the Shepherds

THERE CAN BE FOUND NEXT to Bethlehem, on the road that leads to Jerusalem, a hill on which stands a tower of very great antiquity. This structure was known in ancient times as Migdal Eder, "the tower of the flock"; in Jewish tradition it was said to be the site from which the Messiah would one day be revealed. A passage in the Mishnah[10] leads to the conclusion that the flocks that pastured on this hill were destined to be sacrificed in the temple; and the shepherds who watched over them received special training in the care and nurturing of the flocks under the supervision of the rabbis. In addition, the Passover lambs were required to roam in the pastures of Migdal Eder for thirty days before being sacrificed.[11] These notices point to a clear symbolism regarding the location of Christ's Birth and his destiny to be set apart as God's Lamb for the eternal Passover.

It was from the sky above this tower that the announcement to the shepherds was made:

Now there were in the same country shepherds living out in the fields, keeping watch over their flock by night. And behold, an angel of the Lord stood before them, and the glory of the Lord shone around them, and they were greatly afraid. Then the angel said to them, "Do not be afraid, for behold, I bring you good tidings of great joy which will be to all people. For there is born to you this day in the city of David a Savior, who

---

Samaria in AD 100 and was martyred in 165. His birthplace makes him a native Palestinian and as such deeply familiar with the geography and history of the land. Over this cave has risen the Church and Convent of the Nativity. Another testimony comes from St. Jerome, the translator of the Vulgate, who traveled to Palestine in 386 and spent thirty of his declining years there in prayer, fasting, and study.

10 Mishna, Shek. vii 4.

11 Edersheim, *The Life and Times of Jesus the Messiah*, vol. 1, 187.

is Christ the Lord. And this *will be* the sign to you: You will find a Babe wrapped in swaddling cloths, lying in a manger." And suddenly there was with the angel a multitude of the heavenly host praising God and saying: "Glory to God in the highest, and on earth peace, goodwill toward men!" (Luke 2:8–14)

Once the angelic vision had withdrawn, the shepherds promptly made their way to see the new Child. They arrived in Bethlehem while the city was still steeped in silence and darkness; and when the morning light had broken, they inquired of the keepers of the inn where the holy family was lodging. The innkeepers showed them to the entrance of the cave; and when they entered, they saw the Child of whom the angels sang and offered what little gifts they could—cheese and meat.[12] Then they told to Joseph and Mary their remarkable tale; and the story spread and circulated, particularly among the temple personnel with whom the shepherds normally dealt. Consequently, the news naturally reached the ears of Simeon the elder and Hannah the prophetess, both of whom prepared themselves to see the coming One. And Mary hid all these things within her heart.

The Visit of the Magi

JUST AS THE ANNOUNCEMENT TO the shepherds represented the initial revealing of the Messiah to Israel, so did the visit of the Magi become the Messiah's first revealing to the Gentiles. And just as the angelic voice directed the shepherds to the manger, so did the star guide the Magi to Christ's birthplace. These men were scholars who studied the science of astronomy: "Now after Jesus was born in Bethlehem of Judea in the days of Herod the king, behold, wise men from the East came to Jerusalem, saying, 'Where is He who has been

---

12   Giovanni Papini, *Life of Christ*, 1923, 23.

THE STORY OF JESUS

born King of the Jews? For we have seen His star in the East and have come to worship Him'" (Matt. 2:1, 2).

If we would desire to estimate the date when the Magi visited Christ, we will find that we must deal within a very limited time-frame. We already know that Herod certainly died before the lunar eclipse that took place on March 12 or 13 in the year 4 BC. And since the best date we have for Christ's birth is December 25 in the year 5 BC, then we are left with a three-month time range in which the Magi must have made their appearance, offered their gifts, and returned to their country.

A question that has long been debated among scholars is the nationality of these Magi. Were they Medo-Persian or Babylonian? Both these nations excelled in the study of astronomy as well as in the practice of astrology. But the question is most likely decided by the etymology of the word *magi*, which is of Persian origin. The Magi are mentioned in the works of Herodotus, and scholars have discovered that they were one of the official tribes of the Medo-Persian Empire. Clement of Alexandria, Cyril, Diodorus of Tarsus, and Chrysostom all speak of the Magi as being the intellectual elite of Persia. These men were renowned for their knowledge of the stars and for their ability to relate the movements of the heavens to events on earth. They practiced, in addition, a highly developed form of worship; they recognized one God, believed deeply in prayer, and strove to practice virtue.[13]

It is therefore conjectured that they originally came into close contact with the Jews who were taken into the Babylonian captivity during the sixth century BC. The captive Jews, it is proposed, played a most vital role in the education and religious civilizing of the Persians; they planted in them the spirit of worship, the fear of God, and a belief in monotheism. We must also remember that a large

---

13 W. Hendriksen, *Bible Survey*, 59–62.

portion of the Jews did not return to Palestine after the captivity had ended, but remained in the foreign land, married Persian wives, and spread their religious literature throughout the empire. The Persians consequently inherited from the Jews the eager anticipation of a Messiah-King who would one day appear to liberate His people.[14]

The Magi arrived in Jerusalem with a single question on their lips: "Where is He who has been born King of the Jews?" (Matt. 2:2). The inquiry threw Herod and all Jerusalem into a state of unrest; for Herod, an Idumean usurper placed on the throne by the Roman power, naturally saw any political challenger to his position as a threat to himself and to his dynasty. But the simple-hearted inquiry was the very purpose of the Magi's lengthy journey, which took them over vast expanses of the eastern desert and likely consumed the better part of three months. An overflowing joy must have filled them on being informed by the rabbinic schoolmen that the Messiah was to be born in Bethlehem, a town not far from Jerusalem. Their calculations and the star had spoken truly.

But what was the nature of this star? The astronomers[15] tell us that a conjunction of the planets Jupiter and Saturn occurred in the constellation Pisces around the time of Christ's birth. This conjunction created a brilliant spectacle in the night sky, appearing as a great star with a long tail; and the phenomenon was attributed by astrologers to the fulfillment of a grand cosmic hope. This "star" could easily be seen with the naked eye. But there was a curious idea current at the time which said that a starry phenomenon could also be seen with the heart, if the spirit of the observer had an existential connection with the star; and so a person himself could be moved to and fro by the movements of a special star. This is apparently what occurred to the Magi, who were moved by the hope for a new kingdom and

---

14   W. Hendriksen, *Exposition of the Gospel According to Matthew*, 151.
15   Johannes Kepler, *De Stella Nova*.

a new world. The science of these Persian sages was heathen and tinged with superstition; but we must agree with Chrysostom in saying that God inspired them to use what was good and true in their knowledge to seek Him.[16]

Herod Moves to Slay the Infant Christ

THE RELATIONSHIP BETWEEN HEROD AND the Jews was a stormy one, and the suspicious king had numerous eyes and ears planted throughout the nation to monitor the activity of the people. When the news of the Magi's arrival therefore reached Herod, along with their inquiry about the birth of a "King of kings," he called together the chief priests in alarm and asked them where the Messiah was expected to be born. They recited to him Micah's prophecy: "But you, Bethlehem Ephrathah, / *Though* you are little among the thousands of Judah, / Yet out of you shall come forth to Me / The One to be ruler in Israel" (Micah 5:2). "Then Herod, when he had secretly called the wise men, determined from them what time the star appeared" (Matt. 2:7). Of course, the real intent of his wily questionings was to determine the approximate age of the young Messiah in order to devise his murderous plan. But heaven moved quicker than Herod to protect the Child, and an angel was sent to Joseph in a dream with a message: "Arise, take the young Child and His mother, [and] flee to Egypt" (Matt. 2:13).

When Herod sent the Magi on their way to see the Child, with the request that they bring back word so that he might go and worship Him, the divine counsel had them depart to their country by a different route; and this so incensed Herod that he sent out his soldiers to put to death every male child under the age of two. And

---

16   Chrysostom, *Homilies on the Gospel of Saint Matthew*, NPNF, First Series, Vol. 10, 38.

in case the reader might doubt that Herod could carry out such a reprehensible plan, we present here the words of Canon Farrar from his *Life of Christ*:

> His whole career was red with the blood of murder. He had massacred priests and nobles; he had decimated the Sanhedrin; he had caused the high-priest, his brother-in-law Aristobulus, to be drowned before his eyes. He had ordered the strangulation of his favorite wife, the beautiful Asmonean princess Mariamne, though she seems to have been the only human being whom he passionately loved. . . . His son Archelaus narrowly escaped execution by his orders. . . . Deaths by strangulation, deaths by burning, deaths by cleft asunder, deaths by secret assassination, confessions forced by unutterable torture, acts of insolent and inhuman lust, mark the annals of a reign so cruel that the full range of wickedness cannot be recorded by pen.[17]

The Flight to Egypt

EGYPT WAS NOT A FOREIGN land to the Jews. Many of their nation had taken up permanent residence there for above four hundred years, and the Jewish population of Alexandria was second only to that of Palestine. Philo of Alexandria estimates the Jewish population in Egypt in AD 40 to have been approximately one million, and they were to be found mostly living in "Babylon" (Old Cairo), Alexandria, and Upper Egypt.

Joseph, therefore, took the Child and His mother and went down to Egypt. We may suppose with some certainty that the gold provided by the Magi was enough to cover the expenses involved

---

17   Farrar, *The Life of Christ*, repr. 1965, 20.

in traveling and boarding in Egypt, and also that the guardhouses set up along the roads by Alexander the Great provided a peaceful sojourn for the travelers. Historians have described the possible routes of the Holy Family's journey, especially near the ancient city of Leontopolis in Old Cairo.[18]

Coptic tradition points to a church called Abu-sirga, a modern shrine in the vicinity of Old Cairo, as a renowned resting place for the Holy Family. The family also resided for a time in Babylon of Old Cairo and passed by Gabal at Teir and Assiut on their way. A plethora of districts in Egypt were thus blessed by the footsteps of the Savior as He fled from the wrath of the Idumean tyrant. Just as Joseph the Patriarch went down to Egypt due to the wrath of his brothers and built storehouses of bread for the Egyptians, so did Christ—the Bread of Life—go down to be preserved for a time, in order to give Himself for the life of the world. When David prayed that God would preserve the vine that He took out of Egypt, it was a prophetic supplication for the protection of the Son of Man: "You have brought a vine (Israel) out of Egypt. . . . O God of hosts; / Look down from heaven and see, / And visit this vine / And the vineyard which Your right hand has planted, / And the branch *that* You made strong for Yourself" (Ps. 80:8, 14, 15).

"And [he] was there until the death of Herod, that it might be fulfilled which was spoken by the Lord through the prophet, saying, 'Out of Egypt I called My Son'" (Matt. 2:15). This messianic prophecy, originally spoken by Hosea regarding Israel's exodus from Egypt, is now applied to Christ. The original verse has a memorable beauty to it: "When Israel *was* a child, I loved him, / And out of Egypt I called My son" (Hos. 11:1). Christ did not stay long in Egypt, for Herod died shortly after the escape.

---

18   Paulus & Schubert, cited by H.A.W. Meyer, *Gospel of Matthew*, 65.

The Return to Israel

THE DIVINE VOICE CAME ONCE again to Joseph in a dream:

> Now when Herod was dead, behold, an angel of the Lord
> appeared in a dream to Joseph in Egypt, saying, "Arise, take
> the young Child and His mother, and go to the land of Israel,
> for those who sought the young Child's life are dead." Then he
> arose, took the young Child and His mother, and came into
> the land of Israel. But when he heard that Archelaus was reign-
> ing over Judea instead of his father Herod, he was afraid to go
> there. And being warned by God in a dream, he turned aside
> into the region of Galilee. And he came and dwelt in a city
> called Nazareth, that it might be fulfilled which was spoken by
> the prophets, "He shall be called a Nazarene." (Matt. 2:19–23)

We should not miss the clear parallel here between Moses and
Christ. Moses had fled long ago from the presence of Pharaoh and
returned when summoned by the divine voice: "Go, return to Egypt;
for all the men who sought your life are dead" (Ex. 4:19); and similarly, Christ fled the presence of Herod until He was recalled by
the divine summons. The upshot of this parallelism is the idea that
Christ is the new Moses. Christ is also the new Israel; for just as
the people of Israel went down to Egypt in consequence of a famine
in their land, so did Christ go down to Egypt in consequence of a
deadly persecution in His land.

The word *Galilee* indicates a "circle," and it was indeed a central
point of communication between all the Gentiles living in the surrounding regions. The Galilean countryside teemed with Gentile
shepherds, hence the appellation "Galilee of the Gentiles"—a term of
scorn, because the Gentiles were considered a profane people. Nevertheless, Galilee opened up all the channels of trade to the Gentile
world and thus became a trading district. But the great majority of its

land was used for agriculture, and its people were mainly farmers. To the far north of Galilee could be seen Mount Hermon, standing like a giant among little hills and dominating the northern landscape, its snowy peak gleaming like a crown of ice in the sunlight. On the western horizon could be seen the dark and crimson Mount Carmel; and in the far distance, one could spot the shimmering silvery mass that was the Mediterranean Sea. The peaks of Mount Tabor rose to the southeast, covered by thick forests and surrounded by beaten tracks over which caravans trod.

The city of Nazareth itself, nestled in the heart of a mountain, was a scene of tranquil beauty. To its northeast bubbled a spring or well that served as a rendezvous point for townspeople and a resting place for travelers. The typical Nazarene home had a flat rooftop and a small garden that contained trees bearing figs, olives, dates, and pomegranates. The air of Nazareth was perpetually filled with the fresh aroma of flowers and was home to multiple species of birds displaying beautiful and colorful plumage. Though the inhabitants of Nazareth were poor, its natural resources were rich. In addition, one of three major highways ran through the city, transporting caravans from the coastal city of Acco all the way to Damascus.[19]

Canon Farrar provides us with this interesting description:

> The hills which form the northern limit of the plain of Jezreel run almost due east and west from the Jordan valley to the Mediterranean, and their southern slopes were in the district assigned to Zebulun. Almost in the center of this chain of hills there is a singular cleft in the limestone, forming the entrance to a little valley. As the traveler leaves the plain he will ride up a steep and narrow pathway, through scenery which is neither colossal nor overwhelming, but infinitely

---

19   Edersheim, *Life and Times of Jesus the Messiah*, 146.

beautiful and picturesque. The basin of the valley is divided by hedges of cactus into little fields and gardens, which, about the fall of the spring rains, wear an aspect of indescribable calm and glow with a tint of the richest green. . . . Gradually the valley opens into a natural amphitheater of hills, supposed by some to be the crater of an extinct volcano. And there, clinging to the hollows of a hill, "like a handful of pearls in a goblet of emerald," lie the flat roofs and narrow streets of a little Eastern town.[20]

This brings us to Matthew's remark that He shall be called a "Nazarene." The meaning of the Hebrew word *nasir* or *ne'tseri* is a "shoot" or "branch," and the prophets employed this word in their writings: "There shall come forth a Rod from the stem of Jesse, / And a Branch shall grow out of his roots" (Is 11:1). The word "branch" came to be associated with Nazareth—"My servant the BRANCH" (Zech. 3:8)—and this was taken to mean that Nazareth was a low and contemptible city. Hence the question, "Can anything good come out of Nazareth?" (John 1:46).

But the question immediately arises, why Nazareth of Galilee? Of all the countries sitting under heaven's vault, Galilee was specifically chosen to be Jesus' homeland; and of all the cities of Galilee, Nazareth was chosen to be His hometown. The choice was indeed a deep offense to the academic minds of the rabbis. The idea of the Messiah arising from Galilean Nazareth could only be looked on with horror by Jewish scholars. For the Messiah was to embody the highest wisdom of the nation, but Nazareth to them represented nothing but coarse ignorance. The Galilean country was profaned by the presence of Gentiles and foreigners in its cities, and so, clearly, Nazareth could produce nothing good. Hence the remark to Nicodemus: "Are

---

20   F. W. Farrar, *The Life of Christ*, 24.

you also from Galilee? Search and look, for no prophet has arisen out of Galilee" (John 7:52).

The divine counsel thus willed to use the "offenses" of Galilee and Nazareth in its great plan of salvation, just as it was pleased to use the manger and the Cross: "Behold, I lay in Zion a stumbling stone and rock of offense, / And whoever believes on Him will not be put to shame" (Rom. 9:33). Saint Paul borrowed this verse from Isaiah in order to throw its meaning into bold relief: "He will be as a sanctuary, / But a stone of stumbling and a rock of offense / To both the houses of Israel, / As a trap and a snare to the inhabitants of Jerusalem" (Is. 8:14, 15). "Behold, I lay in Zion a stone for a foundation, / A tried stone, a precious cornerstone, a sure foundation; / Whoever believes will not act hastily" (Is. 28:16). It should be clear to the reader now how the sending of the Angel Gabriel to Nazareth is an integral part of our theology of salvation as it is worked out in the life of Christ.

We have in Isaiah a prophetic and poetic description of the illumination of Galilee:

> *Nevertheless the gloom will not be upon her who is distressed,*
> *As when at first He lightly esteemed*
> *The land of Zebulun and the land of Naphtali,*
> *And afterward more heavily oppressed her,*
> *By the way of the sea, beyond the Jordan,*
> *In Galilee of the Gentiles.*
> *The people who walked in darkness*
> *Have seen a great light;*
> *Those who dwelt in the land of the shadow of death,*
> *Upon them a light has shined. (Is. 9:1, 2)*

Isaiah then quickly lifts the veil to reveal to us the Child who will be born and will bring light to all people:

For unto us a Child is born,
Unto us a Son is given;
And the government will be upon His shoulder.
And His name will be called
Wonderful, Counselor, Mighty God,
Everlasting Father, Prince of Peace.
Of the increase of His government and peace
There will be no end,
Upon the throne of David and over His kingdom,
To order it and establish it with judgment and justice
From that time forward, even forever.
The zeal of the LORD of hosts will perform this. (Is. 9:6, 7)

A human person can barely contain his emotions when reading such moving words as these—words which transcend time and eternity, which describe the light that would burst from the Galilean darkness and cover the world, which reveal a Child who would be God Himself! The young Christ would read passages such as these with a throbbing heart, for He could foresee the final culmination of their message: the Cross.

The Childhood in Nazareth

TO ANYONE WHO LOVES JESUS, the question naturally arises as to what exactly His childhood and early manhood were like. For with the exception of a single report given to us by St. Luke, inserted below, relating the Holy Family's visit to Jerusalem during Passover, we have no direct information regarding our Lord's upbringing.

His parents went to Jerusalem every year at the Feast of the Passover. And when He was twelve years old, they went up to

Jerusalem according to the custom of the feast. When they had finished the days, as they returned, the Boy Jesus lingered behind in Jerusalem. And Joseph and His mother did not know *it*; but supposing Him to have been in the company, they went a day's journey, and sought Him among *their* relatives and acquaintances. So when they did not find Him, they returned to Jerusalem, seeking Him. Now so it was *that* after three days they found Him in the temple, sitting in the midst of the teachers, both listening to them and asking them questions. And all who heard Him were astonished at His understanding and answers. So when they saw Him, they were amazed; and His mother said to Him, "Son, why have You done this to us? Look, Your father and I have sought You anxiously."

And He said to them, "Why did you seek Me? Did you not know that I must be about My Father's business?" But they did not understand the statement which He spoke to them. Then He went down with them and came to Nazareth, and was subject to them, but His mother kept all these things in her heart. (Luke 2:41–51)

Jewish tradition stipulated that when a boy reached the age of twelve, he was to be brought to the temple for testing in order to become a "son of the Torah." Once the title was bestowed, the boy was an official and active member of the Jewish nation, and he was to attend the three major Jewish feasts annually (Ex. 34:22, 23). Christ likewise was presented to the elders and teachers of the temple that He might receive the blessing of the consecratory prayers.[21]

This critical episode in the life of our Lord may suffice to satisfy our curiosity regarding the first thirty years of His earthly life. It shows us that the all-consuming objective of His life was to carry

---

21   Shepard, 51.

out His Father's work. The scene that presents Him sitting among the Jewish doctors, listening and speaking, debating and teaching, is proof enough that He was already fit for such a role at the age of twelve. It also shows how deeply His early years were steeped in the study of the Law, the Prophets, and the Psalms. According to Jewish tradition, as a small boy He would have been taught by His parents, afterward by the town's elders, and finally by His own personal communion with God.

Now, the young Jesus' mind was completely open to the Father's being. He continually grew in the favor and knowledge of God, and His singular focus was to fill His heart with the awareness and presence of God. So when He spoke, it was not as one drawing on knowledge that was above Him, but as one whose mind inhabited the very summit of all wisdom. We must never forget that Christ was Himself "the Word of God," in the sense that He was expressive wisdom itself, whose expressions carried the force of actions. His utterances were at one and the same time word and action.

The activity of His body was the direct consequence of the activity of His mind. The evangelists write that He spoke only what He heard from God; and what He heard from God, He did. Saint John the Theologian writes about Him, "All things that the Father has are Mine. Therefore I said that He will take of Mine and declare *it* to you" (John 16:15). And St. Matthew: "No one knows the Son except the Father. Nor does anyone know the Father except the Son" (Matt. 11:27). The knowledge of the Father and the Son is one and the same, for they are one. Christ's mystical unity with the Father is the key to the mystery of His perfect wisdom.

Thus, Christ never underwent a formal religious education. Hence the bewilderment of the people: "The Jews marveled, saying, 'How does this Man know letters, having never studied?'" (John 7:15). By "having never studied," they mean that He was never discipled by any of the great rabbis, never sat at the feet of an illustrious Pharisee, never imbibed the opinions of the schools. His knowledge, that is, did not come from a human teacher—for it originated in the Father. The years He lived in Nazareth before His manifestation were passed in the silent pursuit of the awareness that all that was the Father's was His. The Father's will, and wisdom, and work—these were all His. The identity of the Eternal Word and the Incarnate Son was one. "I and *My* Father are one" (John 10:30). The Torah was stamped firmly in His heart, and the history of the patriarchs and prophets of Israel was alike to Him a living book. This frame of mind enabled Him to finish the Father's work: "I have glorified You on the earth. I have finished the work which You have given Me to do" (John 17:4).

It is inconceivable, therefore, for us to suppose that the unreported years that Jesus spent in Nazareth between the ages of twelve and thirty were passed without a profound inward movement, without a great flourishing of wisdom, that was the result of a process that began when He was just a small boy. We may imagine that those early years, which for humans are normally a period of mental growth, were for Him a bursting open of spiritual vision that disclosed to Him all truth about reality and what is above nature. This was His "schooling," similar to the school of the prophets; and His teacher was the Spirit of God, who prepared Him to become a Teacher far above the teachers of Israel. He who came to fulfill the Law must necessarily be greater than the Lawgiver, Moses: "You have heard that it was said to those of old . . . But I say to you" (Matt. 5:21, 22). "Before Abraham was, I AM" (John 8:58). "Yet I say to you that in this place there is *One* greater than the temple" (Matt. 12:6).

In consideration of the enormous burden placed on His shoulders by the Father—to be the Light of the World, Redeemer, Savior, and Champion over death—it was necessary that in wisdom and might, and everything else besides, He become the Alpha and Omega, the beginning and end. He needed to combine in Himself all heavenly and earthly knowledge, to become the culmination of all that the patriarchs and prophets were; in essence, He must possess all final authority: "All authority has been given to Me in heaven and on earth" (Matt. 28:18). Thus, the Virgin Birth by the Holy Spirit was the great prerequisite that enabled Him to grant mankind its new birth from His own flesh and bone.

The anthem sung by the angelic choir on the day of Jesus' birth celebrated man's new incorporation into the Kingdom of Heaven—no longer as a servant or a temporary passerby, but as a co-heir with Christ of everything that is God's: "But the saints of the Most High shall receive the kingdom, and possess the kingdom forever, even forever and ever" (Dan. 7:18). Since the day of His birth, therefore, Christ has united in His Person everything needed for humanity to be made worthy to stand before God, blameless, to the praise of His glory.

When Christ reached the age of thirty (the age at which a Levite officially took on his ministerial role), He was finally ready to take up His extraordinary mission. The emotion and conviction of His redemptive vocation began to press on His heart with maximum force; the divine voice inside began to recite His calling with an unrelenting certainty; and the deepest recesses of His mind began to prophesy that the fullness of time had come. Thus, the sacred yoke that the angelic voices prophesied would be placed on His infant shoulders was now to be taken up. He turned His steps resolutely toward Bethabara, where the Baptist was carrying out his preparatory work.

CHAPTER FOUR

The Baptism and Temptation of Christ

John the Baptist Prepares the Way for the Messiah

John the Baptist was charged with a uniquely significant mission. The Jewish nation had succumbed to a sort of despair due to their prolonged wait for a redeemer. The national conscience fell into a stupor; sin had slowly eaten away at their moral fiber, and Satan had wreaked havoc with their worship and destroyed their hopes. But once the call was heard, from the midst of this wasteland, to the near inauguration of a Kingdom, the people's hopes were suddenly rekindled. After being downtrodden for so long under the heel of the Romans, hearing the invitation to salvation revived the spirit of the people. Finally, after they had passed through so many dark days of oppression, the first rays of the "Day of the Lord" began to streak over the horizon. This rekindling of Israel's hope was the foremost task of John the Baptist; and it constituted the most important phase in the preparation for the coming Messiah.

But the most dangerous threat to the success of the Baptist's work, and by corollary to the Messiah's work, was the people's initial confusion of their identities. So when the Baptist first began his announcement of the coming Kingdom, he immediately hastened to add that he himself was not the awaited Messiah, but was rather one sent before Him whose job it was to clear His path. The Baptist's work was foretold by Isaiah the Prophet, who defined his role simply as that of a voice crying out in the wilderness:

> Now this is the testimony of John, when the Jews sent priests and Levites from Jerusalem to ask him, "Who are you?"
>
> He confessed, and did not deny, but confessed, "I am not the Christ." . . .
>
> Then they said to him, "Who are you, that we may give an answer to those who sent us? What do you say about yourself?"
>
> He said: "I *am*
>
> 'The voice of one crying in the wilderness:
>
> "Make straight the way of the LORD,"'
>
> as the prophet Isaiah said." (John 1:19–23)

From this the Pharisees understood him as claiming to be nothing more than the Messiah's forerunner.

However, John the Baptist was not satisfied with merely announcing that the Messiah was coming; he went on to describe what kind of person He would be. He proclaimed that the Messiah was "from above" and "above all," that He was sent by God and spoke in God's place. He also explained that he himself was from the earth and spoke from below; and that though he baptized the people, he was not worthy to stoop and unlatch the sandal of the coming One. "The Father loves the Son, and has given all things into His hand" (John 3:35). The Baptist thus introduced the people to the idea of the Messiah's heavenly nature and that He would baptize with the Holy Spirit. His final analysis of the Forerunner-Messiah relationship was that the Messiah was the Bridegroom, but he was the friend of the Bridegroom; the Messiah would increase, and he must decrease.

The sturdy and ascetic spirit of John the Baptist bore a strong affinity to that of Elijah, yet the two still had different approaches. Elijah appeared as a striking thunderbolt to denounce the false prophets and apostate king to whom he was sent; and he slayed four hundred false prophets by the Kishon River. John the Baptist, on the other hand, appeared as the first sunbeam of a new morning in Israel's history; his mission was to scatter the darkness that had oppressed the people's vision for so many centuries. His booming voice announced that the dawn was breaking, and that the people needed to wake up and open their eyes to the emerging light; for the Lord was nigh, and "the kingdom of heaven is at hand!" (Matt. 3:2). He was sent to restore the people's hope, to remind them of the covenant, and to realize the dreams of their fathers. This was indeed the single proper introduction to the Messiah's advent, for His work was the fulfillment of Abraham's greatest longings since receiving the promise.

All the Baptist's zeal was focused on moving the nation to repentance, with the intention of renewing their minds and cleansing their bodies. Josephus says the following regarding him:

Herod slew John, who was called the Baptist; he was a good man, and commanded the Jews to exercise virtue . . . and so to come to baptism; for that washing would be acceptable to Him, if they made use of it, not just for the remission of some sins, but also for the purification of the body, assuming that the soul was purified beforehand by righteousness. Now, when many came in crowds about him, for they were greatly moved by hearing his words, Herod, who feared lest the great influence John had over the people might put it into his power and inclination to raise a rebellion (for they seemed ready to do anything he advised), thought it best to put him to death to prevent any mischief he might cause, and not bring himself into difficulties, by sparing a man who might make him repent.[22]

John's work was the embodiment of the deepest aspiration of the Old Testament prophets—which was to announce the inauguration of the Kingdom of God. Thus, it would not be wrong to think of the Baptist as aiding the Jewish people in taking their first few steps into the New Testament era; for the briefest statement of his objective was to prepare the people's minds and hearts to receive the coming Kingdom. The evangelists, indeed, speak approvingly and even glowingly regarding John the Baptist; they present his character as so intimately bound up with the Christian gospel that he almost appears to wear the Christian mantle. He, however, had not in his lifetime taken one actual step into the New Testament Kingdom. For after offering many laudations in John's favor, Christ spoke this final verdict regarding him: "He who is least in the kingdom of heaven is greater than he" (Matt. 11:11). Hence, John's tongue ceased from its work the moment Christ took His first steps toward opening the Kingdom: "This joy of mine is fulfilled. He must increase, but I *must decrease*" (John 3:29, 30). And Christ's statement places him in his true position: "I do not receive testimony from man, but I say these things that you may be saved. He was the burning and shining lamp, and you were willing for a time to rejoice in his light" (John 5:34, 35).

The Teacher in the Wilderness

THE BAPTIST LIVED A LIFE of seclusion in the Jordanian desert along the western bank of the Dead Sea. It was a rough existence, full of asceticism, struggle, and total deprivation of all worldly pleasures. He contented himself with whatever bounty nature happened

---

22   Josephus, Antiquities 18.2.116–119.

to produce for him: bits of honey produced by bees living in the rocks, or else flitting locusts, which he would capture, roast, and eat. He also found sufficient covering (as had Elijah) in a hairy coat of camel's hide and a leather belt to gird his waist. This was the attire adopted by those desert ascetics whose occupation in life was to keep nocturnal vigils in prayer and worship. This lifestyle was also the consequence of an inner sorrow John felt for the moral degeneracy of the Jewish nation—a sorrow very similar to the laments of the last prophets of the Old Testament era.

His distress over the nation found its counterpart in Daniel's grief: "In those days I, Daniel, was mourning three full weeks. I ate no pleasant food, no meat or wine came into my mouth" (Dan. 10:2, 3). But the Baptist's heart was perhaps more deeply cut by the people's sins, because he knew they would become the Messiah's burden. Indeed, the darkness of their transgressions had become so opaque that the Baptist felt the pressing need for the Messiah's advent more urgently than ever. The one thing that gave him courage to go out and speak with such fervor was his conviction that the Messiah was really at the doors. It was the inner divine voice that finally prompted him to abandon his lonely abode and appear before the public with his startling message: "Repent, for the kingdom of heaven is at hand!" (Matt. 3:2).

The Baptist therefore did not spare the slightest trace of energy within him till he had fully and faithfully discharged his mission. One of the most startling metaphors he used to jolt the hierarchy of his day was that God would use a winnowing fan to thoroughly clean out His threshing floor and separate the wheat from the chaff; the one would be stored up and the other burned. Only those found worthy could enter the Kingdom of God. And the Baptist vigorously repudiated the idea that the chief rulers and religious authorities— who could boast of only a vain and external piety—would have a privileged place in the Kingdom. *Repentance* was the first credential for entering the Kingdom; and water baptism was the cardinal sign accepted by penitents that they were consecrating themselves for the Messiah's advent.

This was foreordained in Ezekiel: "Then I will sprinkle clean water on you, and you shall be clean; I will cleanse you from all your filthiness and from all your idols. I will give you a new heart and put a new spirit within you; I will take the heart of stone out of your flesh and give you a heart of flesh" (Ezek. 36:25, 26). And Zechariah had predicted that God would do a new work in Israel: "In that day a fountain shall be opened for the house of David and for the inhabitants of Jerusalem, for sin and for uncleanness" (Zech. 13:1). Malachi likewise declared that baptism would one day be used to distinguish the good from the wicked: "Behold, I send My messenger [John the Baptist], / And he will prepare the way before Me. / And the Lord, whom you seek, / Will suddenly come to His temple, / Even the Messenger of the covenant, / In whom you delight. / Behold, He is coming, says the Lord of hosts. . . . / He will sit as a refiner and a purifier of silver. . . . / Then you shall again discern / Between the righteous and the wicked, / Between one who serves God / And one who does not serve Him" (Mal. 3:1, 3, 18).

John the Baptist's Work Compared to the Messiah's Work

JOHN THE BAPTIST'S UNIQUE ABILITY to move an entire nation to repentance, and to submit them to the rite of water baptism, lay in the fact that the people saw him to be a man of authentic virtue and a sincere desire to execute his calling. A few who were especially drawn to him by his simple, honest, and unadorned spirit became his disciples. He laid down no laws for the people except that they should display conduct befitting repentance. A most excellent feature of his preaching policy was the fact that he would never bid a person to abandon their employment, no matter what it was; the person's duty was to carry out that employment in absolute good faith. He applied this policy even to such disreputable occupations as soldiery and tax collecting, and so these types of people were particularly drawn to him. The eye of the Forerunner was always on the heart of the people and not on their station in society or their type of employment.

Now, when we come to compare the Baptist's teaching with that of Christ, we really find it to be only a *preparation* of the heart and mind, and not a *renewal* of them. The requests he made of the people did not touch the deepest essence of humanity as did those of Christ; he could never claim to require the absolute loyalty and self-sacrifice of the people in the way Christ did. Christ did not deliver commands in the same manner as the Torah—that is, leaving it up to the individual to find enough strength and resolve to carry them out. Instead, Christ delivered commands along with the very power of His Spirit, offering the believer special grace to carry them out if he believed with all his heart.

So John the Baptist knew that in order for hearts to be changed, a distinctive power from on high was needed. He therefore left such divine acts to be accomplished by the Messiah: "He who is coming after me is mightier than I" (Matt. 3:11). He did his utmost to lead and guide, knowing that the Messiah alone had the power to renew and transform. In other words, John understood the limits of his mission, and despite the fiery prophetic zeal that dwelt in him, he could not exceed the limitations of a prophet. He could prophesy but not fulfill; he could teach but not transform; he could urge repentance but not lift man to a higher state. He had a settled conviction that the coming One would make all things new, and he was satisfied in sounding the trumpet and waiting in joy for His appearance. His own disciples could not elevate him beyond the modest status he set for himself: "He . . . whose sandals I am not worthy to carry" (Matt. 3:11). John's disciples knew indeed that he was sent by God, but he was only a lamp burning for a time, through the darkness of the night; and that lamp's glow would soon be absorbed and overtaken by the brilliance of the rising sun.

The Baptism of Christ

The baptism of Jordan was a prelude to the baptism of which He would later speak, the baptism of His passion.
FULTON SHEEN, *LIFE OF CHRIST*

FINALLY, CHRIST ARRIVES AT BETHABARA after a long journey from Nazareth. The three-day journey provided Him with ample opportunity to reflect on all the things He was told by His mother— about her encounter with the angel during the Annunciation, and about the prophecy regarding the world's salvation being placed on His own shoulders. He must have traveled contemplating the immense weight of His mission; and yet the Spirit was ever preparing His mind to receive the direct missives of heaven regarding His work, as well as guiding Him to focus on the inner divine voice.

When the hurried reader comes to the story about Christ submitting to John's baptism, it easily gives rise to confusion or misunderstanding in the mind. The event needs precise theological interpretation for a meaningful reading. Now, we cannot imagine Christ approaching baptism in the same mindset as everyone else—that is, for the purification of sin; for He was Himself the Redeemer who had come to purge the world of sin. Nevertheless, to all appearances, Christ approached John's baptism under that very pretext. And up to that point, John might have really believed that Jesus was in need of baptism, if not for the fact that his inward eyes were opened to see the infinite gulf that separated his status from Christ's. And this is expressed at their initial meeting recorded in the Gospel of Matthew: "Then Jesus came from Galilee to John at the Jordan to be baptized by him. And John *tried* to prevent Him, saying, 'I need to be baptized by You, and are You coming to me?' But Jesus answered and said to him, 'Permit *it to be so* now, for thus it is fitting for us to fulfill all righteousness.' Then he allowed Him" (Matt. 3:13–15).

A simple, lowly interpretation of this passage would be that the "righteousness" that needed fulfilling was Christ's abject humility in submitting to the rite as a human being. The loftier theological interpretation, on the other hand, is that Christ came to the baptism *carrying humanity in Him.* He did not approach for His own need, since He was the "Son of the Highest," as declared by the angel of the Annunciation; it was rather for the sake of the humanity He bore in His body that He approached the baptismal waters.

Theology teaches us that the Divine Logos put on a human body in order to renew humanity, or to say it another way, to recreate humanity anew; but before cooperating with the Holy Spirit to grant humanity that new spiritual nature, it was necessary that He first submit to John's baptism of water. For after the baptism was completed and Christ rose from the water, the heavens were immediately opened, and the Holy Spirit came down and rested upon Him.

By the same token, when the Gospels speak of Christ suffering in the body, we say that we suffered *with Him*; when He dies, we die *with Him*; when He is baptized, we are baptized *with Him*. The Son of God is naturally immortal; but, by participating with us in our human condition, He may die with us. And just as His sufferings and death were not for His sake but for ours, so was His baptism not for Him but for us. Everything that Christ underwent in the body, He underwent so that the humanity that was His could be joined to and blessed by the divinity that was His.

The Baptist himself also offers us a beautiful interpretation. He says that Christ approached the baptism so that he (John) might proclaim Him to be the Messiah as man, and that heaven might proclaim Him to be the Messiah as Son of God:

> "I did not know Him; *but that He should be revealed to Israel,* therefore I came baptizing with water." And John bore witness, saying, "I saw the Spirit descending from heaven like a dove, and He remained upon Him. I did not know Him, but He who sent me to baptize with water said to me, 'Upon whom you see the Spirit descending, and remaining on Him, this is He who baptizes with the Holy Spirit.' And I have seen and testified that this is the Son of God." (John 1:31–34, emphasis added)

Once Christ emerged from the waters, the Holy Spirit lighted upon Him in the form of a dove. It was as if the Father was now presenting His perfect oblation—"This is My beloved Son, in whom I am well pleased"—as the sacrifice for the world. This was the voice that revealed the testimony to the Baptist: "And I have seen and testified that this is the Son of God" (John 1:34). And with the support of this dual testimony—of the prophetic voice of the Baptist, and of the heavenly voice of the Father—Christ went out in power to begin His redemptive ministry.

The Temptation

Adam was tempted and defeated by the enemy;
Christ was tempted and defeated the enemy.
ALFRED EDERSHEIM,
THE LIFE AND TIMES OF JESUS THE MESSIAH

AND NOW CHRIST, HAVING RECEIVED His divine mission by the audible voice of the Father and the visible token of the Spirit, went forth with this double testimony as evidence for all to see that God was at work in His ministry. But such a ministry required that Christ face the Adversary in combat as a human being, using those spiritual weapons with which human nature was particularly endowed; and this would provide Him with the certitude of His superior authority over the prince of this world. If Christ came to inaugurate the Kingdom in the midst of this world, then the power and authority of the prince of this world must first be broken—hence the necessity for the face-off in the wilderness. And Christ underwent this great test without the aid of His divine authority, that He might genuinely stand in our place. "In whatever Christ gained the victory, we gained the victory too."[23] Thus, in this fierce battle with evil, humanity rose victorious, for in whatever Christ succeeded bodily, we succeeded verily. The Spirit therefore moved Him into the arena where He would engage in an official confrontation with the enemy—the howling wilderness, Satan's home turf.

In order to further understand the significance of this trial of Christ by the enemy, we may refer to Christ's own comments regarding their relative powers, and in particular, as they are evidenced throughout the period of His ministry (as in the cases of healing illnesses and casting out devils). His words were these: "But if I cast out demons by the Spirit of God, surely the kingdom of God has come upon you. Or how can one enter a strong man's house and plunder his goods, unless he first binds the strong man? And then he will plunder his house" (Matt. 12:28, 29). It is evident that it is Christ Himself who bound the "strong man," the devil; and the "binding" entailed exposing the devil's deceit and stripping his diabolical methods of their power. Saint Luke provides us with an enlightening

---

23   Edersheim, 294.

detail on this point in his Gospel: "When a strong man, fully armed, guards his own palace, his goods are in peace. But when a stronger than he comes upon him and overcomes him, he takes from him all his armor in which he trusted, and divides his spoils" (Luke 11:21, 22). That is, after the strong man has been defeated, his weaponry is stripped and confiscated and his spoils divided.

"Then Jesus was led up by the Spirit into the wilderness to be tempted by the devil" (Matt. 4:1). The temptation on the mount was an event foreordained in the economy of God as a necessary prelude to Christ's earthly ministry. Christ was coming to serve humanity, so He could not allow Satan to roam unbridled and harass mankind, and so to impede His work. Christ had to disarm the strong man of the weapons that were used to secure his seizure of the "house," which was mankind. Satan was *the strong man*, but Christ was *the stronger*. And so, here we have the beginning of the epic battle waged between Christ and Satan over the disputed possession, humanity—a conflict that would reach its climax at the Cross.

"And when He had fasted forty days and forty nights, afterward He was hungry" (Matt. 4:2). Christ's fasting is here made the occasion of the first temptation; in other words, the trial was begun by striking at His *flesh*, since it was the skin of humanity itself that He bore. Christ's union with humanity was what gave Satan the "right," as it were, to tempt Him; and so it was critical that Christ fortify His flesh (humankind) by fasting. And the Gospel's statement that He was "hungry" is an indication that He had reached the uttermost limits of human endurance in depriving the body of food and drink. It was at this point that Satan made his appearance, as he construed it to be the most opportune time to make his introductory attack. For hunger is a type of fleshly desire, and it was precisely this fleshly desire that brought about the fall of Adam and Eve. Satan approaches with a long and successful record in felling humans by the desire of the flesh; and he accordingly appears to Christ wielding his favorite weapon.

"Now when the tempter came to Him, he said, 'If You are the Son of God, command that these stones become bread'" (Matt. 4:3). Here the tempter exploits the state of extreme physical weakness in which he finds Christ to suggest a solution that is at variance with His mission: he recommends the exertion of Christ's divine power to fulfill His own needs rather than the needs of humanity. But to submit to His own will by such an act would constitute a direct violation of the messianic precept: "I have come down from heaven, not to do My own will, but the will of Him who sent Me" (John 6:38). In addition, Satan's timing of this first temptation seems to be cunningly intentional. For had he not just heard (at the Jordan) the voice from heaven declaring Jesus to be God's Son? What more fitting, therefore, than to see direct proof of this declaration by an authoritative act by this Son of God, such as turning stones to bread? Thus did Satan always try to drive a wedge into that perfect unity between Father and Son.

"But He answered and said, 'It is written, "Man shall not live by bread alone, but by every word that proceeds from the mouth of God"'" (Matt. 4:4). Here Christ parries the attack by wielding the word of God before Satan; and His method is meant to be instructive for us as well. By the inherent authority of God's word, man is to throw down the weapons of the enemy. Our ultimate defense is obedience to God's will: "My food is to do the will of Him who sent Me, and to finish His work" (John 4:34). Satan's artifice is to feign sympathy with man's plight and to suggest that a person perform an illicit act (theft, for example) in order to hold onto life and not die. Christ's response, however, is that man's life is not sustained just by bread, but also by God's word.

Finding his weapon against Christ's flesh being torn from his hands and dashed to the ground, Satan proceeds to launch his second attack, this time predicated on Christ's own remark about God's word.

> Then the devil took Him up into the holy city, set Him on the pinnacle of the temple, and said to Him, "If You are the Son of God, throw Yourself down. For it is written: 'He shall give His angels charge over you,' and, 'In *their* hands they shall bear you up, / Lest you dash your foot against a stone.'" (Matt. 4:5, 6)

This is Satan's age-old weapon of employing the word of God for the purpose of self-aggrandizement. We find it also to be the same weapon used by the Pharisees when they demanded of Him a "sign"; but He responded to them that no sign would be given them except that of Jonah the Prophet. In the hands of *the strong man*, God's word becomes a weapon for self-glorification; in the hands of *the stronger*, it is a weapon for repentance. In addition to all this, we may notice the sheer opposition in thought between Satan, who was urging Jesus to reveal His messianic identity by sensational means, and Christ, who would reveal it only by God's appointed road of death and Resurrection.

"Jesus said to him, 'It is written again, "You shall not tempt the LORD your God"'" (Matt. 4:7). Jesus here draws on the story of Israel's rebellion against Moses and Aaron on account of their thirst: "You shall not tempt the LORD your God as you tempted *Him* in Massah" (Deut. 6:16). Satan's crafty suggestion here is that, if God really does rescue His children, and if Jesus is indeed the Son of God, then God ought surely to rescue Him, even were He to fling Himself from the roof of the temple. The temptation was ostensibly aimed at Jesus on account of His title "Son of God"; but Jesus rather says that it was a temptation aimed directly at the Father Himself. The implied question was, is God present or not? Will God keep the promise stated in Psalm 91 or not? It is a temptation to doubt

God's word, a challenge to test whether God hears us or not. Jesus responds that such "trials" of God are futile.

"Again, the devil took Him up on an exceedingly high mountain, and showed Him all the kingdoms of the world and their glory. And he said to Him, 'All these things I will give You if You will fall down and worship me'" (Matt. 4:8, 9). This temptation involved a mental vision of the world's kingdoms without any transportation of the body. It is a special endowment of man that he may peer into the essence of things without seeing the complete outward image: a revelation of the mind and not of the eyes. For if a person were to be perched on an extremely high point on earth, looking down, he would not in fact be able to discern any nations. Now Christ possessed this perspicacity to the maximum degree; and when Luke's Gospel states that this vision occurred in a moment's time, we conclude that it was tantamount to a "rapture" of Christ's mind. Satan's weaponry here is aimed at the Father directly. For in offering Jesus the kingdoms of the world as spoils for submitting to himself (Satan), rather than to the Father, he was actually attempting to undermine the Father's plan of saving the world through the Son's sacrificial death.

Satan was capable of offering the glory of the entire world to Jesus at the cost of a single bow at his feet, for he was indeed the prince of this world: "for *this* has been delivered to me, and I give it to whomever I wish" (Luke 4:6). The reader should understand, however, that the "world" placed at Satan's disposal is not the world of goodness and beauty but the world of sin, futility, and false glory. Our daily prayer is that God Himself will rule the world with love, justice, and grace; and this is accomplished through His children who work for the increase of liberty and peace among humanity. Inasmuch as humanity opens its ears to the voice of truth and love, insomuch will the world progress in goodness and peace.

"Then Jesus said to him, 'Away with you, Satan! For it is written,

"You shall worship the LORD your God, and Him only you shall serve."'" (Matt. 4:10). The words *Him only you shall serve* imply the idea that to accept kingship over the nations of the world, apart from God's rule, is really a form of treason against God. This last temptation is, in fact, the very snare into which Satan himself fell. His ancient opposition to God degraded his once-glorious preeminence over all the angels to a sordid rule over the material world. Christ's response to the final trial was in essence a complete and uncompromising surrender to the Father's will. In place of the delectable items offered by the devil, He chose the road of suffering, of crucifixion and death—and in so doing, defeated those enemies of man.

From a more general scope, the concealed purpose of the enemy in imposing these three temptations on Christ was the disruption of His vocational mission; and this disruption, it was surmised, could be best effected by disrupting Christ's relationship to God—which was characterized by obedience, trust, and faithfulness. Christ's *obedience* to God was tested in the suggestion to change the stones to bread. His *trust* in God was tested when He was tempted to throw Himself down from the wings of the temple. His *faithfulness* to God was tried when all the kingdoms of the earth were offered to Him in exchange for a single prostration.

Hence we find that the dual episodes of Christ's Baptism and temptation are to be read as a single unit, dovetailing into the launch of His ministry. For at the Baptism, Christ is chosen by God and commissioned for the great work; and at the temptation, Christ safeguards this election and commission by showing the utmost obedience, trust, and faithfulness to the Father as Israel's King. In other words, before the ministry could begin, the Father needed to ordain Jesus as His official deputy in founding His Kingdom on earth. Christ was tried and proven; and so all that would occur over the course of His ministry would be on behalf of the heavenly King.

CHAPTER FIVE

Christ Begins His Ministry in Judea

Miracles in Christ's Life

The miracles performed by Christ were intended to be, in effect, manifestations of His Person; and naturally, therefore, they were intimately woven into His teaching. They were a visible commentary of sorts on His dual status as Son of God and Son of Man. They were also meant to turn the minds of the people away from the petty diversions of material life and toward the eternal truths of the Holy Spirit. When Jesus raised a man from the dead, He taught mankind to scorn death and to stand in awe before the Creator of Life. When He gave sight to a blind man, He taught mankind to spurn the limitations of physical life and to seek further knowledge of the Author of Light. We should view miracles therefore as a guide, not for the mind but for the heart, on its journey toward a fuller knowledge of God.

So each miracle is a visible manifestation of God's creative power, and it enables the mind to appreciate God's immanent presence. When, for example, we look at nature, with its quiet movement of sun and earth and oceans, we habitually forget to see God in it; but His fingerprints are all over. We forget to see the miraculous in creation simply because it was always here. But if we were able to place ourselves in a position prior to nature's existence and to watch the creation of the cosmos out of nothing, then we would confess that everything is truly astounding and miraculous. And nature here includes man himself, who has eyes to see—but we never say that God gave man the "miracle" of sight. When, however, a man who was born blind has his sight suddenly restored to him, we call it a miracle, because the stamp of God's power is clearly read on the incident and on the man.

Now, the salient point here is that the power and force that are latent in miracles can be transferred to the believer who makes faith in Christ his chief priority. As He says in the Gospel of John, "Most assuredly, I say to you, he who believes in Me, the works that I do he will do also; and greater *works* than these he will do, because I go to My Father. And whatever you ask in My name, that I will do, that the Father may be glorified in the Son. If you ask anything in My name, I will do *it*" (John 14:12–14). A sincere faith in Christ unites the believer with Him; and consequently, Christ will work wonders through him, as long as he makes his requests with confidence and perseverance: "Whatever things you ask in prayer, believing, you will receive" (Matt. 21:22).

When a believer achieves such a state of cooperation with Christ and grows accustomed to living on a plane above nature, the supernatural things he does are no longer "miracles" but common works. When seen from a higher plane, all miracles appear as God's ordinary workings. Miracles appear as stupendous things to us now because our minds are ruled by natural law; any deed that seems to defy natural law becomes a marvel in our eyes. But once we are lifted to higher planes by faith in Christ, we will recognize miracles as the usual workings of God's Kingdom stealing into our world and functioning not in obedience to the world's laws but by virtue of its own independent authority.

The First Miracle

"THERE WAS A WEDDING IN Cana of Galilee, and the mother of Jesus was there. Now both Jesus and His disciples were invited to the wedding" (John 2:1, 2). It was for good reason that Christ started to manifest Himself to the world in the setting of a wedding feast. The Gospels of Matthew and Mark describe the launch of Christ's ministry by the announcement of the "Kingdom of God."[24] Matthew gives us a further hint into the nature of the Kingdom with these words: "The kingdom of heaven is like a certain king *who arranged a marriage*" (Matt 22:2, emphasis added). Indeed, Jesus Himself compares His entire time on earth to an extended wedding feast: "Can the friends of the bridegroom fast while the bridegroom is with them?" (Mark 2:19). The Lord clearly saw Himself as a bridegroom who came to celebrate the inauguration of the Kingdom with His Bride.

Now, St. John highlights this symbolism by giving us the story of Christ's attendance at a wedding in Cana of Galilee. His status as the divine Bridegroom was indeed unknown until that event; but the mystery started to be unveiled the moment the words were uttered: "They have no wine" (John 2:3). How could a marriage feast go on without wine? There was a common saying among the Jews: "There is no mirth without wine."[25] Joy had departed from Israel! Wine was also seen as a theological symbol of man's joy in the salvation that would come during the messianic era. The idea that the joy of salvation had departed from Israel was a dirge constantly sung by the Old Testament prophets. And John understood this quite well.

"When they ran out of wine, the mother of Jesus said to Him, 'They have no wine'" (John 2:3). This statement is the pivot around which the entire story revolves. Christ comes to the wedding to supply the lack, and Mary reveals her vital role as intercessor. But

---

24 Mark 1:14; Matt. 4:17.
25 Pes. 109a (Talmud).

what is really going on here? What is the true story? The superficial onlookers who are attending the wedding feast assume that the presence of Christ and His circle of friends—who make up a large number—was unaccounted for in the coordinator's planning, and this is what caused the wine vats to run dry.

But if we look deeper into the story, especially with the spiritual eyes of St. John, we find a second meaning running through the events. Christ's presence has not only caused the lack of wine but has also revealed its insufficiency as a "sign." For can there ever be wine at the Lord's table that is not eucharistic? Can a cup of wine from which Christ drinks ever fail to be the Lord's cup? Wine was a symbol of man's fellowship with God. And therefore any wine that passes through Christ's hands must become a full and perfect sign of worship offered to God.

The guests' eyes were on Christ to see what He would do. They had heard the news that had spread to all the surrounding cities regarding Him, especially that of the Baptist's striking testimony to Christ as the Messiah and Bridegroom. Mary's own heart was pulsating in earnestness for some miraculous work, and He delivered according to her desire and much more. But here we read of the one admonition He gave her, which is that she hastened His journey to the Cross. "Jesus said to her, 'Woman, what does your concern have to do with Me? My hour has not yet come'" (John 2:4). The hour of the Cross was set in the Father's plan, and her request for a miracle was an interference in that hour. For to work a miracle is to finally announce His mission; and to do so meant taking the first step in His descent toward death. Any good work He did would be counted against Him by His enemies; so here, in requesting the "sign," the mother was unwittingly announcing to His enemies the beginning of the conflict.

"Jesus said to them, 'Fill the waterpots with water.' And they filled them up to the brim" (John 2:7). These were large ceramic waterpots, each of which held over one hundred gallons; and so filling them to the brim required a considerable amount of time and labor. Thus, in a way, Jesus sets these servants (Greek: "deacons") to a task that is comparable to the ritualistic preparations of a religious service. The fact that the servants filled the pots *to the brim* is an example of Christ's unfailing generosity: "Of His fullness we have all received" (John 1:16). Christ came to inaugurate the era of fullness and grace.

"Draw *some* out now, and take *it* to the master of the feast" (John 2:8). Jesus naturally would see to it that the master of the feast would be the first to taste of the new wine, because Jewish tradition required the host or elder of a dinner feast to initiate the tasting; then the cup would circulate among the guests one by one until it reached the youngest member. But possibly His greater purpose would be to elicit the vocal testimony of the feast's master regarding the superior quality of this wine, which was the fruit of Christ's divine power. Any such sign required power to be poured forth from the Lord. He was the true vine, and the sap that dripped from Him was the true wine. The depth of Jesus' generosity was communicated to the master by the sweetness of the wine; and to many believers afterwards, that generosity is communicated by joyful gaiety in the heart.

Once the master of the feast tasted the new wine, he called for the bridegroom and asked in astonishment why the inferior wine was offered first and the better wine kept till last. It is clear that neither of them knew of the wonderful deed that had transpired. The simple reason for this was that the waterpots—which were reserved for handwashing—were always kept at the entrance of the dwelling. And due to the immense weight of these pots, they were never moved from their position, even after being filled with wine. Therefore, the miraculous change occurred far from the notice of the master and his guests. And here we encounter the mystical sign in this deed: it indicates the changing of all things from old to new. This human bridegroom, celebrating an earthly feast according to the regulations of the law, is now superseded by the divine Bridegroom, who has come to celebrate the heavenly feast according to grace. The traditional water of purification has now become the wine of feasting.

Jesus at the Passover

FROM CANA IN GALILEE, JESUS went down to Capernaum with His mother and disciples for a brief interlude.[26] He had forsaken Nazareth and now made Capernaum His new home city; for He had been dishonored by the city of His childhood and could not do there many wonders because of their poverty of faith. (Joseph is not mentioned anymore, presumably because he was by this point deceased.) And from Capernaum, Jesus makes His way with His new entourage to the holy city to celebrate the Jewish Passover.

The reader must observe that St. John's Gospel is unique in that it pays specific attention to the Lord's early activity in Jerusalem before the launch of His official ministry in Galilee. It was in Jerusalem, in fact, that Christ articulated His most theologically rich teaching; and it was in Jerusalem that He entered into the hottest disputes with the sages of Israel, those proud keepers of religious knowledge. Jesus believed fervently that "salvation is of the Jews"—as He remarked to the Samaritan woman—and so it was to the Jews of Jerusalem that He offered His most telling discourses. But it was to His Galilean disciples that He unfolded the mystery of the Kingdom

---

26 "After this He went down to Capernaum, He, His mother, His brothers, and His disciples; and they did not stay there many days" (John 2:12). "And leaving Nazareth, He came and dwelt in Capernaum, which is by the sea, in the regions of Zebulun and Naphtali" (Matt. 4:13).

of heaven—the true zenith of all religious knowledge—which they received with simplicity of heart.

Jesus typically focused the delivery of His teaching during the Jewish feasts, because the festive rites served as powerful illustrations for His message. There was the Feast of Tabernacles, for example, when the Levites filled the jars of the temple with water to be consecrated and poured out over the altar; and Jesus stood in the temple on that solemn day and cried out, "If anyone thirsts, let him come to Me and drink" (John 7:37). And at the Feast of Dedication, when the golden lampstand was lit to illumine the temple, Jesus said, "I am the light of the world" (John 8:12).

It is a striking fact that St. John viewed Jerusalem as the seminal stage for the delivery of Christ's most important teachings. And the tidings of His words and work went out from Jerusalem and reached Galilee before His arrival there to begin His missionary tours: "So when He came to Galilee, the Galileans received Him, having seen all the things He did in Jerusalem at the feast; for they also had gone to the feast" (John 4:45).

This was not, of course, Jesus' first visit to the holy city. The pilgrimage was a family tradition that had been observed from His earliest childhood; some have conjectured that His family had relatives and a family lodging to harbor them while in the city. In any event, He now comes as One who is visiting His own city and His own special people. He comes bearing the weight of a new responsibility on His shoulders and a new mission in His heart: to gather His people into His arms. "O Jerusalem, Jerusalem, the one who kills the prophets and stones those who are sent to her! How often I wanted to gather your children together, as a hen gathers her chicks under *her* wings, but you were not willing!" (Matt. 23:37).

When He entered the precincts of the temple, Christ's eyes were met by a revolting sight. The outer court was filled with the sounds and smells of animals, of clanking coins, and of merchandise. It was the Court of the Gentiles, which meant that people from all over the earth came to worship in this very area. They came to experience the holiness of Yahweh's abode, but the racket of this marketplace obscured its sanctity. And since Jesus' mission was to save all peoples—the Jew first and then the Gentile—this scene especially wounded Him.

"When He had made a whip of cords, He drove them all out of the temple, with the sheep and the oxen, and poured out the changers' money and overturned the tables" (John 2:15, 16). We can only imagine the look of sheer terror that came across the faces of all those who bought and sold in that temple marketplace. The show of indignant anger the Lord displayed undoubtedly pricked the consciences of all those present and placed their sin in the clearest light. And the mighty deed was not just an act of reform; it had theological underpinnings as well. It was a symbol that the era of animal sacrifice was coming to a close. A temple without sacrifice would be merely an empty shell—an unmistakable declaration that the Messiah had arrived.

Nicodemus

SOON AFTER THE FOREGOING EVENTS, we meet with the first of those sparkling dialogues that are recorded for us between Christ and select individuals in the Gospels. Nicodemus, our Lord's interlocutor, is a Pharisee who represents the finest product of Jewish wisdom and law, and he approaches Christ bearing with him all the grandest hopes of Israel. In the dialogue he is confronted with the central tenets of Christianity—repentance, renewal, and resurrection—concepts that would boggle his mind for three full years until he witnessed their literal outworkings in the world.

Nicodemus initially regards Jesus as only a "rabbi," and he approaches Him with the typical pharisaical mindset. He is not expecting to hear about spiritual regeneration but rather about the older concepts of holiness and moral life. John the Baptist's statements about a kingdom had aroused feelings of anticipation and hope in his breast, and since Christ spoke openly and frequently about the Kingdom of God, he eagerly desired to hear more of His teaching.

Nicodemus directs his steps after nightfall toward the house in which Christ was staying (possibly that of the Apostle John). The late hour of the meeting is so impressed on the mind of John, in fact, that every subsequent mention of Nicodemus' name in the Gospel has appended to it the phrase, "who came to Him by night"—evidently implying that Nicodemus's faith began as a shadowy thing. The Lord receives him with a warm openness and pours out His heart to the Pharisee. And what ensues is a profound conflict of understanding between the old and the new.

Christ's central message to the Pharisee was that, in order to see the "kingdom" he so zealously desired, it was required of him to be "born again," or "anew," or "from above" (all legitimate translations). The reason people could not see the kingdom was the decrepit state of their spirits; people were overrun by the demands of the flesh, and this disabled their minds from comprehending truth. The natural (fleshly) eyes of man are restricted to seeing what is in nature; and so, if man wished to see anything past nature, he would need a new spiritual "birth"—new eyes would need to be born to him.

Nicodemus responds to this new doctrine with a question: "How can a man be born when he is old? Can he enter a second time into his mother's womb and be born?" (John 3:4). It is not an ignorant statement; he is not wondering how an old man can push himself back into the womb. Nicodemus realizes that Christ is referring to changing one's life, and doing it so dramatically that it is tantamount to a second birth. He is staggered at the difficulty of such a thing.

The reader must appreciate the depth of Nicodemus's question. Here is a Pharisee who has spent about sixty years of his life studying Hebrew wisdom, who is a recognized expert among the Jews, and who now asks a question so childlike in its simplicity that it makes it seem as if he had not really been living all those decades. That ego or self he had been studiously building up since he was even conscious of the self is now blown away in the self-emptying nature of that question. It is an admirable humility.

Christ's response is that he must be "born of water and the Spirit," a phrase that could not have been strange to Nicodemus's ears; for everyone had heard John the Baptist's saying that whereas he baptized with water, the Coming One would baptize with the Holy Spirit. God had divinely ordained the Baptist to prepare the entire extent of Judea to hear the sacred formula. It was an unfortunate fact, however, that in rejecting the baptism of John, the Pharisees had also rejected the word of the Holy Spirit in themselves. And in order to prevent Nicodemus from thinking that there could be any admixture or cooperation between the old man and the new man, Christ utters another striking teaching: "That which is born of the flesh is flesh, and that which is born of the Spirit is spirit." He says, in other words, that there can be no "progression" from flesh to spirit; a man can never by any spiritual effort transform his flesh into spirit. The flesh will always be the flesh, and that which is born of spirit will always be spiritual.

And to further aid Nicodemus's comprehension, Christ offers an analogy. He bids Nicodemus to imagine a tree standing in utter calm; then, all of a sudden, its branches begin to sway and bend, and its leaves begin to quiver and make a rustling sound. The observer immediately perceives that the tree has been made subject to a strong wind; the wind's source and substance, however, are invisible. Just so is everyone born of the Spirit. The unseen influence of the Holy Spirit is made evident by certain visible traits: by a person's words, his wisdom, his love, his courage, and his conduct in the world. In short, such a person becomes somebody he could never before have been. This is the effect of the second birth.

The Woman at the Well

FROM THE CONVERSATION WITH NICODEMUS we are transported swiftly by the Gospel of John to another rather long and intricate dialogue, that between Christ and the Samaritan woman. The Jews and Samaritans of the day had been driven apart by insurmountable barriers of animosity and pride; this was likely the reason Christ entered Samaria, in order to communicate to them the Father's love. The city of Shechem was the ancient capital of the land of Samaria, and it was originally the habitation of the Old Testament patriarchs. Shechem was made desolate by the exploits of John Hyrcanus, and in its place was built several miles away the more modern city of Nablus (or Neopolis, "the new city").

The Samaritans were referred to by the Jews as *Kuthim*, a title of disparagement, because they represented the remnants of Israel's ten northern tribes that were taken into captivity by the Assyrians and intermarried with foreign peoples. The historical episode that triggered the bitter feud between Jew and Samaritan was the series of reforms carried out by Nehemiah and Ezra in the fifth century BC to "purify" Jewish blood. They expelled from Jerusalem all who had intermarried with non-Jews. Not the slightest amount of pardon was allowed in the cleansing, despite the fact that the people of Samaria had pleaded earnestly for permission to assist in the building of the temple and for participation in Jewish worship. This complete expulsion from Jewish life kindled feelings of rage in the Samaritan breast that continue to this day.

> So He came to a city of Samaria which is called Sychar, near the plot of ground that Jacob gave to his son Joseph. Now Jacob's well was there. Jesus therefore, being wearied from *His* journey, sat thus by the well. It was about the sixth hour. A woman of Samaria came to draw water. Jesus said to her, "Give Me a drink." For His disciples had gone away into the city to buy food. (John 4:5–8)

Now, the question naturally arises, why did this woman travel all the way to this well to draw water, when the region was studded with wells easier to reach and from which water could more readily be drawn? And why did she choose noontime, which meant going out in the blistering heat of the oriental sun? The answer is simple, though a bit embarrassing. She was a woman of dishonorable reputation, and she took pains to avoid the company of her more blameless peers. The evangelist never expressly states such facts but leaves the reader to infer the truth from the narrative.

It is a remarkable scene. During the heat of midday, Christ approaches this individual whose character was questionable, whose female sex was spoken of by the rabbis in disdainful tones, and who likely held only the position of a servant in her household. And now observe how Christ breaks down the barrier of sex that divided man from woman; He breaks down the racial barrier that divided Jew from Samaritan; and He breaks down the social barrier that divided people of high rank from people of low. "Give Me a drink." It is a request to *receive*; but it is pleased with merely the intent in the other to *give*. A glaring paradox is present here. How can the very Fountain of living water request a draft from a dry cistern? It is because man's deficit can be turned into God's surplus. God puts Himself in need of us in order to eventually fill us.

The woman said to Him, "How is it that You, being a Jew, ask a drink from me, a Samaritan woman?" It was a fair question, and on the face of it, predictable enough. But there was more to it. Her perceptive eye saw that this was a holy man, and she reasoned that any interaction with Him might jeopardize her life of sin. She wanted quickly to stop the light from reaching her heart, and so she received His request with a contrived coldness and used the excuse of her shyness as a woman to repel His approach. But little did she know! The divine pursuit could not slacken, and the holy light could never be refracted by the darkness. She could try to resist the light, but she would be like one who beats the air and who eventually gives up and surrenders to it.

"If you knew the gift of God . . . you would have asked Him, and He would have given you living water." He points to Himself as the "gift" (Gr. *dorean*) given to wayward humanity, using the same word used in the immemorial verse, "For God so loved the world that He gave (Gr. *edoken*) His only begotten Son" (John 3:16). The term "living water" was an old Eastern expression that meant "running water." So in David we read the prayer, "My soul thirsts for You" (Ps. 63:1); it is the cry of one seeking spiritual life as intensely as a man dying of thirst seeks material water.

"Sir, You have nothing to draw with, and the well is deep. Where then do You get that living water?" Finally she allows the discussion to delve deeper! The Lord has made a very generous offer, one that defies reason; for such are God's gifts to us. But how does a sinner come to appreciate the gift of God when she is already satisfied with the gifts of the world? Will the dry bones of Ezekiel's vision live again? At least she has begun to call Him *Sir*—or *Lord* (Gr. *kyrie*)—which is a considerable advancement on *You, Jew*. Christ's skill in changing hearts is wielding its power in her, and she has begun to recognize His lordship over her.

"Where then do You get that living water?" It is a plausible but uninspired question. He has no bucket in which to draw up the water, so how is He supposed to give her any? This is how a typical soul acts. It places certain conditions on a possibility that turn it into an impossibility; and after it disables itself from achieving a good thing, it rests complacent in its inactivity and is relieved that it does not have to try. But the Lord always has solutions that defy such barriers. His ways transcend human capacity and human dreams. He "is able to do exceedingly abundantly above all that we ask or think, according to the power that works in us" (Eph. 3:20).

"Jesus answered and said to her, 'Whoever drinks of this water will thirst again, but whoever drinks of the water that I shall give him will never thirst. But the water that I shall give him will become in him a fountain of water springing up into everlasting life'" (John 4:13, 14). Christ here chooses material water as a metaphor to reflect the watering of a soul. The woman understands the nature of physical thirst, and so she will be led on to understand the nature of spiritual thirst and how it is satisfied. Physical thirst, once slated, soon drives a person to seek to be slated again; spiritual thirst, however, once slated, is permanently satisfied, for it is watered from the springs of eternal life.

And when Christ referred to "the water that I shall give him," He pointed to Himself as that water. He is the refreshing stream which, once poured on the human heart, totally quenches its thirst. The things of the world then lose their stranglehold on the soul. So Christ here plucks at a sensitive cord whose calming sound reverberates to the very depths of a heart grown tired with the pursuit of worldly pleasure. The more the heart drinks from the cistern of worldly pleasure, the more it thirsts; and as this futile process continues, despair begins quietly to creep in. And when Christ said that this water of life would cause a person to *never thirst*, the myriads on myriads of saints in heaven would have responded with a thunderous "Amen!"

With this moving promise the Lord succeeds in inviting the woman to a better life. She makes a request for this perfectly satisfying water. Her arms have grown weary of heaving two full pails of water such a long distance every day, and she would be glad to have her own thirst quenched. Jesus then says to her, "Go, call your husband, and come here." Yes indeed: she must bring the man she was living with and present him to Christ. The Lord makes this request to test her dedication to receiving the gift and to see how far His message had penetrated her conscience. The Lord's real focus is on the woman's own faith, not on her husband or her family, for it is through her faith and repentance that He intends to save the rest. He is prepared to forgive her sin, and therefore, He places this obligatory condition on her. She must decide.

And since this sin is the one obstacle to the offered gift, her confession will be her healing. As Christ previously hinted, once she drinks of this water, it will become a fountain within her, sending up fresh water both for her husband and for her town. He already knows her response: "I have no husband." It is her great shame. But Christ places His hand on the wound very gently and compassionately, like a physician applying anesthesia to a patient's injury before surgery. The Lord gradually takes her step by step till she reaches the point at which she says the unsayable. He has awakened her conscience.

Christ's immediate response is the acceptance of her confession. "Jesus said to her, 'You have well said, "I have no husband," for you have had five husbands, and the one whom you now have is not your husband; in that you spoke truly.'" This was the support she needed in order to overcome her deep reluctance. The Lord always speaks "a word in season to *him who is* weary" (Is. 50:4). Her deed was not good, but her confession was good, and it was accounted to her a noble act of truth. In thus showing how thoroughly He understood her life, the Lord begins to lift the veil concealing His Person by a little. For she had had five previous husbands, and we need not inquire into the sordid details of such a record if Christ Himself did not see fit to do so. One thing, however, is clear. It was a life full of betrayal and exploitation, and this she confessed even to her entire town: "Come, see a Man who told me all things that I ever did. Could this be the Christ?"

The Early Galilean Ministry

Healing of the Nobleman's Son

N ow after the two days He departed from there and went to Galilee" (John 4:43). After the Divine Sower had scattered the seed of the Word in Samaria, He tarried two days to make sure the seed had settled, then went up to Galilee. "And there was a certain nobleman whose son was sick at Capernaum. When he heard that Jesus had come out of Judea into Galilee, he went to Him and implored Him to come down and heal his son, for he was at the point of death" (John 4:46, 47). There is a consensus among scholars that this nobleman was a servant of Herod Antipas, tetrarch of Galilee. Some believe that he might be the Chuza of Luke 8:3, or possibly the Manaen of Acts 13:1.

The evangelist hurls us at once into the pulsating drama. The nobleman says to Him, "Sir, come down before my child dies!" The father's patience has completely run out. He is thrown into a wild hysteria over his sick son, and in his panic he forgets to employ the usual rules of courtesy. Whatever treatments the son was put through have proved futile, and he now totters on the edge of death. A son, so tender, so young, and so close to the heart of his compassionate father! Just like Martha, this nobleman had no idea that Christ's authority extended to the grave, and that Christ's word could recall those who had fallen under its dominion.

We may notice that the evangelist does not concern himself with the nobleman's identity, or with the son's name or age, or any like detail. It matters not whether this is a Jew or a Gentile, rich or poor. The one startling feature is the tyrannical grip of *time*—down to the very seconds—on the heart of one who is weak in faith. The Gospel always stresses the importance of faith without miracles; but this nobleman comes begging for a miracle without requesting faith! In his eyes, Christ is nothing but a wonder-worker. Today, we have adopted a similar view of the saints. They are extolled primarily for their miracle-working capabilities, and we take interest in them mainly for the favors they can do for us.

"Jesus said to him, 'Go your way; your son lives.' So the man believed the word that Jesus spoke to him, and he went his way" (John 4:50). There were three reasons that spurred Christ to say these words. First, the nobleman had undertaken a journey of at least 25 kilometers to see Him, and he came with a trusting attitude that the healing would take place. Second, the son was critically ill. This was a case of life and death put into Christ's hands, and so He was bound to judge in favor of life. Third, the father came to make his application to Christ with extreme earnestness, and this is God's express desire. If the pleas of the poor widow enabled her to prevail over the unjust judge (Luke 18), would not the pleas of this heartbroken father prevail over the righteous Judge?

The nobleman[27] receives the words uttered by Christ like an order delivered by a superior magistrate. We may imagine him making an official salute, offering a reverential bow, then turning

---

27   The Arabic translates this man's role as "royal officer," which conveys the sense that he served in a high government or royal court. Edersheim calls him a "court-official."

and starting his journey home in obedience to the command. And in his hands, or his heart rather, he is entrusted with a royal jewel that he is to safeguard until he reaches his final destination. But the danger loomed over the father's head the entire way home, for he had only the healing *word* with him, and not the healer Himself. He had to trust that Christ's word carried power in spite of His physical absence. The nobleman thus represents every person who receives and believes and submits to the Gospel and carries it with him like treasure in his heart—even though the Master of the Gospel is physically absent.

"And as he was now going down, his servants met him and told *him*, saying, 'Your son lives!'" (John 4:51). This was a watershed event in the inner life of the father. He journeyed back to his home wondering how exactly the healing would take place. But when he learned from the servants that his son had been healed in the same hour the thing was said by Christ, then it could not have been a natural recovery. Christ was the Savior indeed; this the nobleman would now believe, not with a casual faith, but with absolute trust. But let me now ask you a question, my dear reader. Shall we also supplicate the Almighty merely for our personal benefit? Shall we seek the Lord of Life only for bodily healing? Even if we take this approach, Christ will not reproach us: "The one who comes to Me I will by no means cast out" (John 6:37) and a "smoking flax he will not quench" (Matt. 12:20). He is the Good Shepherd, and He will hunt for a single missing sheep. Did He not save the Samaritan woman, and through her, in one day win all of Samaria?

The Synagogue at Nazareth

THE WRITERS OF THE SYNOPTIC Gospels present the imprisonment of John the Baptist as the event that triggered the opening of our Lord's ministry in Galilee.[28] Saint Luke—quietly passing over the early ministry in Judea, which only St. John relates for us—states that He returned from the wilderness "in the power of the Spirit"[29] to commence His work in Galilee. "And news of Him went out through all the surrounding region. And He taught in their synagogues, being glorified by all" (Luke 4:14, 15). The Gospels of Matthew and Mark clarify that the "surrounding region" mentioned by Luke is in fact Capernaum. Capernaum became the country from which Christ launched His Galilean ministry: it was there that He began teaching the Galileans, and His first Galilean miracles were wrought there. This eventually caused great consternation to the inhabitants of Nazareth.

And so it became an unfortunate fact that, although Christ's teaching was well received by the synagogues of Galilee, it was rejected by the synagogue at Nazareth. Saint Luke alone records for us the passage from Isaiah that our Lord read in the synagogue that day. The entire scene is drawn up as a kind of royal proclamation, befitting the opening of our Lord's ministry to the world. The congregation of Nazareth, however, could not reconcile the idea that the Man thus inaugurating His messianic office is also the son of Joseph the carpenter, with whom they had all grown up.

"So He came to Nazareth, where He had been brought up. And as His custom was, He went into the synagogue on the Sabbath day, and stood up to read" (Luke 4:16). It was our Lord's custom to visit the synagogue of any city He went to, and it appears that He was regularly given preference when it came to the reading and preaching. He became the bridegroom and adornment of the Galilean synagogues; He could not enter a synagogue without becoming its guest of honor. Luke records for us the astonishment of even

---

28   Mark 1:14; Luke 3:19, 20.
29   Luke 4:14.

the inhabitants of Nazareth themselves.

Regarding the order of worship in the Jewish synagogues of the first century, it was required of the reader to stand on an elevated platform so the listeners could hear his voice; but the office of teaching was carried out while the person sat. "I sat daily with you, teaching in the temple, and you did not seize Me" (Matt. 26:55). The service itself was opened by the recitation of the *shema*,[30] the centerpiece of Jewish faith, which confessed the oneness of God. Next came the *tephillah* prayers or the twelve benedictions. Then followed the heart of Jewish worship: the reading of Scripture. An excerpt from the Torah was first read in Hebrew, followed by a translation of the passage into Aramaic. A passage from the prophets was then read, according to the order of their lectionary. However, it seems that in the first century some freedom was given to the reader to choose the prophet he preferred. After the prophecy was read, a short prayer was said, then the sermon was delivered. If a noteworthy person was present, he would be asked to deliver the sermon.[31] Finally, the *kaddish*, the sanctification of God's name, was prayed.

And He was handed the book of the prophet Isaiah. And when He had opened the book, He found the place where it was written:
"The Spirit of the Lord *is* upon Me,
Because He has anointed Me
To preach the gospel to *the* poor;
He has sent Me to heal the brokenhearted,
To proclaim liberty to *the* captives
And recovery of sight to *the* blind,
To set at liberty those who are oppressed;

---

30   "Hear, O Israel: the Lord our God, the Lord *is* one" (Deut 6:4).
31   See Acts 13:14–16.

To proclaim the acceptable year of the LORD."
(Luke 4:17–19)

By standing before the congregation at Nazareth and delivering such a stately and impressive reading of this prophecy, Jesus was clearly taking the role of the Messiah foretold by Isaiah and proclaiming the fulfillment of the promises in Himself. Thus, He was presenting Himself as the newly appointed King of God's people—who is sent to heal, to liberate, and to console the brokenhearted. And when Isaiah wrote, "he has anointed me," the anointing referred to the priests and prophets of the Old Covenant. But now, the anointing was performed directly by the Holy Spirit in the Jordan, and the words of ordination to the messiahship were spoken directly by God the Father.

The closing statement of the prophecy mentions the "acceptable year of the LORD." This refers of course to the Year of Jubilee, which occurred once every fifty years. This was a year of liberation and restitution in which all debts were cancelled and all slaves were given their freedom. Fields were given their rest by lying fallow, and the field workers were allowed to return to their homes. "And you shall consecrate the fiftieth year, and proclaim liberty throughout *all* the land to all its inhabitants. It shall be a Jubilee for you; and each of you shall return to his possession, and each of you shall return to his family" (Lev. 25:10). It was a symbol of the era of salvation, which Christ had now come to inaugurate. Scholars have investigated the date of the Year of Jubilee in Christ's time, and their results have yielded the date of AD 26 or 27. If we recall that Christ was born about 4 BC, and that He was thirty years old when He read this prophecy, we reach the conclusion that this year was historically a Year of Jubilee—the perfect moment to announce that God had returned to rule His people in the Person of Christ.

"And He began to say to them, 'Today this Scripture is fulfilled in your hearing.' So all bore witness to Him, and marveled at the gracious words which proceeded out of His mouth. And they said, 'Is this not Joseph's son?'" (Luke 4:21, 22). The audience was immediately struck by speech so filled with authority and grace; the power in Christ's words induced a temporary and involuntary awe in the listeners' minds. But then they remembered that He was only the carpenter's son; they remembered too that He had performed impressive works all over Galilee except in His own town of Nazareth. So they began to disdain those initial feelings of admiration that had seized them; they began to disdain Christ Himself. Jesus—the great rock of offense! Yes, He was a carpenter and the son of a carpenter. Yes, He was not an impressive sight. Yes, He was a man of sorrows, forsaken and stricken. Yes, He had taken the form of a servant. But what He did no man had ever done: commanding demons, calming boisterous seas, healing disease, restoring sight, raising the dead. Yes, He was the "son of Joseph the carpenter," yet He was crucified, buried, and rose on the third day.

And so, if you wish to believe on Him, you have ample reasons. And so, if you wish to reject Him, you also have ample reasons. But how extraordinary are the rewards of faith!

> He said to them, "You will surely say this proverb to Me, 'Physician, heal yourself! Whatever we have heard done in Capernaum, do also here in Your country.'" Then He said, "Assuredly, I say to you, no prophet is accepted in his own country." ... So all those in the synagogue, when they heard these things, were filled with wrath, and rose up and thrust Him out of the city; and they led Him to the brow of the hill on which their city was built, that they might throw Him down over the cliff. Then passing through the midst of them, He went His way. (Luke 4:23, 24, 28–30)

Jesus Begins to Work in Capernaum

JESUS HEALS A DEMON-POSSESSED MAN

It had become apparent to those who followed the Lord's career that He often began His work in a certain area with the expulsion of demons. His work always agreed with His teaching. For the crux of His teaching regarding salvation was the forgiveness of sins, and the purpose of casting out demons and healing the sick was also the forgiveness of sins. His miracles, in other words, put the theory of salvation into visible and palpable form. In St. Luke's Gospel, *healing* is synonymous with *forgiveness*. "Your faith has made you well" (Luke 8:48) is interchangeable with "Your faith has saved you" (Luke 7:50). And this theological truth is further illustrated by Luke in his recording of Christ's response to His critics: "Which is easier, to say, 'Your sins are forgiven you,' or to say, 'Rise up and walk'?" (Luke 5:23). Forgiving sins and healing the lame are equivalent acts.

"Now in the synagogue there was a man who had a spirit of an unclean demon. And he cried out with a loud voice" (Luke 4:33). Luke is writing here for a Greek audience, so he must distinguish a demonic spirit from the Holy Spirit; and it is clear that the demonic spirit was responsible for the victim's fits of screaming. In such cases of possession, the evil spirit seizes the victim's spirit, and the result is a physiological illness that is unresponsive to the conventional forms of medical treatment. The possessed individual may, for example, become totally blind or mute or deaf; but the moment an effective prayer is said over the person, the demon is overthrown, and the person is totally cured.

"Let *us* alone! What have we to do with You, Jesus of Nazareth? Did You come to destroy us? I know who You are—the Holy One of God!" (Luke 4:34). The demon thus recognizes the ascendant authority of Jesus. It throws its victim onto the ground and comes out of him in a convulsive fit. Indeed, the casting-out of an unclean spirit that has oppressed its victim for many years can only be a tumultuous event. The spirit's control over the person's senses and drives must be torn away; the person performing the exorcism must himself have a very robust spiritual life in order to triumph in the struggle. The miracle is performed, and the crowd is stunned at Jesus' capabilities. Jesus thus saves the man, and the evangelists illustrate for us the fact that the salvation Christ brought to the world was not just an effect of the Cross and Resurrection but was in fact interwoven into His daily ministry.

JESUS OFFICIALLY CALLS PETER, ANDREW, JAMES, AND JOHN TO THE APOSTOLATE

The evangelists provide for us this singularly interesting event that occurs toward the beginning of Christ's ministry. Jesus skirts the shore of the Lake of Gennesaret one morning, and there He spots two pairs of fishing partners who are docking their boats after a long and unsuccessful night of fishing. As they wash and repair the nets, He asks them to set out a little in a boat; and from that watery pulpit, He begins to preach to the people the "word of God" (Luke 5:1). In order to avoid the press and jostle of the crowds, it was Jesus' custom to teach from a boat as the people stood on the shore listening, or else to sit on an elevated platform, such as a mountainside, and preach to the people below. His favorite teaching posture was sitting.

This would, indeed, be the first time Peter heard publicly preached that word which would become his life's vocation. Luke specifies the boat as belonging to Peter, and it is possible that Christ chose to perform this miracle in Peter's boat so that he who was to become the chief fisher of men would the more readily abandon His old calling in favor of the new.

"When He had stopped speaking, He said to Simon, 'Launch out into the deep and let down your nets for a catch'" (Luke 5:4).

According to the rules of fishing, nets were not to be used in deep waters—only fishing lines with weights and bait—because deep-sea fish fed on the plants located at the bottom of the sea. Christ caused these experienced fishermen to pause and wonder: What kind of teacher is this who controls the path of fish? "Simon answered and said to Him, 'Master, we have toiled all night and caught nothing; nevertheless at Your word I will let down the net'" (Luke 5:5). Peter tells the Lord that they will not rely on their vast experience but on His word alone.

The "deep" did not yield anything to them, but it would to Him. And there is a mystical double meaning that runs all through the narrative. Mankind had toiled through the night of the world's history and had come up spiritually empty. But once the Word of God enters the world, the fish will no longer be drawn into the nets by the usual rules of the trade, but rather by a special power from on high. This brings hope to souls who have grown weary with the system of this world—a world that gives with its right hand and takes away with its left. God is our refuge, who gives us good things beyond what we ask. And at His word we let down our nets and hope in Him every day.

Without having much hope in themselves, they relied on Christ's word, and they cast the net over the right side of the boat. The right-hand side in Jesus' teaching symbolizes the power of God: "I have set the LORD always before me; / Because *He* is at my right hand I shall not be moved" (Ps. 16:8). As soon as the net was cast, a large swarm of fish was taken up in its folds. Peter had passed his first test. He would learn thereafter how to cast the net of grace into the sea of the world, and on the Day of Pentecost, he would draw in three thousand souls. The other disciples also rushed to help pull in the large catch, for their labor and spiritual development would also reap benefits from their obeying Christ's call. It might seem at first that the purpose of this miracle was an external one—to put Jesus' power on display. But the greater miracle was His entrance into the deep of these disciples' hearts. For Christ spoke to their hearts without using words. "What do you think? Have you experienced in your lives a catch such as this? Is it worth more to follow Me now or to persist in your regular life of angling, in which so much energy and time is spent for naught?"

"When Simon Peter saw *it*, he fell down at Jesus' knees, saying, 'Depart from me, for I am a sinful man, O Lord!'" (Luke 5:8). Simon received the name of Peter the moment Christ consecrated him to the life of discipleship. Luke's Gospel first gives him this name at the end of this story, because it is then that Peter recognizes Jesus' lordship and suddenly feels small and worthless in His presence. "And Jesus said to Simon, 'Do not be afraid. From now on you will catch men.' So when they had brought their boats to land, they forsook all and followed Him" (Luke 5:10, 11). This is the first apostolic experience of the four leading disciples: Peter, Andrew, James, and John. Here, at the beginning of the road, they reached the ultimate aim of faith. For they needed to first "forsake all" in their hearts before they could start forsaking all things in the world.

Jesus Heals the Afflicted

A LEPER

In the narrative of the life of Jesus, after He has finished calling the four fishermen-disciples to their new apostolic vocation, He proceeds to perform acts of mercy and healing for the afflicted children of Israel. A man approaches Him who is, in the medical language of St. Luke, πλήρης λέπρας—"full of leprosy"—indicating that the disease was no longer in its beginning stages but had advanced to an extreme degree. To the ancient mind, to recover from such a severe form of leprosy was tantamount to being raised from the dead. The Jews believed that leprosy was the consequence of some egregious sin, and therefore, one of the signs of the messianic age would be the healing of lepers. When the Baptist sends his disciples to ask if Christ is indeed the One to come, He replies, "Go and tell John the things you have seen and heard: that *the* blind see, *the* lame walk, *the* lepers are cleansed" (Luke 7:22). One of Christ's first "messianic" acts of healing, therefore, was the healing of this leprous man.

Considering the prohibitions placed on lepers, this man's approaching Christ comes as quite a surprise to the onlookers. But when the leper sees the only Person who can heal him, he knows it is his one and only chance. The man comes to Christ and asks with admirable courage and respect, "Lord, if You are willing, You can make me clean" (Luke 5:12). The request touches the Lord's heart, and it stimulates an inner desire to heal already present in His heart. In the face of this absolute trust, Jesus immediately rewards the man's faith: "Then He put out *His* hand and touched him, saying, 'I am willing; be cleansed.' Immediately the leprosy left him" (v. 13). The Lord *touches* him, in order both to restore strength to the shriveled members and to restore hope to the emaciated soul.

Christ then commands the healed leper to go and make an offering to the priest. The purpose of this is multifold: to comply with the Mosaic laws; to present a testimony to the priesthood that the messianic age had dawned; and finally in order that the man may receive official certification that he is now free of the affliction and can once more mingle with common society.

A PARALYZED MAN

Next we come to a healing that directly speaks to the devastating effects of sin in a person's life and to the saving power of forgiveness. We have here a paralyzed man whose body is about to demonstrate faith with a voice louder than any words can express. "Now it happened on a certain day, as He was teaching, that there were Pharisees and teachers of the law sitting by, who had come out of every town of Galilee, Judea, and Jerusalem" (Luke 5:17). These specialists in the dogma of Judaism had come from the main centers of Palestine to monitor the teachings of the new Prophet from Nazareth.

"Immediately many gathered together, so that there was no longer room to receive *them*, not even near the door. . . . Then they came to Him, bringing a paralytic who was carried by four *men*. And when they could not come near Him because of the crowd, they uncovered the roof where He was. So when they had broken through, they let down the bed on which the paralytic was lying" (Mark 2:2–4).The typical oriental home of the time had a low, flat roof, in the middle of which was a large opening that was usually covered during winter and uncovered during summer.

The friends of the paralyzed man lower him through this opening to the very feet of Christ. The Lord states, "Son, your sins are forgiven you" (Mark 2:5). The scribes bristle with resentment at the presumption of these words, for only God can forgive sins. And their objection is correct: forgiveness is solely God's work. But here is the Son of God sitting before them, and He and the Father are one. What the Father forgives, the Son forgives also—that the Father and Son might be glorified together.

"When Jesus perceived their thoughts, He answered and said to them, 'Why are you reasoning in your hearts? Which is easier, to say, "Your sins are forgiven you," or to say, "Rise up and walk?"'" (Luke 5:22, 23). The answer, of course, is that both are impossible to say, because no human being has the ability to offer either to another human. "He said to the man who was paralyzed, 'I say to you, arise, take up your bed, and go to your house'" (Luke 5:24). The man rose up, with all the burdens on his conscience and limbs lifted, and went home praising God. The Pharisees' tongues, however, became paralyzed, for they could not speak against the clear work of heaven they had just witnessed.

THE PARALYTIC AT THE POOL OF BETHESDA

Without having exact knowledge of the chronological order of the events in our Lord's life, we know at least that during these earlier years, Christ healed a paralytic in Jerusalem. "After this there was a feast of the Jews, and Jesus went up to Jerusalem" (John 5:1). It is a matter of debate which feast it was that marked this seminal event. Cyril and Chrysostom both think it was the Feast of Pentecost. Other Church Fathers, along with some modern commentators, think it was the second Passover attended by our Lord, which would place us in the spring of AD 28.

Christ "goes up" alone, without His disciples, in the interest of preventing a scene. His interactions with the Jews lately have caused some heat, and so He must enter Jerusalem under concealment. Jesus enters the temple and walks by a pool, around which lie a "great multitude of sick people, blind, lame, paralyzed, waiting for the moving of the water" (John 5:3)—the last category of which includes the man who is about to be healed. Here we are back to the theme of water, which was visited before in the stories of the wedding in Cana, Nicodemus, and the Samaritan woman. The reference to the *moving* of the water invokes the concept of *living water*—a mystical symbol of Christ.

The verse in John's Gospel that refers to an angel disturbing the waters of the pool is absent from a number of important manuscripts. Chrysostom quotes the verse, however, and makes the pool a forerunner of the baptismal font and the action of the angel a foreshadowing of the action of the Holy Spirit in baptism. The Greek word used here for pool, *kolumbethra*, was indeed the traditional term used by the early Church for the baptismal font. In effect, this is an infusion of divine grace into an Old Testament rite. John is implicitly reminding us of the rich history of water-healing dispersed throughout the Old Testament.

"Now a certain man was there who had an infirmity thirty-eight years. When Jesus saw him lying there, and knew that he already had been *in that condition* a long time, He said to him, 'Do you want to be made well?'" (John 5:5, 6). Note the question: *Do you want to be made well?* The Apostle Paul discusses this most complex of ethical problems—the conflicted will. "What I am doing, I do not understand. For what I will to do, that I do not practice; but what I hate, that I do" (Rom. 7:15). Paul expounds on the conflict between good and evil that rages within the natural man. There is the law of sin, which dominates the members of the flesh; and there is the law of righteousness, which dominates the spirit. And in the natural man, he explains, the law of sin prevails: the will is broken, and the spirit is downcast.

But there is for Paul a third law, which is the law of Christ. It is the power of the Holy Spirit, freely bestowed on man, activated when a person seizes the shield of faith and submits to the commands of Christ. Once a person confesses his sins and trusts in the promises of Jesus, he receives forgiveness without any argument or debate. If Christ did not give up on this man with a thirty-eight-year-old disease, why should sinners give up on themselves? "A bruised reed He will not break, / And smoking flax He will not quench" (Matt. 12:20).

Jesus' question to the man is a critical one: Can a man, after thirty-eight years of paralysis, really desire to be healed and live a better life? Christ recognizes that after being in this diseased condition for so long, and after failing repeatedly to enter the pool, the man might well have a completely deadened will. And Christ is not asking him about the instinctual wish for health and self-preservation that governs both man and beast; He is referring to the will to triumph over sin. A life of abandonment and sin must have somehow led to this man's paralysis; and in asking this question, Christ must have seen a residuum of goodwill present in the man. And notice that Jesus does not ask about his faith. He must first revive the man's will, and then the renewed will can revive his faith. For faith is a product of the will.

"The sick man answered Him, 'Sir, I have no man to put me into the pool when the water is stirred up; but while I am coming, another steps down before me.' Jesus said to him, 'Rise, take up your bed and walk'" (John 5:7, 8). As soon as the word was spoken, the languid limbs were strengthened, the flaccid muscles were made strong, and the man carried his bed with the vitality of a youth. "The words that I speak to you are spirit, and *they* are life" (John 6:63), Jesus said. If such words have the power to move dead limbs and awaken dead souls, why are we slack in storing them in our hearts? Sickness was once a form of bodily chastisement; but now in Christ it can be transformed into glory for God—when it is borne patiently and with thanksgiving.

The man immediately went and told the Jews what Jesus had done for him, which led to the first open confrontation between Christ and the religious leaders. "For this reason the Jews persecuted Jesus, and sought to kill Him, because He had done these things on the Sabbath" (John 5:16). Their long-hidden spite is now made into official hostility; shifting and questionable motives have now become undisguised malice. It seemed that Jesus chose to do His works almost exclusively on the Sabbath, and such an affront they could not tolerate. The theologians of Israel had for centuries wrangled about the question of whether or not God Himself kept the Sabbath. And in AD 95, the chief rabbis held council together, and a noteworthy decision of the gathering was the doctrine that God did observe the entirety of the Law, because He would not or could not breach the limits of His own creation.

Christ's answer was aimed directly at their frivolous thinking: "My Father has been working until now, and I have been working" (John 5:16). God, that is to say, is not bound by the restraints of time and location; an eternal God is not subject to a transitory law. The idea must be exploded; for if God were ever to cease from His work, then creation itself would melt away. And Christ goes further in making Himself a partner in God's creative work. He is its redeemer and renewer: "God . . . has in these last days spoken to us by *His* Son, whom He has appointed heir of all things, through whom also He made the worlds . . . [and] had by Himself purged our sins" (Heb. 1:1–3). He who restored sight to the blind, and brought back a dead man after four days in the grave, and healed a multitude of sicknesses and diseases, was engaging in work as original as creation itself.

The claim that God was Jesus' own Father was an unsettling provocation to the Jews. To apply the phrase *Son of God* to this young prophet from Nazareth seemed to the minds of the hearers a revolting blasphemy. And it was this very title which caused them to deliver Jesus up to Pilate: "Therefore, when the chief priests and officers saw Him, they cried out, saying, 'Crucify *Him*, crucify *Him!*' Pilate said to them, 'You take Him and crucify *Him*, for I find no fault in Him.' The Jews answered him, 'We have a law, and according to our law He ought to die, because He made Himself the Son of God'" (John 19:6, 7).

The Election of the Twelve

"NOW IT CAME TO PASS in those days that He went out to the mountain to pray, and continued all night in prayer to God" (Luke 6:12). This blessed little morsel of Scripture, Christ's night-long retreat for prayer before the calling of His disciples—related incidentally only by Luke—is an indication of the link between quietude and closeness to God. This passage is the foundation for the Church's tradition of nocturnal vigils, as well as the midnight praises performed in monasteries. It is the transformation of the darkness of earth into the light of the spirit. One of the Church's midnight praises begins with the words, "Arise, O you children of the light."[32] Believers remain awake into the small hours of the night, consecrating their hearts as altars for the offering up of a sacrifice of praise.

"And when it was day, He called His disciples to *Himself*; and from them He chose twelve whom He also named apostles" (Luke 6:13). The succeeding verses make it clear that a large number of disciples, seventy and possibly more, had followed Him up to this point; and when He has summoned them into His presence, He picks twelve from among them to be His personal attendants. We may also infer from the passage that at this point the rest of the disciples descend the mountain, and Jesus remains alone with the twelve at the top. He calls them by name to His personal discipleship and begins to call them "apostles" (Gr. *apostoloi*)—indicating His future intent to send (Gr. *apostello*) them to the ends of the earth.

Our Lord's election of the twelve disciples was intended, firstly, to give birth to that body which would be His eternal presence on earth. It was also intended to begin the hardening process of the material that would go to make up the foundation over which God's Kingdom would be erected. He did not choose them to become merely substitute teachers in His place; they were not merely to deliver a verbal message to people. Their task was to relay Christ as a Person to the rest of humanity. Christ was to be the foundation, the gate and the law of the new Kingdom: "having been built on the foundation of the apostles and prophets, Jesus Christ Himself being the chief cornerstone" (Eph. 2:20). The apostles were not sent to work of themselves, but Christ was to work *through* them.

---

32   This reference is to worship in the Coptic Orthodox Church.

The question naturally arises, why twelve? Over the course of its history, the nation of Israel gradually succumbed to discord and disunity; following the exile, only two of the original twelve tribes survived—Benjamin and Judah—while the other ten were lost among the Gentile nations. The choosing of the twelve, therefore, pointed to the gathering of the entire body of the Hebrew nation around Himself, and the disciples were assigned as heads of the tribes (Matt. 19:28). He called each disciple by name, knowing the unique traits of each and their potential contributions to the ministry. Christ even knew the nature of Judas: "Did I not choose you, the twelve, and one of you is a devil?" (John 6:70). Why was Judas chosen, we may ask, since Christ knew that he was a thief and a sower of discord among the others? All we may say is that Christ bore patiently with him until the very last moment: "Jesus said to him, 'What you do, do quickly'" (John 13:27); and we conclude that Judas was tolerated till the end so that the ensuing events would occur.

There were certain apostles, such as Peter and John, who possessed exceptional personal qualities and who consequently played decisive roles in the apostolic work. They were living proof that human nature possesses unique potentials that may be used for the world's benefit. For when they accepted the Christian Faith, they lived out its truth in remarkable ways and thus revealed the Lord's wisdom in choosing them. And the rest of the apostolic band proved themselves to be worthy vessels as well.

Another question that arises is, why uneducated men? Jesus could have selected disciples from among the teachers of Israel who became attached to Him, such as Nicodemus, or from the numerous scribes and Pharisees who secretly sympathized with His cause. But these disciples possessed a unique spirit of simplicity and childlikeness that was dear to God: "In that hour Jesus rejoiced in the Spirit and said, 'I thank You, Father, Lord of heaven and earth, that You have hidden these things from *the* wise and prudent and revealed them to babes. Even so, Father, for so it seemed good in Your sight'" (Luke 10:21). A simple and childlike spirit is an object of scorn to the world; yet by Christ it is esteemed great riches.

Christ therefore imposed on them no formal rules of fasting, solitude, or the like; on the contrary, He urged them to mingle with the world and to teach it the truth. He called Himself a bridegroom walking among the bridegroom's friends. As He responded to the Baptist's disciples' question regarding fasting, "Can the friends of the bridegroom mourn as long as the bridegroom is with them? But the days will come when the bridegroom will be taken away from them, and then they will fast" (Matt. 9:15). One cannot take the old patch of the Pharisees' teaching on asceticism and sew it onto the new robe of New Testament grace. The new wine of the Spirit's joy cannot be poured into the old wineskins of Old Testament chest-thumping and ash-tossing. The spirit of the New Testament, in other words, cannot be nourished on the doctrines of the Old Testament.

And so, by elevating the concept of a festive union between the bridegroom and his friends in the disciples' consciousness, Christ was discrediting the teaching of the Pharisees with its emphasis on rigid ceremonialism and moral exclusivity. Theirs was the negative approach; Christ's was the positive. He sought to drive home basic principles in the disciples' minds and to train their spiritual senses to detect and absorb the work of grace. They would learn the art of personal restraint, not by compulsion, but by enlightenment. Anger would be replaced by forgiveness; revenge replaced by patience; every negative thing replaced by its positive counterpart.

During the initial stages of the ministry, therefore, the disciples' obedience to Jesus was based on the confidence they had in His strength of presence. But little by little, their daily life with Him provided them with a deeper insight into His personality, His thoughts, and His deeds. Slowly, His character molded their characters; His vision expanded their vision; His will shaped their will—much in the way heat is conducted from a warm body to a cold body. Happily, we gradually detect a change of character in the disciples. Their mode of speech and conduct becomes an icon—even if a hazy and faded one—of Christ Himself.

The Sermon on the Mount

If anyone will piously and soberly consider the sermon which our Lord Jesus Christ spoke on the mount, as we read it in the Gospel according to Matthew, I think that he will find in it, so far as regards the highest morals, a perfect standard of the Christian life.

AUGUSTINE OF HIPPO,
ON THE SERMON ON THE MOUNT

AROUND SPRINGTIME OF THE YEAR AD 28, still in the early days of Christ's ministry in Galilee, while the Lord was being followed by a multitude of people, He ascended a mountain near Capernaum and sat down on a level place. His disciples came and sat at His feet while the people eagerly found places to sit near Him in anticipation of His words. And the sermon He delivered on that mountaintop was destined to become one of the shining pinnacles of the entire New Testament.

As the quotes referenced above indicate, the consensus among Church Fathers and scholars is that the driving theme of the sermon is the moral requirement for citizenship in God's Kingdom. And from the outset, we may notice the striking absence of certain religious elements in the sermon. There is no mention of religious creeds, of priesthoods, of sacrifices, or of any of the plethora of rites that conferred holiness in the Old Covenant. Instead, the sermon constitutes a key phase in Christ's inauguration of the New Covenant: it demonstrates how the new teaching of God had its seeds buried in the Old Covenant, and how the people of God were now to move from the era of law to the era of gospel joy. The Christian Faith was to find its genesis in a Jewish faith transformed by spirit and grace.

The heart of ancient Israel's Hebraic theology was encapsulated in a short but weighty formula: "Hear, O Israel, the LORD our God, the LORD is one." The Sermon on the Mount was intended to have no less authority as an expression of faith in the believer's heart. It must be noted, however, that Christ did not present the sermon as a detailed syllabus for religious study. It was not a method or program of any kind. It was rather the announcement that God's Kingdom was at hand. And the Kingdom was not to be founded on the basis of a school but on the basis of a brotherhood. The point must not be lost on the reader that the Sermon on the Mount was immediately preceded by the calling of the twelve disciples. Their devotion to their new Lord bound them together in a spirit of brotherhood, and it was over this filial bedrock that the Kingdom of God was built.

One of the touching qualities of Christ's ministry was His sensitivity to the human need in the crowds that followed Him. On one occasion, for instance, His preaching lingered late into the evening, and the people grew faint with hunger; so Christ divided the small loaves and two fish to feed them all. On another occasion, the people began transporting their sick and afflicted to His side, and so He stayed late into the night performing acts of healing. Here, the pining multitude comes in need of hearing some words of consolation; thus, Jesus sits for many hours at a time, satisfying their need. His heart was not unfeeling toward their groaning. So He opens His discourse with the Beatitudes, a list of spiritual axioms that deliver the mercy and reassurance so desperately needed by those oriental ears.

Blessed are the poor in spirit, for theirs is the kingdom of heaven.
This blessing is not pronounced on those who struggle to feed themselves, but on those who are aware of an acute spiritual need inside
them that they cannot satisfy. It is a pressing need within the human
heart that simply cannot be met by people or things or the world, but
only by the Spirit. If a child cries out in hunger, its mother hastens
to feed it. And if the soul cries out for feeding, the Spirit will hasten
to feed it. This lowly meekness of spirit is the first step to finding the
Kingdom.

Blessed are those who mourn, for they shall be comforted.
Grief will meet its end in God's Kingdom: "God will wipe away every
tear from their eyes" (Rev. 7:17). Mourning is a sign of man's exile
on earth, and it points to man's consolation in God's Kingdom. It
was long believed the Messiah's career would include comforting the
grief-stricken and drying up their tears:

> The Spirit of the Lord GOD *is* upon Me, / Because the Lord
> has anointed Me / To preach good tidings to the poor; / He
> has sent Me to heal the brokenhearted . . . / To console those
> who mourn in Zion, / To give them beauty for ashes, / The oil
> of joy for mourning, / The garment of praise for the spirit of
> heaviness. (Is. 61:1–3)

Blessed are the meek, for they shall inherit the earth.
Jesus here echoes Psalm 37, promising the inheritance not of any
fleeting terrestrial land but of an unshakable portion in God's new
world. The ancient promise to Israel was of a visible land, which
they gained, but over which they eventually lost sovereignty. For the
Christian, however, the inheritance of a small piece of the world is a
thing of very slight value. One lesson of the Sermon on the Mount
is that anything not directly connected to the Kingdom of God is in
Christ's eyes a trifle and an irrelevancy. The meek will gain a generous

portion of spiritual blessing here, and a hundred times more in the hereafter of God's Kingdom.

Blessed are those who hunger and thirst for righteousness,
for they shall be filled.

The "righteousness" commended in this beatitude is not the righteousness of the Law but rather that of Christ. In fact, for the New Testament, Christ is the soul's food and drink. "I am the bread of life. . . . If anyone eats of this bread, he will live forever" (John 6:48, 51). "If anyone thirsts, let him come to Me and drink" (John 7:37). "He who comes to Me shall never hunger, and he who believes in Me shall never thirst" (John 6:35). One of the greatest discoveries of man, as well as one of the greatest revelations of God, is the startling truth that God Himself can be our food and drink.

Blessed are the merciful, for they shall obtain mercy.

Mercy is one of God's attributes; it is a fundamental aspect of His being. Any mercy therefore shown by man to man is a replica or reflection of God's mercy. When a person shows mercy, he is reflexively speaking of God. Creation is the work of His hands, and the mercy He shows completes His creative work. When God commands man to be merciful, then, He is allowing man to participate in finishing His handiwork. Christ here reveals how far superior mercy is to law and sacrifice: "Go and learn what *this* means: 'I desire mercy and not sacrifice.' For I did not come to call the righteous, but sinners, to repentance'" (Matt. 9:13).

Blessed are the pure in heart, for they shall see God.

Purity of the heart is the state in which God can see His image clearly reflected in us; and we in turn, by our transparency of heart, can see Him too. God takes the initiative in the process: "Create in me a clean heart, O God" (Ps. 51:10). And St. Paul relates his experience on this point: "We all, with unveiled face, beholding as in a mirror the glory of the Lord, are being transformed into the same image from glory to glory" (2 Cor. 3:18). Thus, purity of heart is exercised by directing one's face toward Christ, until the heart within us is transfigured, and until Christ too is transfigured in our heart.

Blessed are the peacemakers, for they shall be called sons of God.
The Scriptures make it clear that Christ's principal work is to restore peace between man and God. And a worldwide peace can pervade and bless humanity only through the sons of peace. But God's peace is resisted, and the sons of peace are persecuted. But Jesus promised the disciples that if anyone accepted their peace, it would be given; and if anyone rejected it, it would return to the disciples and increase in their hearts. The peacemaker must necessarily possess a very generous store of love and patience in order to persuade stony hearts to accept God's peace. He who preaches peace must become like God, and so Jesus bestows on them the title "sons of God."

Blessed are those who are persecuted for righteousness' sake,
for theirs is the kingdom of heaven.
The righteousness spoken of here is that gained from a faith in Christ's Cross and Resurrection. If we confess faith in Christ's righteousness, we are deemed to be ignorant and fools in the world's eyes. We in addition become a target of the devil's schemes, because we become obstacles to his aims and a nuisance to his followers. The world cannot tolerate a person who has stepped onto the road of truth and holiness, and it resolves to destroy him. And so the person who endures such persecution for righteousness' sake becomes a worthy citizen of the Kingdom of God.

These are the eight foundational premises of the Sermon on the Mount; and the discourse, rich in edifying words, magnetic in its pull on the soul, extensive in scope and penetrated with divine light, made a powerful impression on its listeners: "When Jesus had ended these sayings . . . the people were astonished at His teaching, for He taught them as one having authority, and not as the scribes" (Matt. 7:28).

The Compassionate Jesus: Acts of Mercy

ACCORDING TO THE EVANGELISTS MATTHEW and Luke, following the Sermon on the Mount, Jesus enters the city of Capernaum and proceeds to show mercy to the multitudes that follow Him by healing their sick and raising their dead. The first supplicant who approaches Christ is a Roman centurion. He comes to intercede for a servant who languishes in extreme illness, on the brink of death. Saint Luke indicates that a delegation of Jewish elders is sent to deliver the centurion's request, while St. Matthew states that the centurion himself goes directly to Christ. Notwithstanding the slight difference in detail between the two accounts, the core of the story and the lesson to be drawn are the same.

The episode is an important one, because it serves as an authoritative guide on which a church policy may be constructed regarding the treatment of those who are strangers to ecclesiastical life and to religion in general. Here is a Roman centurion who is essentially a pagan, but who is confessed by the Jewish elders to be a builder of their synagogue and a friend to their nation. The fact should astonish us. He is an extremely wealthy man; he has secured the permission of King Herod to build a synagogue for a people whose race and religion are repugnant to his own; and he nevertheless shows such a confident faith in Christ that it merits the praise of Jesus Himself.

The centurion expresses his faith in the form of an analogy. He says that, just as he commands his soldiers to do this or that and it is done, so may Christ command His servant to be healed, and it will be done. Jesus is astonished at the comparison; it shows a faith in His power expressed in terms of Roman military discipline. Christ naturally compares such a vibrant trust with the limp and lifeless faith of the scribes and Pharisees: "'I say to you, I have not found such great faith, not even in Israel!' And those who were sent, returning to the house, found the servant well who had been sick" (Luke 7:9, 10).

Following this miracle, Jesus travels to Nain—a city which Josephus informs us is on the eastern side of the Jordan in Idumean territory. On approaching the gate of the city, Jesus is met by a mournful assemblage of townsmen carrying a coffin. The deceased is the only son of his mother, who is also a widow and is now left desolate. The general lament raised by this group reveals how dear the widow is to the town's inhabitants.

"When the Lord saw her, He had compassion on her and said to her, 'Do not weep'" (Luke 7:13). Any man could say these words while lacking the means of providing the needed comfort; but Christ had the means. He has the means not only to wipe away tears and sorrow but to eradicate the source of them altogether. So, after Jesus spoke, He acted. The Author of Life drew near to touch the coffin, and death and darkness fled away that same instant. The young man's soul returned from the abyss to clothe itself again in mortal flesh. Since the coffin was open, as was the Jews' custom at the time, the revivification of the body was immediately apparent; it sat upright in its burial clothes, and the youth turned his gaze on an awestruck crowd.

There was a price that needed to be paid for the resurrection of this dead man; and the price was Christ's own death. Christ's death, in fact, purchased every resurrection ever to occur from the beginning of time to its end. The forceful rescinding of nature's laws accomplished in this miracle astounded the onlookers, and the people declared that God had truly visited His people in the form of a wonder-working prophet. And what was most staggering was that Jesus did not call on any power from on high to assist Him in the work, but commanded the miracle to be done on His own authority. And it was done.

The Embassy of the Baptist

"THEN THE DISCIPLES OF JOHN reported to him concerning all these things. And John, calling two of his disciples to *him*, sent *them* to Jesus, saying, 'Are You the Coming One, or do we look for another?'" (Luke 7:18, 19). John's two disciples approach Jesus in a state of turmoil, because their leader—a man so dearly beloved and deeply respected—had been thrown into prison and awaited an impending death. Some Fathers and commentators have attempted to protect John's reputation by saying that he had no genuine doubts about Jesus at all, but sent his disciples to Jesus simply as a way of encouraging them to hear His words. But it is not the Bible's method to hide the flaws of its saints. Were not Moses and Peter, both leaders in religion, severely rebuked for their error? But the Baptist's doubts were just another form of that "offense" Christ had to endure from the scribes, the Pharisees, the priests, the disciples, and even from the members of His own family.

This was a sorrowful question, sent out from a dark and dismal dungeon, at a time when news was circulating that the enemies of John at Herod's palace were seeking retribution from him and were plotting his death. The soul of the Baptist—whose voice had once roared in the free winds of the desert—was now withering in that solitary darkness. He was Elijah, and he had fallen into the hands of Jezebel. He naturally turned his thoughts to the bridegroom he had so joyously announced. *Where is He now, and where am I? Has He not heard of my suffering? Why has He left me to waste away in this prison? Is He perhaps not the One whom we have been waiting for after all?*

John had understood everything about Christ with the exception of one thing: the Cross. That death from which the Baptist shrank was itself the Savior's aim and purpose. If the Christ was moving toward His own Crucifixion, was it so strange that He allowed for the imprisonment of His forerunner? But the Baptist's forlorn disciples come to Jesus with the searing question, "Do we look for another?" which was partly complaint and partly a plea on John's behalf. And they arrived at a time when multitudes of sick and blind were being healed. It was one of the great hours of the Messiah. It was as though the pages of the Prophet Isaiah were being quickly flipped, and all those prophetic foreshadowings were being brought to life by Jesus' hands.

"Jesus answered and said to them, 'Go and tell John the things you have seen and heard: that *the* blind see, *the* lame walk, *the* lepers are cleansed, *the* deaf hear, *the* dead are raised, *the* poor have the gospel preached to them'" (Luke 7:22). *The blind see.* It was a common motif in the prophets that when the Messiah arrived, the blind would have their sight restored. Jesus presses this point firstly because it was an unmistakable sign to John that He was indeed the Anointed One. But what was probably Jesus' greatest work, and the messianic marker most distinct in Isaiah, was that He preached the good news to the poor. This in itself weighed as much as all the other healings combined.

"When the messengers of John had departed, He began to speak to the multitudes concerning John: 'What did you go out into the wilderness to see? . . . For I say to you, among those born of women there is not a greater prophet than John the Baptist'" (Luke 7:24, 28). In Jesus' eyes, John was the greatest because he came not to deliver prophecies in the same fashion as the rest of the prophets, but to affix the final seal on prophecy and to hand the prophetic office over to Him who was the very spirit of prophecy. The former prophets forecast the coming of Christ, but John prepared His way. The former prophets spoke mystically through revelation, but John pointed with his finger directly to the true Light. The former prophets cried woes upon Israel, but John announced the arrival of God's Kingdom. The former prophets spoke longingly of the Messiah from a distance, but John placed his own hand on Christ's head in the baptismal waters, and witnessed the Spirit's descent upon Him, and declared that this was truly the Son of God.

The Woman Who Was a Sinner

"THEN ONE OF THE PHARISEES asked Him to eat with him. And He went to the Pharisee's house, and sat down to eat" (Luke 7:36). It might seem strange to us that such a hospitable invitation would be extended to Jesus by a Pharisee. But the truth is that a number of the pharisaical sect did in fact appreciate His ministry and began to believe in Him. It is likely that this invitation was extended following a Sabbath service at the local synagogue, because it was the custom for the wealthier Pharisees to invite prominent members of the Jewish congregation to dine at their homes. It is also likely that this invitation was extended to Jesus in all sincerity. However, as the story shows, the common elements of hospitality were woefully neglected, and Christ was given a cold reception.

The usual arrangement of such a supper was for the guests to recline on the floor around a low table placed in the center. The guest typically sat or reclined on a low, flat cushion, called a divan, with his head positioned near the table and his feet extending out behind him. Now at a certain point during the meal, "A woman in the city who was a sinner ... stood at His feet behind *Him* weeping; and she began to wash His feet with her tears, and wiped *them* with the hair of her head; and she kissed His feet and anointed *them* with the fragrant oil" (Luke 7:37, 38). The clause "in the city" indicates that her sin was publicly known; however, the text calls her not a sinner, but one *who was* a sinner. She had extricated herself from her former life of dissipation; and now, in a spirit of thanksgiving and deep humility, she purchases a flask of oil, and searches diligently for Christ, and presents to Him her gift.

"When the Pharisee who had invited Him saw *this*, he spoke to himself, saying, 'This Man, if He were a prophet, would know who and what manner of woman *this is* who is touching Him, for she is a sinner'" (Luke 7:39). An article of the Mosaic Law declared that the person who made contact with an adulterous woman would himself become unclean. So when the Pharisee saw Jesus accepting the woman's touch, he took it as a sign that this was no prophet after all; a true prophet, he reasoned, would have confessed aloud that this woman was a defilement. Little did he know that Jesus all the while was reading the murmurings of his heart.

Christ proceeds to offer a parable as a corrective to the Pharisee: "There was a certain creditor who had two debtors. One owed five hundred denarii, and the other fifty. And when they had nothing with which to repay, he freely forgave them both. Tell Me, therefore, which of them will love him more?" (Luke 7:41). It was a scenario taken from the heart of society at the time, bloated as it was with money-lending and usury, but unfamiliar with the forgiving grace depicted therein. The creditor of the parable forgives both a large and a small debt equally, just as Christ forgives sins both large and small by virtue of the same shed blood. The Pharisee replies to Jesus' question cautiously: "I suppose the *one* whom he forgave more." He is clearly reluctant to acknowledge a mercy so profound and unknown to him.

Using this parable, Christ opens a case between Simon and the woman. Simon, who in his heart accused the woman of misdeeds, is the plaintiff; and the woman, who for so long has been an object of reproach, is the defendant. As it turns out, Simon was neglectful of three important obligations. He was obligated to provide Jesus with water for His feet after a long journey, and did not; the woman's tears served as the cleansing solution instead. Simon was supposed to give Jesus a welcoming kiss and did not; the woman's kisses were an effective replacement for this expression of love. Simon was supposed to anoint Jesus' forehead with oil, a balm to soothe the harsh effects of the oriental sun, and did not; but the woman rubbed oil on His feet. Thus, it was made clear to Simon's conscience—without a spoken verdict—who the guilty party was and who the innocent.

"Then He said to the woman, 'Your faith has saved you. Go in peace'" (Luke 7:50). The entire scenario serves as a remarkable example of the love sinners have for Christ, and equally as an opportunity for Christ to demonstrate His love for sinners. She was a woman who had squandered the choicest days of her life in dissolute living and had every reason to finish her time in despair. But she discovered Jesus; she became a disciple to Him in heart, though not in status, and offered a sincere repentance. She sealed her repentance at His feet and offered her faith along with the oil, a freewill offering of the soul accepted by Christ and witnessed by all those present.

Although her sin was great, her position was dire, and the forgiveness needed was immense, yet love tipped the scales of probability. And it is the same Jesus who promises to bring us near. We may need to sell everything in order to purchase love. Let us not miss the opportunity.

CHAPTER SEVEN

The Later Galilean Ministry

Sabbath Controversies

A t that time Jesus went through the grainfields on the Sabbath. And His disciples were hungry, and began to pluck heads of grain and to eat. And when the Pharisees saw *it*, they said to Him, 'Look, Your disciples are doing what is not lawful to do on the Sabbath!'" (Matt. 12:1, 2). Several passages of Scripture are dedicated to the stormy controversies that occurred between the Pharisees and our Lord touching the question of the Sabbath. The keeping of the Sabbath was a central mandate of Jewish life. History tells us, for example, that during the days of the Maccabees, men, women, and children were willing to go to their death rather than to fight on the Sabbath day.[33] We also learn that in later years, during the Roman siege of Jerusalem, the Roman general Pompey was able to exploit the Jews' inactivity on the Sabbath in order to successfully carry out his attack.[34]

Christ's reproof of the scribes and Pharisees, however, was due not to their breaking of the Sabbath but to their failure to appreciate the positive aspects of the holy day. Their fanatical zeal made them

---

33   1 Macc. 2:31–38.
34   Joseph. *Ant.* XIV, 4, 2.

forget that the Sabbath was a day for rejoicing, a day for prayer and good works, a day of thanksgiving and worship. The *Mishnah* itself describes the copious prohibitions that became encrusted around the Sabbath as so many "mountains hanging by a thread" due to their utter baselessness.[35] In the Gospel of Matthew, Christ's invitation to take up His yoke and rest is placed immediately before the chapter on the Sabbath controversies; it is a kind of preface, comparing His light yoke to the galling burden of sabbatical regulations, invented by the scribes and Pharisees. Of course, Jesus was not advocating neglect of the Sabbath. He was attempting, rather, to disengage it from the pharisaical obsession with rule-keeping and to preserve it as a day for the benefit of man.

"He said to them, 'Have you not read what David did when he was hungry, he and those who were with him: how he entered the house of God and ate the showbread which was not lawful for him to eat'" (Matt. 12:3, 4). Christ's method was often to lay before His accusers the clear words of Scripture, that they might realize they were protesting God's own word—that is, God Himself. The Book of Samuel describes David and his men entering the tabernacle and requesting food from the priest, who, having nothing to offer them except the showbread, which was meant only for the priests, freely gave it to them. It was a case in which David clearly broke a religious regulation, but Scripture does not utter a single word of reproach against David for his actions. Jesus here gives them a double lesson. First, they are found ignorant of sacred history and of the Torah. Second, their quick habit of judging others cancels the whole spirit of Scripture.

"If you had known what *this* means, 'I desire mercy and not sacrifice,' you would not have condemned the guiltless" (Matt. 12:7). The Lord draws on the wisdom of Hosea the Prophet, who railed against

---

35   *Mishnah, Hag.* I. 8.

the religious leaders of his day. They had also drowned themselves in the ceremonial minutiae of animal sacrifice, but heedlessly cast away the most essential aspect of the law: *mercy*. And He makes the declaration that, if a man were pressed to make a choice between mercy and sacrifice, he ought to follow God, who always prefers mercy. God can dispense with sacrifice; He can forgo a cold and lifeless ritual; but He cannot tolerate the oppression of the innocent. And if the temple rendered innocent the priests who broke every Sabbath by their sacrificial slaughtering, then the Christ—who is greater than the temple—by His very presence made the disciples innocent of plucking grain on the Sabbath.

"And He entered the synagogue again, and a man was there who had a withered hand. So they watched Him closely, whether He would heal him on the Sabbath, so that they might accuse Him" (Mark 3:1, 2). The Sabbath controversy is now removed to the synagogue at Capernaum. This was His home synagogue, to which He frequently went to pray, and to which a good deal of afflicted humanity flocked in order to seek His aid. On this particular Sabbath, a man in need of healing was present. But this was likely not an accidental affair; it was a plot, deviously orchestrated by the Pharisees and Herodians with the intent of proving His guilt. The Greek word[36] used by St. Mark to indicate their "watching" implies a close surveillance with the purpose of attacking an enemy. Saint Mark employs it to display the state of mind in which we find the Pharisees and Herodians. Their relation to Christ has now reached a new point of bitter opposition.

Christ knew well the menacing thoughts stirring in his enemies' minds. He accepts the challenge, and furthermore aims at exposing to full view the silent murmurings of their hearts. He commands the man with the withered hand to stand in the midst of the synagogue.

---

36 παρετηρουν

The assembly clearly witnesses the heartbreaking scene of a man with a lifeless arm. An apocryphal legend states that the man was a day laborer and that the palsied limb was his right hand; thus his affliction made him incapable of any work or self-support. It was a sight that would elicit human tears; but the Pharisees thought it preferable for the man to live paralyzed and die paralyzed rather than for anyone to violate the Sabbath. But Christ now enters the scene to disrupt the unbending dogmatism of these religious leaders and to upset the scales of hypocrisy that intentionally set up the dilemma at its beginning.

"He said to them, 'Is it lawful on the Sabbath to do good or to do evil, to save life or to kill?'" (Mark 3:4). Jesus presents them with this critical question, but not just for this particular case; for He could easily have placated them by waiting till the next day to perform the healing. But He is laying down a universal rule. The Sabbath, along with the rest of Moses' Law, cannot be made to conflict with the well-being of man. That is the very reason they were established in the first place. Christ thus exposes the scribes and Pharisees to the full extent of their blindness. In doing so, He rescues both the Law and the Sabbath from their iron grip and puts the Sabbath back into the service of mankind's salvation. Jesus then orders the man to stretch out the withered hand, and it is immediately healed.

"Then the Pharisees went out and immediately plotted with the Herodians against Him, how they might destroy Him" (Mark 3:6). The Pharisees are thrown into a frenzy of anger; Jesus' words have trapped them in an inextricable web, and their reputation before the people has deeply suffered. They immediately quit the scene of their defeat in shame and begin to consort with the Herodians. The Herodians were a loosely organized political group whose defining mark was loyalty to Herod Antipas and to Rome. The relationship between the Pharisees and Herodians was generally one of sharp animosity; but now they are united by a common enmity to Christ. From this day forward, a gray cloud is cast over the sunnier days of Jesus' ministry.

This event in the synagogue of Capernaum also marked the end of Jesus' open ministry in Galilee. His enemies had misinterpreted Him as being a religious scholar whose personal views on the Law and traditions of Israel had threatened to subvert their own authorized teachings. In reality, Jesus confessed the full authority of the Law, but He aimed at elucidating God's true intentions through it for the good of humanity. And He accompanied His new teaching with signs and miracles in order that His words would carry a more compelling legitimacy with the teachers of Israel. But the offense they could not brook was Jesus' refusal to concede to their own distorted interpretations of Sabbath law. Thus, the Pharisees now saw that cooperation with the Herodians for His destruction was the only way forward. It is a sad day for Jesus, because He sees the price for their obstinacy branded on their foreheads; and it is a price He will one day have to pay on the Cross. In such a state of indignant sorrow, Jesus leaves the synagogue of Capernaum, never to return again.

The First Parables

ONE DAY, IN THE EARLY period of Christ's ministry, Jesus sits in a boat and orders the disciples to put out a little into the sea. As the people gather on the shore to hear His words, He proceeds to deliver His teaching in a new form: the parable. The disciples are naturally perplexed. They ask the reason for this unprecedented method. Jesus enigmatically responds, "Because it has been given to you to know the mysteries of the kingdom of heaven, but to them it has not been given" (Matt. 13:11). He desires to initiate His chosen followers into the secrets of the Kingdom, but there are many who would make ill use of such knowledge. The dullness of heart among the general people is one barrier to clear speech, but the malice and cunning of the scribes and Pharisees is an even greater hindrance.

A parable is not meant, however, to hide the truth. It is intended to simplify and clarify the truth about God's Kingdom; it is an aid to help the believer to a deeper spiritual understanding. But that knowledge can only be claimed by one who receives the Bridegroom. The scribes and Pharisees had rejected Him, and in doing so, they had nullified their right to perceive the truths contained in Christ's parables.

He begins by describing a scene familiar to all the listeners. A farmer goes out to throw seed on his field. The seed is God's word, and the soil is man's heart. Some seeds fall by the wayside and are immediately devoured by birds; this refers to the heart which, when the word is heard, at once expels it by force of the lies and suggestions of Satan. Some seeds fall on stony soil and sprout a little plant, which, when exposed to the scorching rays of the sun, dies for lack of roots. And this refers to people who adopt the Faith when the road is easy; but when the road gets tougher, they abandon the way. Some seeds are cast into thorny soil and are choked to death. This refers to the heart that chokes the word of God by the unremitting cares of this world and chasing after riches. Finally, some seeds fall on fertile soil and yield a crop. And this of course refers to the heart that receives God's word and has health and strength enough to bear spiritual fruit.

Christ then begins delivering another parable, in which a man sows good seed in his field, but, while the servants are asleep, an enemy steals in and seeds the same field with tares. The servants ask if the master would prefer them to pull up the wheat immediately; but he responds no, it is better to allow the wheat and tares to flourish together. At harvest time, they will both be pulled up and dealt with accordingly. The master is Jesus, and the field is the world. Christ comes to sow His good seed, the new creation, in this old world. The flourishing of the wheat points to the growth of God's children. The children of God are not planted in order to be immediately harvested; they are to fill the world meanwhile with love and mercy and peace. They are placed on earth not just to prepare themselves for the Kingdom of God but also to prepare the world around them for the acceptance of that Kingdom. The enemy is Satan, who plants his own seed—false gospels, false prophets, and false hopes—in the world. But at the end of the age, the true and the false will be revealed.

Jesus moves on to the parable of the mustard seed, in which He sets before their minds an image common to every farmer in first-century Palestine. The Kingdom of God is compared to a mustard seed, which, though very small, is sown by the farmer and eventually grows into a stately tree. And Christ chooses this plant specifically for its rapid growth. A farmer may plant it and witness its growth every single day. Scholars say the mustard tree would grow to an average of three meters high in Palestine, and some were sturdy enough even to have their boughs climbed by a human. Jesus here draws our attention to the fact that, just as the farmer sees the mustard seed sprout and grow without his intervention, so would the Kingdom of God continue to grow every day, even without the agency of human intervention.

Jesus utters several more parables, then asks the disciples a question: "Have you understood all these things?" "Yes, Lord," they respond. Then He says, "Therefore every scribe instructed concerning the kingdom of heaven is like a householder who brings out of his treasure *things* new and old" (Luke 13:51, 52). At their answer of "yes," Christ places on them the responsibility of being the scribes of the New Covenant.

Calming the Tempest

JESUS HAS CONCLUDED HIS TEACHINGS, and just as the sun begins to dip below the horizon, He orders His disciples to steer the boat to the other shore. The Gospels include the interesting detail that a few smaller boats accompanied Him on the journey; these smaller vessels likely bore certain men and women in addition to the twelve who had abandoned their daily lives to follow Christ. The graphic detail with which the whole narrative is recorded in the Gospel of Mark drives us to the inevitable conclusion that this is the account of an eyewitness—possibly St. Peter, or possibly St. Mark himself. A story that includes so many minute details could not be the invention of a forger.

"And a great windstorm arose, and the waves beat into the boat, so that it was already filling" (Mark 4:37). The Sea of Galilee is flanked by mountainous heights on its northern and eastern shores; these heights send down strong gusts of wind into the Jordan Valley. In addition, chilly blasts pass from the western to the eastern boundaries of the sea, which further stir up its waters. The inexperienced sailor would typically experience some anxiety at such testy waters. But when the waves become so violent that they throw the boat around like a toy, even the most confident and sturdy sailor may lose his nerve. On this particular day, the sea is especially boisterous. The squall that descends on them is so violent, in fact, that the boat begins to flood from the inside, and the disciples are thrown into a panic. They rush to the Master with the exclamation, "Do You not care that we are perishing?"

Jesus then rises from His area of repose and answers the ferocity of the elements with an equally fierce rebuff: "Peace, be still!" At once the stormy waters collapse into a calm silence. Christ does not perform this sign just to prove His ascendancy over nature; He wishes to make a very clear point about His gospel: He possesses sovereignty over every turbulence in our world. His power surpasses not only that of water and gale but also that of every other thing in life that can overpower man, whether it be personal trials, disease, or crises. He demonstrates to the disciples that He is Lord of creation and director of the cosmos. But He does not demonstrate His supremacy in order to widen the gap between Himself and us poor human creatures. For He has given His majestic power to us, the Church, that we may carry on His work by virtue of His authority. He has given us everything: His riches, His glory, and even His inheritance in the Father.

"He said to them, 'Why are you so fearful? How *is it* that you have no faith?'" (Mark 4:40). The question naturally leads us to infer that Christ expected them to rebuke the wind and sea themselves. Every act that Christ performs by *authority* has been given to us to perform by *faith*. Since the Son of God became incarnate and made us children of God, the ability to use His authority has become a bona fide human right. If we have inherited the curse of sin through Adam, then we have inherited righteousness and holiness through Christ. The physical journey the disciples took in the boat on that day was also a spiritual journey into the mystery of who Christ is.

"And they feared exceedingly, and said to one another, 'Who can this be, that even the wind and the sea obey Him!'" (Mark 4:41). The terror that gripped the disciples was not a fear of Christ or even of the miracle; it was a natural dread that filled them at being in the presence of an unexpected and unknown power they had never before witnessed. When God's power is suddenly manifested, man will prostrate in fear. The disciples' fear of the boisterous waves displeased Christ, but their fear of the divine presence was seemly and right. Saint Matthew says that the disciples "marveled" at the miracle, while St. Mark says they "feared." To marvel is a more transient emotion, whereas fear rises from the depths of one's being.

The episode ends with a critical question posed by the disciples to each other: *Who can this be?* A host of scholars and wise men have attempted to provide an answer but, alas, unsuccessfully. The question itself is a foretaste of the answer the evangelists give in the rest of their Gospels. *Who can this be?* Well, to all appearances, here is a humble human figure, sleeping in a boat, seemingly unaware and careless as to the storm that is threatening everyone's life. But He rises with unperturbable calm and bids earth and sky to obey His will. *Who can this be?* It is a question classically treated by professional theologians, but it may be correctly answered by anyone who believes in the mystery of the Incarnation. The evangelists seem to record the question with one eye on Bethlehem and one eye on the empty tomb. *Who can this be?* This is a mystery, almost a riddle, decipherable only by the person who reads the Gospel while looking up.

Jairus's Daughter and the Bleeding Woman

AS JESUS' BOAT NEARS THE shores of Capernaum, He is immediately met by a great crowd of people who have come to meet the renowned teacher. He has crossed back and forth several times across the Sea of Galilee, and He teaches each time from within the boat as it floats very near the beach; His intent is to avoid the press and jostle of the crowds. But in this instance, the crowd has been watching His every movement and is already anticipating His arrival. He disembarks from the boat, and the multitude, astonished at the news of a recent miracle performed in the region of the Gadarenes and eager to get a glimpse of the young prophet, press and squeeze without a thought for His comfort.

A cleavage is suddenly made in the crowd, because a special envoy has arrived. Jairus, a ruler of Capernaum's synagogue and hence a person of some standing among the Jews, comes to Jesus in a state of visible agitation. Forgetting his title and position, he flings himself at Jesus' feet and tells Him with broken words that his daughter, his only daughter, lies at death's door. If Jesus will only come and lay His hand upon the girl, pleads the ruler, she will be made well. O Jairus! You, the representative of that nation that was rejecting the One sent to it, are now begging for mercy in your time of need! But Jesus immediately consents to the request and begins walking toward Jairus's home.

At this point, a woman who possesses a faith greater even than that of Jairus makes her way stealthily through the throng to see, if possible, whether she might touch Him. She has suffered for years from a distressing malady and has exhausted all her funds in seeking medical care. As her hope in physicians died, a new faith in Christ has been kindled in her heart. Once she has reached Jesus, she stoops in humility and touches the fringe of His flowing robe. Her modesty and the shame of her disease compel her to act in complete secrecy, but she is determined to steal from Him, unknown, the blessing for which she longs. God's riches are inexhaustible, and His stores cannot be pilfered except by one who already has a large account in his or her bank of faith.

At the touch of His robe, she immediately feels her body restored to health. It is not a mere conjecture; she is certain of the healing. Bodily healing that comes by the aid of medicine is often slow, sporadic, and uncertain; but divine healing is clear and absolute. And is not this brave woman's act an illustration of Christ's remark that the Kingdom of heaven shall be taken by force? Our faith in Christ permits us to "plunder" the blessings of God. This bleeding woman stormed Christ's warehouse of divine goods, and God has granted us as well the right to enter His presence and take what we need by a stalwart faith.

Christ immediately turns and asks, "Who touched Me?" The

woman's faith draws out the power latent in Christ's divinity before He even realizes she is there! This is a remarkable discovery of the evangelists' and worthy of a place in the Church's theology: that the power of God through faith is available more openly and immediately to us than we could ever conceive. Christ's question, however, catches the woman by surprise, and she comes, trembling yet grateful, and reveals to Christ all that has transpired. There are some who imagine that Christ was offended by the touch of one who was ceremonially unclean. But such a conception is totally unworthy of the Son of God—who came specifically to raise a woman like this and to make her a member in His Church.

"He said to her, 'Daughter, your faith has made you well'" (Mark 5:34). Can we not call this woman the apostle of plundering faith? Has she not taught us, even more than the rest of the apostles, that a believer has the absolute right to ransack divine things, even if she be levitically unclean? In any event, this woman plundered God's storehouse and took healing, purity, and holiness as her spoils. And Jesus rewarded her boldness by drawing her nearer to Himself with the tender appellation "daughter."

As Christ turned to resume His way to Jairus's habitation, some of Jairus's servants came to him with the report that his daughter had finally died; and they added, with a touch of irony, "Why trouble the teacher any further?" The announcement had filled the synagogue ruler's heart with agony; but Christ, perceiving his profound despair, immediately planted hope in his heart by declaring, "Do not be afraid; only believe."

Christ then took with him the inner circle of His disciples, Peter, James, and John—the three who went with Him up the Mount of Transfiguration and into Gethsemane—and arrived at the ruler's house. He was met by the weeping and wailing of those women who were hired to raise a clamor of sorrow at funerals. Their task was to announce the coming of that dark reaper who flashes his sickle and takes his victims regardless of age or status. The scene was covered in a veil of death that served as a real challenge to Christ's presence—a challenge He would meet again with Lazarus.

"He said to them, 'Why make this commotion and weep? The child is not dead, but sleeping'" (Mark 5:39). The crowd's response was to laugh and sneer at the comment, as though Jesus could not tell the difference between sleep and death. But here was One who knew death very well: "By death He trampled upon death"; and if it seemed that He made light of it, it was because He had broken its thorn: "O Death, where *is* your sting?" (1 Cor. 15:55). He entered the gloomy chamber with the family, pulled aside the curtain that enclosed Hades, and reclaimed the girl's soul with the words, "Little girl, I say to you, arise." And she immediately rose. An awful amazement gripped all those present, but Jesus quietly bade them give her some food. He then warned them not to publicize what had happened. The miracle was clearly messianic in nature, and He did not want the circumstance to rile up the scribes and Pharisees against Him at that time. It was better that the family treasure up the wonderful act in their hearts and allow it to peacefully reveal to them the true identity of the One who had saved them.

The Mission of the Twelve

THE REMAINDER OF THE TIME Christ spent in Galilee (circa AD 28) was devoted to the instruction and spiritual formation of the twelve disciples. They closely followed His steps—seeing, hearing, pondering, asking questions, and preparing for their future role as evangelists. Every now and again Jesus would question them on what they had learned; they must comprehend the things they were witnessing. Finally, they were ready to be sent to all the districts of

Galilee to teach what He had taught. They were not yet ready to preach on the mysteries of salvation—that would be delayed until they received the Holy Spirit. Their only task was to announce the arrival of that which everyone in Israel had been pining for: "The Kingdom of heaven is at hand!" This short-term preaching trip was to be a foretaste of that apostolic work they would undertake one day throughout the whole world, and it was also meant to establish the Kingdom of heaven *within* them.

That wise scholar Bengel calls the apostles the "princes of Christ's Kingdom," and indeed they occupy a place more honorable and illustrious than the kings of the earth. The Church's tradition has reverently tracked their missionary trips across the globe and has turned their martyrdoms into feast days. For, as we say, the blood of these martyrs—after Christ's blood—is the seed of the Church. The mission was not expected to be an easy affair. Luke tells us that Jesus alluded to this mission right before His arrest in Gethsemane: "He said to them, 'When I sent you without money bag, knapsack, and sandals, did you lack anything?'" (Luke 22:35). And with similar words He sent out the seventy apostles on their mission: "Go your way. . . . Carry neither money bag, knapsack, nor sandals; and greet no one along the road" (Luke 10:3, 4).

The moment this commission fell from Christ's lips, they were considered "apostles." And in Acts, they are always referred to as apostles and never as disciples—the latter term being reserved for the new believers (Acts 6:1). The apostleship given to these disciples came with a grave responsibility. It was given with the understanding that its authority and power issued directly from Christ's name. An apostle was expected to live continually in truth and spirit; and if ever he were to abandon the life of holiness and righteousness, or misuse his stewardship of the Name, he would be stripped of his apostleship and become a target for the evil one: "Then some of the itinerant Jewish exorcists took it upon themselves to call the name of the Lord Jesus over those who had evil spirits . . . and the evil spirit answered and said, 'Jesus I know, and Paul I know; but who are you?' Then the man in whom the evil spirit was leaped on them, overpowered them, and prevailed against them" (Acts 19:13, 15–16).

The Gospel writers assume here that the reader knows that Christ had already chosen His twelve disciples at a previous point in His ministry. Now, however, their names are officially and methodically introduced to the reader—not because they are only now being called by Christ, but because they are being *sent* by Him to preach. In the New Testament, the names of the twelve apostles are listed in four different catalogues: one each in Matthew, Mark, Luke, and Acts. When the names are arranged into vertical columns and placed into parallel tables for comparison, a few striking facts become apparent. The twelve can be divided into three ranks or subdivisions of four names each; and in none of the four lists will a name (or its equivalent) be found to wander from its subdivision. The foremost name in each rank is also constant: Peter, Philip, and James the Less hold the first place in their respective ranks across all four lists.

The Gospel of Luke divides the instructions given by Christ to the apostles into two different stages: the first (in chapter 9) to the twelve, and the second (chapter 10) to the seventy. The Gospel of Matthew presents all the instructions as one unbroken speech (chapter 10). Saint Mark is content with simply saying that Jesus sent them out two by two.

These twelve Jesus sent out and commanded them, saying: "Do not go into the way of the Gentiles, and do not enter a city of the Samaritans. But go rather to the lost sheep of the house of Israel. And as you go, preach, saying, 'The kingdom of heaven is at hand.' Heal the sick, cleanse the lepers, raise the dead, cast out demons. Freely you have received, freely give." (Matt. 10:5–8)

They went out from Christ's presence brimming with enthusiasm and in possession of an extraordinary power for the newly appointed ministry. They carried out the service with spirits aflame, and the work gained a further impetus from their gift to cast out demons and heal the sick. The signs that accompanied their preaching would give people the sense that a uniquely new happening was afoot. The apostles did not deviate from the simple announcement that the Kingdom was at hand—but the inner meaning and nature of that Kingdom they left to Christ someday to reveal.

Jesus restricts their preaching to the region of Galilee and expressly forbids them from entering Samaria because the announcement of the Kingdom needed to be delivered to the chosen people; the hearts of the Jews required illumination before they could become a light to the heathen world. The apostles themselves, moreover, needed their hearts primed in the ways of the Holy Spirit. To take just a single example, when Christ sought to enter a Samaritan city on His way to Jerusalem, He met with a cold refusal. Taking sharp offense at the insult, the sons of Zebedee asked Christ for permission to call down fire from heaven to burn the city. But Christ checked their hasty anger; their zeal was not yet seasoned with the salt of grace. In regard to the Gentiles, Christ prohibited the twelve from preaching to them because it was an entrenched assumption that, in order for a Gentile to be accepted by God, he must first become a Jew. Thus, Christ spared the twelve apostles the painful controversy that would one day engage St. Paul and the church of Jerusalem.

The Feeding of Five Thousand

PASSOVER HAD BEGUN TO DRAW near when the apostles had returned from their mission, and great swarms of pilgrims could now be seen heading toward Jerusalem from all over the country. Christ, however, decided not to make His way there just yet, in order to avoid the obnoxious controversies that had beset His earlier visits to the city. His focus was now to prepare the apostles for their future ministries. He sought therefore a quiet place in which He could retire with the apostles, to hear the accounts of their recent ministry and to instruct them further in the principles of service. "Then the apostles gathered to Jesus and told Him all things, both what they had done and what they had taught. And He said to them, 'Come aside by yourselves to a deserted place and rest a while.' For there were many coming and going, and they did not even have time to eat. So they departed to a deserted place in the boat by themselves" (Mark 6:30–32). But upon discovering His whereabouts, the multitudes came to Him, seeking His healing touch and desiring to hear the word of God.

As the hour grew late, it was past the ordinary time for supper; and the multitude, being in a deserted place, and having no access to food anywhere, grew hungry. The disciples went to Jesus and urged Him to allow the people to visit nearby villages for food and lodging. The barrenness of the scene is a distant echo of the ancient Israelites' sojourn in the wilderness of Sinai. Manna fell from heaven to feed the people then; but no manna need fall now, for the true manna was with them. And the people were to feed on this miraculous bread. The disciples' minds were too restricted to perceive the solution to the people's hunger. The story thus becomes a doctrinal lesson for the Church: that even were the Church to find herself poor, without a single drop of oil or grain of wheat, she is still responsible for feeding her sheep. The Church must not forget the oil and flour of the widow of

Zarephath that was placed in the Church's account; nor should she forget Peter's fishing net that was brought up full; nor may she forget the twelve baskets Christ commanded to be collected and put away into the Church's storage rooms to be kept for hard times.

Jesus orders His disciples to divide the multitude into groups of fifty and have them all sit down on the grass. The rearrangement of the people could only have heightened their curiosity as to where the disciples planned to find food to feed so many mouths. All eyes were turned to Christ as He stood in their midst, raised His eyes to heaven, spoke a blessing over the bread and fish, and divided them. As Christ proceeded to divide over and over, yet without any depletion of the loaves or fish, it became apparent to the people that they were witnessing a mystical sacrament. Jesus would hand the blessed food to the disciples, who filled their baskets and passed it along to the people, but then returned to find Jesus breaking the same loaf yet again without depletion. This was a eucharistic bread, which the organs of the people could digest and consume, yet which bestowed spiritual blessings on the recipients.

"So they all ate and were filled, and twelve baskets of the leftover fragments were taken up by them" (Luke 9:17). The episode of feeding the five thousand, along with the abundance of leftover fragments, serves as a beautiful illustration of the principle that physical properties can be transformed into spiritual life. Jesus bursts the boundaries of mathematics and physics. If we assume that each of the five thousand participants received one loaf of bread and one fish, it means that five became five thousand. And what if we were to posit five thousand million hungry mouths? What if they were an infinite number? Christ would have multiplied all the same. Here is a clear indication of Christ's creative power and of His divinity. Here is the Alpha and Omega. Would not such a Person be worthy to become Lord of humanity? Indeed, St. John's Gospel tells us that the men who were fed attempted to seize Jesus by force to make Him their king. But Christ foiled this benevolent plot by commanding the disciples to prepare the boat and depart across the sea. Before He could accept the dignity of royalty, He must first accept the shame of the Cross.

Jesus Walks on the Sea

"IMMEDIATELY JESUS MADE HIS DISCIPLES get into the boat and go before Him to the other side, while He sent the multitudes away" (Matt. 14:22). This verse directly follows the miracle of the feeding, and it strikes us with its sense of urgency. We may ask, why did Jesus take such swift action in sending away His disciples, then dismissing the multitudes singlehandedly? As we have said, John's Gospel relates the deep feelings that agitated the men who were fed and their resolution to set Jesus up as their king. And in all probability, the disciples joined the movement; it was through the disciples' hands that the miracle was accomplished, and to their minds, the messianic age was now breaking through. In order therefore to forestall this scheme, being irreconcilable as it was with Christ's own purposes, He ordered the disciples into their boat and sent the satisfied crowds away to their homes.

He immediately retires to a nearby mountain in search of a few precious hours of solitude and prayer. He had just come through a temptation. The very tests by which He had silenced the devil in the wilderness—changing stone to bread for bread's sake, and seeking glory for glory's sake—Satan now brought to Him once more by the agency of the simple people's clamoring for His kingship. The danger hidden in the temptation was that it threatened to nullify the Cross; and therefore, Christ used His full authority to stamp it out before it could get off the ground.

As the hours drifted by during Jesus' quiet retirement, the waves stirred more boisterously on the Sea of Galilee, and the disciples' boat was storm-tossed. The vessel was headed in a westward direction toward the cities (such as Capernaum) that dotted the western shore; the wind, however, was blowing in the opposite direction, from west to east. And the disciples, meeting such a forceful headwind, strained every muscle to row through it. But nature proved too strong, and every meter gained by rowing was lost to the wind. They were at least three to four miles out from shore; though Jesus could not hear the cry of their voices from the mountain, He could hear the cry of their hearts in His soul. And He began to move.

Jesus drew near to the boat, walking on the water. It was the fourth watch of the night, meaning that it was the darkest hour. The disciples quivered with fear at the uncanny sight. The waters were stirred up by natural and possibly also by satanic forces; yet Christ strides through, superior to all opposition. Satan had once tempted Christ to jump from the temple's roof and fly through the air on angelic wings. But Christ now performs a more difficult feat—not for the sake of show, but for the sake of rescue. Here is a picture worthy to be displayed on the pediment of every church for the comfort of troubled souls. The waves of this world roll and beat against the Church, but she ever waits for her Master to arrive, even if at the fourth watch of the night. And when He does approach, we will not stare aghast as if at a ghost, but we will take hold of Him and entreat Him to enter our vessel!

"Jesus spoke to them, saying, 'Be of good cheer! It is I; do not be afraid.' And Peter answered Him and said, 'Lord, if it is You, command me to come to You on the water.' So He said, 'Come'" (Matt. 14:27–29). Peter, with his impetuous yet sincere love, climbs over the side of the vessel and begins to walk toward Jesus over the stormy waters. But as he peers into the blackness of the troubled winds, his faith and body sink. Christ immediately grasps His disciple by the arm and pulls him up with the gentle rebuke, "O you of little faith." It is difficult for Peter and for us to live near God while feeling the weight of gravity pulling us toward the earth. If we live by bread alone, what will happen when that bread runs out? If we feel secure only when standing on solid ground, how will we be lifted up? And how can we walk on water with heavy feet?

Peter half believed that Jesus was a phantom, but the storm was clearly no phantom. The stormy elements made him forget that he had a stronger support before him. He might have walked at first by faith, but then the dark clouds concealed his faith and blurred his vision of Jesus. He began to doubt Christ's presence, and the doubt sank him. Jesus' command to Peter to come onto the water is also a command to us to put our faith in His word. He stands amidst life's thunderstorms, holding out His hand toward us and bidding us to walk.

The moment Jesus entered the boat, the wind and waves ceased their violent lashing. The disciples responded by paying homage to Him and declaring that He was indeed the Son of God. This was simply the natural response. If the wind and water become prostrate before Christ, shall not man too?

Peter's Confession and Rebuke

AFTER A TIME JESUS BRINGS His disciples to the region of Caesarea Philippi, a quiet place far from the bustle of Galilee. This city sat at the northernmost end of the land of Naphtali, on the border of Syria, in the shadow of snow-capped Mount Hermon. It bore the name of Philip (brother of Herod Antipas) to distinguish it from the other Caesarea that sat on the Mediterranean shore at the foot of Mount Carmel. When they reach this spot of repose, Jesus puts to them a question: "Who do men say that I am?"

The question came at the conclusion of a period of prayer—a small notice provided to us by Luke, meant to indicate the significance of the impending discourse. Jesus likely prayed for the opening of the disciples' minds to a critical truth. He asked what the crowds thought of Him, because the entire success of His mission was contingent on the people's recognition of Him as One who was specially sent from God. He had just recently fed the crowds with a miraculous production of loaves and fish, and so the people's excitement had raised His reputation to its zenith.

So what exactly were their thoughts? Some people had said He was John the Baptist risen from the dead. The Baptist's sudden death had sent shock waves through the nation, and many had expected him to rise from the dead to take vengeance. This was at least the rumor that had reached the ears of Herod. Some again said He was Elijah or a great prophet, for wonder-working became common currency in the days of the prophets. But such conjectures were poor attempts at the truth. With implicit dissatisfaction at these answers, Jesus turns the question on them: "But who do *you* say that I am?"

Peter is the quickest to respond: "You are the Christ, the Son of the living God." Jesus then blesses Peter (who now receives that name), because the revelation came not by some inner workings of Peter's mind, but by a direct enlightenment from God. Thus, Peter had received the primary election to understand the truth and to declare it. And so the faith and doctrine of the Church would find its germ in the faith and doctrine of Peter's statement. The faith and doctrine are not Peter's but are originally God's, given about Christ. It was therefore fitting that the primitive Church was first spread under Peter's leadership and that Peter became a liaison of sorts between the stringently Judaic and liberally Gentile streams of early Christianity.

Jesus sternly warns them not to spread this revelation among the people, because the time was not yet ripe for its proclamation. And in case the disciples thought that the messiahship meant just a dainty enjoyment of honor and homage, Jesus breaks some foreboding news: "The Son of Man must suffer many things, and be rejected by the elders and chief priests and scribes, and be killed, and be raised the third day" (Luke 9:21). This moment is the first introduction Jesus gives to His disciples to the concept of suffering. Thus far, the gospel they had heard from His lips entailed faith and repentance; now it was to include pain. They had been cherishing false hopes of an earthly glory; but now Christ must lead them on deeper into faith, to a faith in a Messiah who suffers for His people's deliverance.

It is ironic: Jesus needed to first convince the disciples of His authority over disease, death, and the devil before He could tell them that He was to suffer. The first half of His ministry focused on teachings regarding Himself; the second half of His ministry focused on suffering. The first half revealed His authority, while the second half revealed His suffering glory. It was Peter's confession—"You are the Christ"—that signaled the successful close of the first phase of His ministry; and now Jesus straightway opens the second phase with the foretelling of His sufferings.

But despite Jesus' clear and unmistakable language about His impending death, the disciples simply could not understand a word He said. They were all along entertaining thoughts of a magnificent earthly kingdom that He was inaugurating, and especially of the privileged places they would occupy around His throne. All this talk of suffering and dying was to them no more than a hazy nightmare they needed simply to scatter from their minds. No wonder, then, that they slept through His agony in the garden, they fled at the approach of His enemies, and they disbelieved at the news of His Resurrection.

Peter again is the first to speak. Emboldened by Christ's praise and feeling himself elevated to the position of adviser to the Messiah, he takes Jesus aside and passionately objects to His predictions. "Far be it from You, Lord; this shall not happen to You!" (Matt. 16:22). But Jesus' response was firm: "Get behind Me, Satan! You are an offense to Me, for you are not mindful of the things of God, but the things of men" (Matt. 16:23). Jesus sees the clear effects of Satan's work on the mind of Peter, because Peter's rebuke recalls to Him the temptation in the wilderness: "Bow to me and I will give You the world." Moreover, Peter's rebuke did not accord with Jesus' intent to build the Church on the rock. Peter imagined he was the favored disciple upon whom Christ would build His Church through acts of might. Never did he imagine that the Church would be built on Jesus' death. At one moment, Peter is speaking by inspiration from the Father, and in the next moment, he is speaking by the inspiration of the devil. His intentions were good, but he lacked understanding.

In order to lay stress on His statements, Jesus delivers the great principle, "If anyone desires to come after Me, let him deny himself, and take up his cross, and follow Me" (Matt. 16:24). Christ does not impose obedience or self-denial on any person, but to follow in His footsteps implies both. He who finds self-denial for Christ too burdensome may be destroying his own soul by his obstinacy. The world is indeed a pleasant place with attractive wares: public honor, accolades, money, feasts, and so on; but at the end of the road awaits death. So what does it profit a man to run after all this, yet to lose his soul in the process and die? Either a man will destroy his ego willingly, or his ego will destroy him unwillingly. It is best to surrender one's soul to Christ, that we may pass with Him through the straits of death and rise with Him in the beautiful splendor of the eternal inheritance.

The Transfiguration

IT WAS AT THIS JUNCTION in time, in the wise purposes of Jesus, that He chose to manifest Himself in transformed glory to His three most favored disciples, that they might see His true majesty and hear the Father's loving approbation of Him from heaven. Even we the readers need the moral support provided by this scene in order to endure the accounts of harrowing pain that are to follow. Our minds will be taken into places where God's Messiah will have His back stripped naked, the flesh torn apart, and the blood sprayed about by flogging. Our nerves are pulled taut when we are made to remember the vivid and awful Crucifixion, the hammering of the nails, and the giving up of the spirit.

Scholars are divided on the identity of the mountain that serves as the setting for the miracle. Some believe that Mount Hermon answers best to the description in the Gospels, while others believe that Mount Tabor in Galilee was the scene of the event. In any case, Jesus desired to pass a peaceful night in the presence of His three chosen disciples, and He takes them to ascend the mountain. As time passes, the sun disappears below the horizon; night overtakes them and creates a deep and stern silence on the mountaintop. The frigid serenity of the place provided the ideal conditions for the ascent of a human soul to grander spiritual heights. Jesus is in the midst of His disciples, praying, as they begin to witness a halo of light slowly emerging from Him.

His appearance (not His nature) was immediately transformed. His face shone "like the sun," to display the true magnificence He shared with the Father before it was hidden in the Incarnation. That divine glory never left Him but was only concealed, so it was necessary that the disciples receive a momentary glimpse of it. It was as though He were telling them without words, "Behold, this is who I truly am. Remember this; for you need this vision of glory to sustain you through the agony that this body will soon inflict upon Me."

In Hebrew, this type of radiance is referred to as the *shekinah*, and it is understood to represent the divine presence. It is a light unlike that of the sun or moon or any earthly body, because it is far more powerful, though it causes no harm to the eye. It penetrates all things—body, mind, heart, and conscience. It is also known in Greek as the *doxa* or glory of God. So when we sing, "Glory to the Father, the Son, and the Holy Spirit," we are pleading for that light to penetrate us, for God's presence to surround us. When Christ says, "I am the light," He means that He embodies the glory of God.

And it was a vision they were never to forget. Peter later writes, "For we . . . were eyewitnesses of His majesty. For He received from God the Father honor and glory when such a voice came to Him from the Excellent Glory: 'This is My beloved Son, in whom I am well pleased.' And we heard this voice which came from heaven when we were with Him on the holy mountain" (2 Pet. 1:16–18). John also writes in his prologue, "And the Word became flesh and dwelt among us, and we beheld His glory, the glory as of the only begotten of the Father, full of grace and truth" (1:14). Saint Paul was likewise struck by a glorious vision of Christ—not from a mountain, but directly from heaven—shining more powerfully than the sun.

The disciples then found Christ flanked by two Old Testament figures—Moses and Elijah. In the still silence of that night, they could make out the words being exchanged between those august figures and Christ. They were conversing about His coming death in Jerusalem. The very presence of Israel's great lawgiver and Israel's great prophet was a clear sign that the One between them was the long-awaited Messiah. Jesus wanted His three disciples to witness this unique conference, composed of the greatest figures from both Testaments, revealing a united faith and an unbroken continuity between what was and what was to come.

Now Peter, who was by this time tired, dazed, and dumbstruck by the vision, stammers as he presents the idea of setting up tents for the three holy men standing in light. It could have been done, but that would be to confuse heaven and earth and to conflate the Old and New Testaments into a meaningless heap. The Gospels give us the appropriate response to Peter's feeble idea: "A cloud came and overshadowed them; and a voice came out of the cloud, saying, 'This is My beloved Son. Hear Him!'" (Mark 9:7). The three were not to be covered by tents of fabric, but by a tent of heavenly light, a cloud descending from above and expressing things that surpassed the understanding of the listeners. The Father's voice spoke from that cloud to convey to the disciples—to the Church and to the world—the blessing of the Son. God, who centuries before had given us Moses and Elijah, was now giving us the gift of His only-begotten Son.

Descent from the Mountain and Healing of the Epileptic Boy

JESUS LEFT THE SCENE OF the sublime event on the mountaintop in order to descend again into the field of pastoral labor and the concerns of humanity. He was reentering a world that oscillated between praises and threats, between acceptance and rejection, where even friends and family were guilty of a total misapprehension of His cause. Though He had received heaven's official approval through the Father's voice, the disciples still could not understand His need to suffer and die. And ever since then, genuine faith in Christ has never relied on perception, analysis, or the agreement of the logical mind. For faith to live, one must give a chance for the spirit to take up its superior role in life and for the Holy Spirit to reveal the eternal things.

It was the morning of the day following the Transfiguration when Jesus descended the mountain with His three disciples to rejoin the nine who had been waiting at the foot. And they found the nine surrounded by a crowd of people with diseases who had come to be healed. A man approaches Jesus and pleads for his epileptic son. "Teacher, I implore You, look on my son, for he is my only child" (Luke 9:38). The boy was seized by a hostile spirit that caused him to foam at the mouth and would injure him by violently flinging him about. The father's first course of action is *prayer*; he comes first to Jesus, then the physician's role would follow.

"'I implored Your disciples to cast it out, but they could not.' Then Jesus answered and said, 'O faithless and perverse generation, how long shall I be with you and bear with you? Bring your son here'" (Luke 9:40, 41). It is a singular point here that Jesus does not underscore the father's faith or the disciples' lack of faith; rather, He laments a lack of faith in *that generation*. The father hardly believed that the disciples were capable of healing his son, and the disciples themselves had scarcely any faith in their own ability to do so. The devil could sit and gloat about his triumph, for it was the all-around faithlessness of the people that gave him the power to abuse God's creation.

When they brought the boy and he saw Christ, the hostile spirit cast him to the ground and made him suffer an agonizing convulsion. The father in his desperation again implores Jesus, "If You can do anything, have compassion on us and help us.' Jesus said to him, 'If you can believe, all things *are* possible to him who believes.' Immediately the father of the child cried out and said with tears, 'Lord, I believe; help my unbelief!'" (Mark 9:22–24). Christ's answer here reveals for us a divine law: that man's faith and God's hand are connected by an immutable bond. The father's quivering faith weakened Christ's ability to heal. Jesus' rule was always to seek the person's faith before healing; so here, the father's faith was sought on the boy's behalf.

Christ here makes one thing clear: faith is everything. The words Jesus spoke when He performed His miracles were the very essence of the gospel; they formed the content of the Church's doctrine as well as the Christian's creed. Notice the evangelists' brilliance in recounting the story. To a dry intellect it might appear that the words exchanged between the man and Jesus were simply wedged into a story whose primary importance is the miracle-working. But in fact, the incidental words dropped in the middle of the story form the very basis of the miracle; and they express, moreover, the principles by which the Church must exist. We are forever indebted to St. Mark for inscribing these words.

Jesus then rebukes the unclean spirit; it convulses its victim once again, gives out a shriek of horror, and departs. Jesus then lifts the boy up and restores him to his father. The disciples, confounded and humiliated by their failure, ask Jesus privately, "Why could we not cast it out?" And the Lord replies, "This kind can come out by nothing but prayer and fasting" (Mark 9:28, 29). The devil is powerless against a robust and genuine faith. This is the reason the Church has established seasons of prayer and fasting to fortify her believers. Collective prayer fortifies the Church, while individual prayer fortifies the believer. Likewise, as collective fasting protects the Church, so private fasting preserves the believer.

The Dispute as to Who Would Be the Greatest and Christ's Warning against Sectarianism

"THEN HE CAME TO CAPERNAUM. And when He was in the house He asked them, 'What was it you disputed among yourselves on the road?' But they kept silent, for on the road they had disputed among themselves who *would be the* greatest" (Mark 9:33, 34). It is likely that this contention was carried on mainly between Judas and Peter.

Judas was the greatest in age, and according to Jewish custom, the eldest always received preference in every aspect of life. When seated for a meal, for example, the place at the right hand of the father was reserved for the eldest, and the youngest sat at his left hand. Peter, however, prided himself on occupying the first place in the Master's trust—a fact Judas resented because he held the money bag and so was entitled to the greatest trust. Tradition preferred Judas, but common sense preferred Peter. Christ would judge the case by a different standard entirely: humility. Instead of advocating for one side over the other, He chose to give them a much-needed lesson.

"Then Jesus called a little child to Him, set him in the midst of them, and said, 'Assuredly, I say to you, unless you are converted and become as little children, you will by no means enter the kingdom of heaven'" (Matt. 18:2). He brought the child as a living illustration of the Kingdom principle that the first shall be last and the last first. He desired the image of the humble child to be stamped onto the disciples' minds and to form a mystical connection in this triple symbolism: child, Christ, Kingdom. The "ideology" of a child—simplicity, innocence, purity—should inspire a Christian leader. The "first" in Christ must be free of the love of power, of control, of primacy. "And when He had taken him in His arms, He said to them, 'Whoever receives one of these little children in My name receives Me'" (Mark 9:36, 37).

Following on the heels of this dispute was another contentious issue that had occupied the disciples' attention. "John answered Him, saying, 'Teacher, we saw someone who does not follow us casting out demons in Your name, and we forbade him because he does not follow us'" (Mark 9:38). This comment might seem abruptly inserted here without relation to the previous incident, but in fact, they are related by one important clause: *in Your name*. The question at hand gives rise to a vital principle. The view held by the disciples was that they could dogmatically forbid or repudiate certain persons because they were not followers of their band. But Jesus is clearly displeased with the notion and offers a strong reproof against it.

He then lays down the basis for dealing with those of differing doctrinal positions who labor for Christ's name. "Do not forbid him, for no one who works a miracle in My name can soon afterward speak evil of Me" (Mark 9:39). The condition for fraternity and cooperation among different doctrinal groups is that they all share a common reverence for Christ's name. Whether they are driving out demons, or healing disease, or teaching doctrine, they are united through the name of Jesus. Then He utters a remarkable statement: "For he who is not against us is on our side" (v. 40). As long as the person (of a different doctrinal confession) does not oppose us, or what we do, or what we believe, then he is on our side. And we all work for the common good—Christ's ministry.

Now, when certain Christian peoples transgressed this law for their personal gain, the oneness of the body was shattered; and the many splinter groups and denominations that resulted from the division turned on each other and began to *oppose each other in Christ's name*. Each claims absolute loyalty to Him while openly flouting His literal command. How long can such a sad state of affairs persist? Such discord is a shame to believers and an offense to the Faith! Can these dissensions be justified? Is ecclesiastical division really enacted for Christ's sake? But when the dictum, "For he who is not against us is on our side," is abandoned, then love is flung to the ground and trampled on. Dear reader, I beseech you, for Jesus' sake, always seek for the unity of the Church and shun needless quarrels!

CHAPTER EIGHT

The Final Judean and Perean Ministry

Jesus at the Feast of Tabernacles

"Now the Jews' Feast of Tabernacles was at hand" (John 7:2). Josephus tells us that the Feast of Tabernacles was the most anticipated and jubilant of the Jewish festivals.[37] It comprised seven days of feasting, along with a final "great day" of completion and rest. This feast fell on the Hebrew calendar during the month that corresponds with our October, and it was the last major feast of the Hebrew year. The Jews spent the days of this feast living in tents or booths constructed of branches, in remembrance of the forty years their ancestors spent in the wilderness after their departure from Egypt. During the festivities all the priests served their courses in turn. Seventy bulls were offered in sacrifice for the seventy nations of the world. Each day the Law was read, and each day the temple trumpets blasted twenty-one times.[38]

For nearly two years now, Jesus has been planting the seeds of the Kingdom all over Galilee, and in the last six months He has purposely avoided going up to Jerusalem on any of the three great Jewish feasts. On this occasion, however, He decides to go up. He must

---

37   Josephus, *Antiquities*, VIII. 4.1.
38   Farrar, *The Life of Christ*, ch. 39.

continue the work He started there among the Jewish pilgrims as well as among his religious opponents. He needs to silence the suggestion that He fears ministering to the people where the Sanhedrin convene, though He evidently sees it prudent to avoid unnecessary conflict with the rulers of Jerusalem.

His brethren understood none of His plans. They had invited Him to accompany them in their travels to Jerusalem; but when He refused the request, they assumed it was because He intended to take refuge in quiet concealment. "His brothers therefore said to Him, 'Depart from here and go into Judea, that Your disciples also may see the works that You are doing. For no one does anything in secret while he himself seeks to be known openly. If You do these things, show Yourself to the world.' For even His brothers did not believe in Him" (John 7:3–5). Jesus' brethren reveal a striking lack of sympathy with Him. Since He was absent at the most recent Passover, their words carry an implied rebuke. Now, say they, is the time for Him to make His grand appearance at the capital and to claim all the disciples who have believed in Him—disciples from every part of the world, including some even from among the Sanhedrin. They urge Him, from impure motives, to launch Himself into the spotlight on the greatest Jewish stage.

Christ's defense is that He must not precipitate the course of events before their due time. The *hour of the Cross*—which would be the hour of His revelation to the world—could only be determined by the Father. Any sudden movement He might make to perturb the rulers of Jerusalem could upset Jesus' calm submission to the Father's plan. "My time has not yet come, but your time is always ready" (John 7:6). *Their* time was ever present and ready, because they could go up to Jerusalem at any time merely as visitors. Jesus could no longer approach the city except in preparation for the Cross. He then offers a striking though subtle reproof to these brethren: "The world cannot hate you, but it hates Me because I testify of it that its works are evil" (John 7:7). The world did not hate them, because their actions were in agreement with the world. They did not believe in Him, and neither did He believe in them. Hence, while on the Cross, He committed the care of His mother to John and not to His brethren.

After these brethren had left for Jerusalem, He was free of the worry that a public appearance with them might cause; so He went up privately. His motive for going was not to join in the common festivities but to carry out a higher purpose. As He arrives, the people are already engaged in fervent controversy regarding His teaching as well as His inexplicable absence from Jerusalem. "Now about the middle of the feast Jesus went up into the temple and taught. And the Jews marveled, saying, 'How does this Man know letters, having never studied?'" (John 7:14, 15). The most difficult of all Jewish teaching was the detailed exposition of the Law, and it was this that perplexed the multitudes. No man could expound the Law (as Jesus was doing) without citing the rabbinical authority under whom he learned, and the authority must be a known and certified name. So Jesus cites His authority: "My doctrine is not Mine, but His who sent Me" (John 7:16). Jesus did not receive this teaching from a rabbi but directly from God.

On each of the seven days of the feast, the high priest would go to the pool of Siloam and fill a golden bowl from its water. He would then pour the water over the brazen altar at the time of the morning sacrifice, and the water would flow through channels lined with silver till it emptied into the Kidron Valley. The ceremony would be accompanied by a chorus singing the praises of Isaiah along with the Psalms. The ritual ceased on the eighth day, since all work was prohibited on that day, and Jesus used the opportunity to proclaim a transcendent truth. "On the last day, that great *day* of the feast, Jesus stood and cried out, saying, 'If anyone thirsts, let him come to Me and drink. He who believes in Me, as the Scripture has said, out of his heart will flow rivers of living water'" (John 7:37, 38).

"The Pharisees and the chief priests sent officers to take Him" (John 7:32). The murmurings of the people reached the ears of the rulers in Jerusalem, and the Sanhedrin immediately dispatched a cohort of officers to seize Him. The officers confront Jesus with their warrant of arrest, but He has something unexpected to tell them: "I shall be with you a little while longer, and *then* I go to Him who sent Me" (John 7:33). They are sent by the Sanhedrin, but He is sent by God. Their mission is one of arbitrary aggression, while His mission is to deliver love and peace and joy. The officers return to the council of Pharisees and chief priests empty-handed. After being upbraided by the council for their failure, they can only confess, "No man has ever spoken like this man!"

The Woman Caught in Adultery

AFTER THESE EVENTS, JESUS GOES up again to the Mount of Olives, as was His custom, in search of silence and prayer. The Mount of Olives plays a prominent role in the Gospel narratives. It is the place Christ went each night during the turbulent days of Holy Week, and it was the scene of His arrest. The Garden of Gethsemane was situated on the mountain's slope facing Jerusalem.

Early in the morning, Jesus descends from the mountain and enters Jerusalem to teach the people in the temple. But now the scribes and Pharisees, Christ's hardened enemies, approach and cast a woman caught in adultery at His feet. They demand a verdict: should she be stoned for her sin? Christ's opponents sought a watertight case, one in which a judge could not possibly avoid a clear indictment. And they believed they had found it in the fact that this adulteress was caught "in the very act."

Jesus is thrown here into a grave dilemma. On the one hand, if He judges according to the letter of the law, the woman will be killed at His word and before His eyes. This would destroy the message of love, mercy, and redemption that He came to make a part of the new life. He came to raise mercy above judgment and to institute repentance as a way of life for sinners. On the other hand, were He to judge that she be pardoned, He would be in clear violation of the law—a violation as bad as that perpetrated in these accusers' hearts. The Law of Moses was the supreme arbitrator in the minds of the people; if He were to so flagrantly defy its orders, then He Himself would be in danger of its judgment.

"Jesus stooped down and wrote on the ground with *His* finger, as though He did not hear. So when they continued asking Him, He raised Himself up and said to them, 'He who is without sin among you, let him throw a stone at her first'" (John 8:6, 7). Before the vehemence of these opponents and their throbbing obsession to see the woman killed and Jesus defeated, He calmly stoops to write something in the sand with His finger, as though totally unaware of their shouts. He gives time for their angry voices to die down and prepares to breach their consciences. He did indeed accept the whole of the Law of Moses, for He came not to abolish it. He came to fulfill it; that is, He came to fill up what was lacking in it, that henceforth we might follow the "law of perfection" and not the "Law of Moses." In order for a sinner to be stoned following the Mosaic code, it was required that someone announce the sentence and someone carry it out. Both of these should be innocent of sin; otherwise they too would be needing a stoning.

John the Evangelist, in his mystical way, presents Christ here as the righteous Judge and as the new Lawgiver. With a single indirect comment, He rescinds the demands of the Mosaic Law. It was a law that judged external incidents but could not judge the conscience. It could not rectify character, and it could not correct or purify human behavior the way the law of Christ does. These accusers thirsted for blood. They cared nothing for the life of this woman, who, as a human being, had every bit as much right to live as they did. And the only support they had in this inhumane and sanguine plot was the Law of Moses!

When the accusers were faced with this truth that lay concealed within the Law of Moses—and they who were posing as the executors of the Law of Moses must also bend to its demands—they abandoned the trial they had opened with stricken consciences. It was a just and irrefutable point: how can one sinner atone for another's sin before God? Their bones shook under Jesus' steady gaze, and the eldest of them to the youngest retreated in humiliation.

Did Jesus not say, "I did not come to judge the world but to save the world" (John 12:47)? Jesus came to redeem sinners, not to kill them. And the redemption would come at the price of His blood. When we hear Him speak to the woman at the end of this episode and tell her, "Neither do I condemn you; go and sin no more," this is a judgment that comes at His own expense. Her life is spared because His will be taken. He sentenced Himself to death by setting her free.

When Jesus rose from the ground, He found that these self-appointed prosecutors had quitted the scene. They had lost the case. The accusers had become the accused, and the judges were found to be under the very sentence they sought against their victim. The Law of Moses was indeed incapable of producing a worthy judge in all Israel, since not a single person was innocent of its demands. And so its obsolete status had already begun to show. The Law could judge the sinner but could not redeem him. As Augustine says, in Jesus' words "go and sin no more," He condemned the sin but acquitted the sinner.

The authority in Moses' Law was fueled by sin, because sin gave the Law something to judge. The authority in Christ's law was fueled by grace, because grace provided a way to mercy.

"Neither do I condemn you; go and sin no more." The woman leaves the scene of the trial empowered by this statement of exoneration. She did not deserve the mercy because of her deeds; she deserved it because she was in Jesus' presence. The presence of God sheds immense grace on a person, even when it is not sought for. Witness the unrequested grace received by the Samaritan woman, or this adulteress, or even St. Paul himself. Jesus makes it clear that she must not return to her former life, and He implies that He will be her support. What hope must have filled this woman's heart in that moment!

The Man Born Blind, Part One

"NOW AS JESUS PASSED BY, He saw a man who was blind from birth. And His disciples asked Him, saying, 'Rabbi, who sinned, this man or his parents, that he was born blind?'" (John 9:1, 2). This is a question that has troubled humanity from the beginning. But if we consider the several factors that contributed to the rise and spread of sin in the world, a satisfactory response to the query might be within reach. Let us begin by listing the several reasons for man's suffering.

Firstly, man has *abandoned God* and forgotten his spiritual nature. These used to provide him with a measure of immunity from the threats he faced from the animal world—predators, parasites, bacteria, viruses, and so forth—as well as from the psychological hardship he undergoes from living in an unpredictable environment.

Secondly, we add to this the factor of *time*, which, due to its tendency to break things down rather than build them up, compounds the effects of nature's threats and subjects man to disease and old age.

Thirdly, there is the factor of *labor*, wherein man has had to expend enormous amounts of physical and mental energy in order to eat his daily bread and make life sustainable. This constant expenditure of living capital has the effect of wearing out a man's limbs and bringing him closer to the grave.

Fourthly, man must grapple with the *natural disasters* of the world—earthquakes, wildfires, famine, drought, frost, and so on.

Finally, there are the sufferings that come as a consequence of man's own decisions. The damaging effects of certain harmful foods, alcohol, drugs, sexually transmitted diseases, and the like are all testament to man's free choice to harm himself.

There are also other types of suffering of which a person is totally innocent, as in the case of hereditary disease. Neither the baby, the father, nor the mother has voluntarily caused the suffering; it is imposed on the child by reason of a random error that occurs during embryological development. The hardship results from a breakdown in the laws of biology, not the laws of morality. This fact lessens man's responsibility in the case and increases God's responsibility. Such was the case of the man born blind. He does not approach Jesus or the disciples asking for healing. Jesus, instead, taking full responsibility for the problem, goes to the man and heals him. Hence, Christ's verdict, "Neither this man nor his parents sinned, but that the works of God should be revealed in him" (John 9:3).

We happen to find, notwithstanding all this, a work of reparation rendered by nature to help compensate for the losses she causes to humanity. Even more, we find that God Himself offers special compensations and consolations that far surpass the sorrows man must endure.

In the case of nature, we ought to recognize that none of the workings of the natural order are immune to error. Error in nature is actually itself a law; it must happen. Every natural law has its exceptions and defects, because perfection is found nowhere but in God.

But nature strives to compensate for her deficiencies. So, when a person is born lacking a certain faculty of the body, the other faculties pull together to try to achieve what the missing faculty cannot. In the instance of a man born blind, his other four senses will become heightened in their awareness and strive to make up for his loss of sight. The other senses simply require time and training. The same process of reparation occurs if the person loses two or three or even four of his senses. We have the famous case of Helen Keller, who became a witness and evangelist only by using her sense of touch.

Thus, to some extent, nature may be absolved of her frequent errors due to the law of reparation built into her. A disabled person may insist on his right to be compensated by nature by recruiting the abilities and faculties he has been given—by patience and hard work, and with a triumphant spirit. Even on a societal level, humanity identifies those members who are specially talented and capable, and puts them into the service of helping those who are less fortunate. Science and technology have marvelously accelerated our ability to bridge the gaps in man's life; the examples of that would fill a multitude of volumes.

In the case of God's compensation, we must realize, first of all, that life is a *gift* given by God and not a *right* that can be demanded by the recipient. It is a gift and will always be a gift until the day it returns to the Giver. It follows that all the features of one's life, including physical and mental health, are also gifts. These are not "rights" to be expected by any man, even were he to receive them all in full measure; and, were he to be deprived of any one of them, it should not be seen as an unfair stripping of his rights. The proper response to these gifts is not expectation but thanksgiving. One must be thankful and know that such free gifts may be withdrawn at any moment.

This is all from man's point of view. Now, from God's point of view,

He is the Father of all humanity, and so man's concerns become His too. Just as a mother nurses her baby so it may live, so does God nurse humanity drop by drop. Now, if a father or mother naturally pays special attention to a disabled child, how much more will God look after His unfortunate ones! It is impossible to list the multitude of mercies God shows to impaired and afflicted humanity. All we can do is affirm the truth in that verse from Isaiah: "In all their affliction He was afflicted, / And the Angel of His Presence saved them" (Is. 63:9).

So we may fairly ask, is it better to have God as compensator for a missing limb or to possess all one's limbs without God? Is there an accurate scale to compare the sadness a person feels at losing his sight to the joy he feels in receiving an inner vision that transcends all?

The Man Born Blind, Part Two

"HE SPAT ON THE GROUND and made clay with the saliva; and He anointed the eyes of the blind man with the clay. And He said to him, 'Go, wash in the pool of Siloam' (which is translated, Sent). So he went and washed, and came back seeing" (John 9:6, 7). All Jesus' other works of healing were a reversal of disease, whereas what we have here is not healing per se but creation. The mention of "clay" transports our minds back to Genesis and reminds us of how God made man out of the dust of the ground. This man was born without eyes. When he was just a small lump of "clay" being formed in his mother's womb, the laws of embryology failed to develop him into a perfect baby. A bit of new clay, therefore, in his Creator's hands was sufficient to give him new eyes. The command to wash in the pool of Siloam points to baptism; the oldest mystical term for baptism was "illumination."

The man himself thence became a "sign." He used to sit in a well-known spot and to solicit the aid of the public who passed by. The neighbors therefore began to doubt the miracle and to wonder if he was really the same man. But it was a miracle difficult to mistake. Would not the man himself speak up on behalf of One who gave him eyes and supplied him with the light of life? "They said to him, 'How were your eyes opened?' He answered and said, 'A Man called Jesus made clay and anointed my eyes and said to me, "Go to the pool of Siloam and wash." So I went and washed, and I received sight'" (John 9:10, 11). This man was put in a tough spot. He bore witness to Jesus—not joyfully, as to a benefactor, but nervously, under the threatening glances of his questioners.

"They brought him who formerly was blind to the Pharisees. Now it was a Sabbath when Jesus made the clay and opened his eyes" (John 9:13, 14). These Pharisees were a small representative body of the Sanhedrin that lingered about Jerusalem, as well as every major city of Palestine, with the authority to try certain cases of the law. And here they must deal with an infraction of the Sabbath. The Talmud had prohibited the application of any medicine to the eyes on the Sabbath,[39] as well as the mixing of water and dirt.[40] Christ was therefore in violation of at least two Sabbath regulations. Yet, according to Jesus' divine conviction that the Father continued His work on the Sabbath, He proceeded to do the good work. He constantly ignored pharisaical rules and even overlooked certain parts of Moses' Law, considering the life and soul of man to be of inestimably more value than both Law and Sabbath.

"They said to the blind man again, 'What do you say about Him because He opened your eyes?' He said, 'He is a prophet'" (John 9:17). The man's testimony is evidence of the light that had penetrated his soul simultaneously with the physical light entering his

---

39 Jeros. Gemara 14, cited in Lightfoot, R. H., *St. John's Gospel* (Clarendon Press, 1956).

40 Sefaria 24:3.

eyes. He felt the effects of both. And so he does not claim that Jesus is simply a good man or a physician, but that Jesus is One come directly from God. The eyes are not a simple appendage of the body but draw their roots from the most inner recesses of the brain; they are, moreover, crafted from highly specialized tissues and nerve endings delicately interwoven together to provide us with sight. The man who felt a power that could restore such complex biology also felt the power move his soul. Consequently, he confessed Jesus as Son of God and bowed before Him in worship.

The cabal of Pharisees demanded to know who had opened his eyes, not because they were interested in studying the sign, but only to ascertain whether or not the Sabbath was broken. This is what is meant by the precept *the letter kills*, because they had resolved on Christ's death as a result of their legalistic mindset; but *the spirit gives life*, for Christ's word was always filled with spirit, light, and life. The man's response later in the interchange has a trace of indignation in it: "He answered them, 'I told you already, and you did not listen. Why do you want to hear *it* again? Do you also want to become His disciples?'" (John 9:27). This the Pharisees could only answer with mad reviling.

"So they again called the man who was blind, and said to him, 'Give God the glory! We know that this Man is a sinner'" (John 9:24). The saying *give God the glory* was a technical phrase in Jewish law used to bind the defendant under a legal oath to utter the truth under pain of divine reckoning. It was a threat, because the man was now liable to being expelled from the synagogue and severed from the community. The man's response was undaunted: "Whether He is a sinner *or not* I do not know. One thing I know: that though I was blind, now I see." The sun cannot be extinguished by a puff of human breath. But this is precisely what the Pharisees sought to do in pressuring the man to repudiate One who had created new eyes for him and enabled him to finally see the light, the people, and the beauty of the world.

After a bit more wrangling, the man made this confession: "Since the world began it has been unheard of that anyone opened the eyes of one who was born blind. If this Man were not from God, He could do nothing" (John. 9:32, 33). The Pharisees found themselves stuck. They had attributed his affliction to his parents' sins; had God not granted him sight, their assumption would have stood unchallenged, resulting in a deep wound to this man's reputation. But the patent restoration of this man's sight constituted the vindication of his parents' lives and the refutation of the Pharisees' ideas. This complete flipping of the case revealed the Pharisees' implacable hatred for the blind man, especially given that he had become a witness to Christ. It also reveals this man's devotion to God and his fearless disregard for the threats of the Pharisees, especially given that they had cast him out.

"Jesus heard that they had cast him out; and when He had found him, He said to him, 'Do you believe in the Son of God?' He answered and said . . . 'Lord, I believe!' And he worshiped Him" (John 9:35, 39). The Pharisees had expelled the man from their presence, and so Jesus went to look for him to speak with him. His own parents had disowned him, fearing to receive the same consequences. The Good Shepherd would not abandon the lost sheep, and He tracked it down in order to return it to the Father's flock. The blind man had first thought this was just a prophet; but now he had learned and believed that He was the very Son of God, who had given him a key to the Kingdom of heaven.

Jesus at the Feast of Dedication

IT IS NOW WINTERTIME, AND about three months have elapsed since the Feast of Tabernacles. That feast having taken place mid to late October, the evangelic chronology brings us to the month of December. The Gospel of John gives us no indication that Jesus left Jerusalem during the three-month interval; rather, it brings us right up to the next Jewish feast: "Now it was the Feast of Dedication in Jerusalem, and it was winter" (John 10:22). The historical beginnings of the Feast of Dedication appear in the Book of 2 Maccabees, which recounts the victories of the Maccabean family over foreign usurpers. Judas Maccabeus, the heroic representative of a powerful family, expelled the Syrians, who had seized control over the Jews and had introduced idolatrous worship into the temple. Judas Maccabeus then rebuilt the altar and rededicated the entire temple to Jewish worship, an event the Jews have celebrated annually ever since. The Hebrew word for the feast is *Hanukkah*, indicating "dedication," while the Greek word indicates "renewal." Josephus refers to it as the "Feast of Lights."[41]

Jesus begins a discourse here that is in reality a continuation of the incident that occurred with the man born blind. It is about the Good Shepherd and His relationship to His own sheep. The man whose sight was restored had confessed to being one of His, and so the Pharisees, considering themselves keepers of the flock of Israel and opponents of Christ, excommunicated him on the spot. To thus abuse the poor man so quickly, without any legal justification, was the most egregious act perpetrated by the Pharisees against God's people. "All who *ever* came before Me are thieves and robbers, but the sheep did not hear them" (John 10:8).

"Most assuredly, I say to you, I am the door of the sheep." He likens Himself to the door not of the "flock" but of the "sheep," putting the symbol on a personal and individual level. He will nurture not just a church of congregations but a church of individuals. He forms a covenant not with a nation but with the individual soul. Here is not

---

41 *Jewish Antiquities* xii. 7, § 7

a national leader like Moses or Joshua, called to free the state from its political foes, but a personal leader, called to free the soul from its servitude to sin.

"I am the good shepherd" (John 10:11). The Greek word for "good" here is *kalos*, which is customarily used to point not to God's eternal goodness (indicated by Greek writers by the word *agathos*) but to a more earthly and practical goodness. In the Gospels, the Lord's eternal attributes are typically preceded by the Greek word *alethos*, meaning "true"—as in the cases when Jesus calls Himself the true vine, true bread, or true light. His career as shepherd is not eternal but based on the temporal needs of humanity. In other words, the goodness of the Good Shepherd is determined not by what He *is* but by what He *does*. Hence Christ's comment, "The good shepherd *gives His life for the sheep.*"

Jesus implies as well a personal superiority to all the temporal shepherds who rose during Israel's history. There was Moses: "Where *is* He who brought them up out of the sea / With the shepherd of His flock?" (Is. 63:11). There was David too: "He also chose David His servant, / And took him from the sheepfolds . . . to shepherd Jacob His people" (Ps. 78:70, 71). But these and all like temporal shepherds were at the same time part of the flock, as David himself confesses: "The LORD is my Shepherd" (Ps. 23:1). An earthly shepherd could die for the sake of his flock's survival, but the power of his life would end there. The Good Shepherd, on the other hand, willingly lays down His life that He may grant that life to the flock.

He goes on to make a statement that startles His Jewish listeners even more: "I know My *sheep*, and am known by My own. As the Father knows Me, even so I know the Father" (John 10:14, 15). The two statements are symmetrical. Their juxtaposition is meant to imply that the mutual knowledge between Him and His followers is equal to the mutual knowledge between Him and God. His intimate relation to the Father colored, in fact, His whole perspective on life: "At that day you will know that I *am* in My Father, and you in Me, and I in you" (John 14:20). "If you keep My commandments, you will abide in My love, just as I have kept My Father's commandments and abide in His love" (John 15:10).

As usual, our Lord's words caused a division among the audience. The split occurred between the outspoken critics who saw themselves as custodians of the law and those who with hesitating faith avoided a public declaration of approval. The critics' claim that He "has a demon and is mad" demonstrates the extent to which their ears were blocked to the voice of God. And we should not wonder at their impertinence; the type of "teaching" they had grown accustomed to was chatter about the irrelevant minutiae of their law and a preoccupation with political news. Their inward eyes were blinded to whatever truth might have radiated from Christ. The same threat faces us today as well. When a shepherd of the people loses sight of the essence of the Faith, forgets the call to repentance and holiness, and becomes lost in the details of this world, his shepherding vocation is severely impaired.

Jesus is then directly accosted by His adversaries, who have finally lost their patience: "How long do You keep us in doubt? If You are the Christ, tell us plainly" (John 10:24). The annual recurrence of the Feast of Dedication served to inflame the nation's hope that someone like Judas Maccabeus would rise and lift the Roman yoke from off their necks. Since Jesus habitually spoke in terms of "salvation" and "deliverance," their suspicions were raised that He might be claiming to be the one. And so, in their conflicted minds, they were continually stuck between acceptance and rejection of His claims. Jesus responds to their question and says that He has told them as much, but they did not believe because they were not of His sheep and would not hear His voice. It is His final assertion—"I and *My*

Father are one"—that causes them to pick up stones to stone Him.

After another short exchange of words, "they sought again to seize Him, but He escaped out of their hand" (John 10:39). Had not Jesus said that no one could steal a single sheep from His hand? If then the wolf had not the ability to steal the sheep, how could it expect to catch the Shepherd Himself? He went away, leaving them grasping at the wind.

The Perean Ministry Begins

AFTER AN EXTENDED STAY IN Jerusalem, Jesus returns to Galilee to conduct His final ministrations there. It is now time to bid farewell to His beloved homeland for the last time. He prepares to embark on the final journey toward Jerusalem, which is introduced by St. Luke with these words: "Now it came to pass, when the time had come for Him to be received up, that He steadfastly set His face to go to Jerusalem" (Luke 9:51). The words *the time had come for Him to be received up* indicate that the period of public service assigned by the Father had neared its close. From this point on, the days no longer move slowly, as they had at the beginning of the Gospel, but quickly. The overarching theme that connects the happenings of this period is Christ's calm but firm resolve to finish His work in Jerusalem.

Samaria lay between Galilee and Jerusalem, and Jesus therefore sends messengers ahead of Him to prepare for the passage through Samaritan country. Due to the age-old enmity between Jews and Samaritans, a Jew traveling through the region had to make prodigious preparations for the journey, including providing enough food to last the whole way. One could never be sure to find a single Samaritan in the land who would offer food to a Jew who was intending to reach Jerusalem. Jesus' messengers entered the country, "but they did not receive Him, because His face was *set* for the journey to Jerusalem" (Luke 9:53). Jesus' disciples take offense at the rejection; filled with retributive anger, they ask Jesus for permission to call down fire from heaven to consume the insolent people. But Jesus immediately disarms their wrath; His mission, He says, is not to destroy men's lives but to save them.

Due to the Samaritans' refusal to allow Jesus and His disciples passage through their territory, they are compelled to cross the Jordan and pursue a southward course through the country of Perea.

One of the first steps taken by Christ during this Perean ministry is to send out seventy apostles to preach all over the countryside. Much of the instruction given for this mission mirrors the words spoken to the twelve when they were sent out at an earlier date. Jesus tells them not to take any extra supplies, to follow a certain protocol when entering people's homes, and to announce that the Kingdom of God is about to appear. To His instructions Jesus adds the remark, "The harvest truly *is* great, but the laborers *are* few; therefore pray the Lord of the harvest to send out laborers into His harvest" (Luke 10:2). Jesus has sown the seed, and now He charges the apostles—as well as the Church—to reap what He has sown. It is an invitation to continue the ministry with zeal, for whatever is not reaped by the Church will be gathered by the enemy. The Church must multiply her laborers in order to harvest the maximum crop possible before the end of this life.

The seventy return from their mission with a jubilant spirit, reporting to Jesus the extraordinary results of their work; this in turn lifts Jesus' spirits tremendously, as He has been reassured that the burden of ministry is being transferred to capable hands. Then, having warned them of the dangers of vainglory and urged them to find pleasure simply in the fact that their names were recorded in the Book of Life, He utters a prayer of thanksgiving in their presence, that they might learn from whence their help comes. He then encourages them with the intelligence that all authority has been put into His keeping, and that the mutual "knowing" between the Father and the Son is of a unique and inextinguishable kind. He blesses their eyes and ears for having seen and heard things that were not unveiled even to the great kings and prophets of the past.

The Good Samaritan

"AND BEHOLD, A CERTAIN LAWYER stood up and tested Him, saying, 'Teacher, what shall I do to inherit eternal life?'" (Luke 10:25). In response to this question, Jesus offers the Parable of the Good Samaritan. We learn of it only from the Evangelist Luke, who has provided the Church with one of the most powerful in her repertoire of stories—and one most emphatic in denouncing the age-old blight of racism. It was a story told simply, on the spur of the moment, from the depths of Jesus' heart; and it sprang from the pain Christ felt at man's coldness to his fellow man. It has become the quintessential representation of Christ's love and a powerful tool in the hand of the teacher and minister.

The parable possesses a universality that is essential to the evangelistic spirit that would take Christ's name to Judea, Samaria, and the ends of the earth. Or, to put it another way, it demolishes the enmity that springs from difference of race and color, and lays the foundation for St. Paul's famous dictum: "There is neither Greek nor Jew, circumcised nor uncircumcised, barbarian, Scythian, slave *nor* free, but Christ *is* all and in all" (Col. 3:11).

The lawyer who poses the question, "What must I do to inherit eternal life?" is of course unaware that he is addressing Life itself—the life that was hidden in God but made manifest on earth in the fullness of time. This is a Pharisee whose specialty is the Mosaic

Law; hearing of Jesus' rising reputation, he has decided to come and test Him. Jesus does not answer the lawyer in the same way He answered the Samaritan woman: "I who speak to you am He." He rather takes the lawyer by the hand and helps him interpret the law. "What is your reading *of it?*" When the lawyer answers correctly— "'You shall love the LORD your God with all your heart, with all your soul, with all your strength, and with all your mind,' and 'your neighbor as yourself'"—Jesus bids him to live out his response. But the lawyer confesses his ignorance in not knowing who his "neighbor" is. And so follows the remarkable tale.

An unnamed man, presumably a Jew, is traveling from Jerusalem to Jericho. The journey is at least seventeen miles in extent, and the road is surrounded by multiple rocky outcrops, behind which (according to Josephus[42]) thieves used to hide. The man fell among thieves; they took everything he had—including the clothes on his body—beat him mercilessly, and left him naked and nearly dead on the road. A priest, who was either going to the temple in Jerusalem or was just returning from there, approaches the poor man on the road. Being content with his own safety, he walks past the man and thus loses an opportunity to show love. A Levite then approaches. A Levite was lesser in rank than a priest but still held in esteem by the people, because he was the custodian of the rites of temple worship. Considering that the care of a bleeding man was outside his circle of responsibilities, he also steps aside and ignores the fallen victim.

A Samaritan finally arrives at the scene and beholds the victim with genuine human compassion. He applies wine to the wounds to cleanse them and oil to ameliorate the pain; these were the best ambulatory services a person could provide in those days. He then lifts the injured man onto his animal and takes him to an inn where he may provide additional care. He stays the night at the inn to help

---

42   Josephus, *The Wars of the Jews*, Bk 4, 474.

the man; and at daybreak, he hands extra money to the innkeeper and charges him with the victim's care until he should return from his journey. And he promises to reimburse the innkeeper for whatever expenses he incurs in attending to the man's needs.

"So which of these three do you think was neighbor to him who fell among the thieves?" Jesus leaves the judgment of the case to the lawyer. The question puts him in a slightly embarrassing position, because Jesus puts him in the place of the victim and a Samaritan in the place of the agent of mercy and humanity. The lawyer, however, cannot bring himself to utter the word *Samaritan*, and so he responds, "He who showed mercy on him" (Luke 10:37). Jesus wrests this reluctant confession from the lawyer's mouth by the sheer logic of the case. He intentionally contrasts the goodness that can be found in a Samaritan with the callousness of the priest and Levite—despite the fact that Samaritans were profane and abhorrent to Israel. The lawyer probably left Him unchanged by the parable. It required Christ's death on the Cross to ultimately dissolve the hatred that lurked in man's heart against his fellow man, and to change mankind that dwelled in "Jerusalem, and in all Judea and Samaria, and to the end of the earth" (Acts 1:8).

The Visit to Mary and Martha

"NOW IT HAPPENED AS THEY went that He entered a certain village; and a certain woman named Martha welcomed Him into her house" (Luke 10:38). We are still on the road leading up to Jerusalem; Jesus has taken a temporary discursion into a city we know from John 11:1 to be Bethany. This little town sat in Jesus' deepest affections, and it was here He often retired for rest and reprieve. Jesus and His disciples were received into a home with the most excellent hospitality; the owner of the dwelling was a woman named

Martha. This woman was in charge of preparing the supper, and she had apparently been caught up in a frenzy of activity in discharging her task.

"And she had a sister called Mary, who also sat at Jesus' feet and heard His word" (Luke 10:39). Mary was content to leave the toil to her sister and sit at Jesus' feet, in the fashion of a disciple sitting at the feet of a great teacher.[43] We learn from John 12:3 that she also anointed the Lord's feet with oil while listening to His words. She doubtless sat exchanging questions and answers with the Master, and He encouraged her devoted attentiveness. Here we find Jesus engaged in one of His remarkably progressive acts, because one of the many prohibitions of that era was the teaching of women. In this scene Christ opens up the possibility of learning for women as well as the future role of women in the Church's ministry. We read of several women following Christ during His ministry, attending the Crucifixion, bearing testimony to the Resurrection, and being the first to speak to the risen Lord.

In the Gospel narrative, it is clear that Martha was oriented toward active service and hospitality, while Mary was oriented toward discipleship and teaching. Now, the Church needs both orientations. It is apparent that Christ acted in this way to demonstrate the indispensable role of teaching and scholarship for women in the era of the New Testament, as well as the complementary role of active service. Jesus obviously was not concerned about the food they were about to eat. He once taught five thousand people for an entire day straight without eating, until the disciples finally realized they had no food. Such was the power of Christ's teaching that it often led people to forget to eat. We may conclude that life with Jesus Christ involves two "plates": the plate of the Word and the plate of material

---

43 St. Paul writes, "I am indeed a Jew, born in Tarsus of Cilicia, but brought up in this city at the feet of Gamaliel" (Acts 22:3).

food. We may eat of both; but, when we feed on the first plate without paying heed to the second, miracles will follow.

"But Martha was distracted with much serving, and she approached Him and said, 'Lord, do You not care that my sister has left me to serve alone? Therefore tell her to help me.' And Jesus answered and said to her, 'Martha, Martha, you are worried and troubled about many things'" (Luke 10:40, 41). When the Lord repeats a person's name twice before addressing him or her, it is a signal either of reproach ("Simon, Simon, Satan has asked to . . .") or of sympathy, as in the present case. In general the repetition is a call to heightened attention to an especially significant message. ("Truly, truly, I say to you . . .") Christ is calling Martha to see the inner turmoil caused by her outer restlessness. She was possibly kneading and baking, frying and cooking, when any leftover loaf of bread would have sufficed. A vital principle is here revealed to us: that excessive worry over externals will lead to inner discord. Internal discord in turn prevents the mind from working peacefully, and this then leads to a hypercritical attitude. This is why, in the spiritual life, a greedy ambition to achieve multiple lofty goals can distress the heart and mind. But when a person sets for himself reasonable goals, he may pursue them with a steady heart.

"'But one thing is needed, and Mary has chosen that good part, which will not be taken away from her'" (Luke 10:42). Mary's choice to receive life-giving words at Jesus' feet hints at Martha's real need. When one's material needs consume all one's attention, nothing more will be sought after; the demands of physical life can totally colonize the mind. Jesus desired to redirect Martha's concerns toward spiritual things. She had prioritized food over Him, although a bare morsel of bread in His hands could turn into lamb. Spiritual life has its own logic. And that logic tells you that, if you are in need of many things and there is One who is the source of all things, you must seek that One, and the many will be provided to you. In Christ we find the mystery of sufficiency and of surplus. So, if sufficiency in everything is what you desire, and surplus too, then empty your heart of its clutter and offer it to Him.

The Lord's Prayer

"NOW IT CAME TO PASS, as He was praying in a certain place, when He ceased, *that* one of His disciples said to Him, 'Lord, teach us to pray, as John also taught his disciples'" (Luke 11:1). The prayer that the Lord was to bequeath to His disciples as a result of this request, known famously as "the Lord's Prayer," was from the dawn of Christianity the first doctrine taught to newly baptized believers.

Our Father in heaven
At the very beginning of the prayer, the deeply intimate relationship that ties the Christian to God is revealed. Jesus spoke in Aramaic, and the Aramaic form of "father"—which is *abba*—is here placed as if proceeding from the mouth of a small child. It is the first word a child learns to use when calling on its father, and it is the same word Jesus uses to call on God. *Abba* reflects Jesus' deep trust in God, and it reflects our trust as well. This opening address fills the entire Lord's Prayer with a special boldness. So bold is it, in fact, that many ancient liturgies request God's consent to hear the prayer before it is uttered by His people.

Hallowed be Your name.
This hallowing of God's name is the same theme heard by Isaiah in the temple when God was hailed by the seraphim.[44] Every announcement of God's presence immediately issues in the sanctification of His name. When Isaiah *saw* God sitting on the throne, he *heard* the

---

44   Isaiah 6:1–4.

seraphic song, "Holy, holy, holy . . ." This request to hallow God's name serves as a mystical preparation for the petitioner to witness God's glory. As such, it is an eschatological yearning of the heart for God's coming. We hallow God's name daily as an attempt to lighten the pain of our exile, or as an ameliorative for the strife and toil in our lives. We have adopted the seraphim's task, and we will not stop until "all the earth be filled with the glory of the LORD" (Num. 14:21).

Your Kingdom come

Hallowing God's name leads naturally to the proclamation of His name on earth. In particular, we proclaim Him as a King—King in the hearts over which He has reigned. It is a marvelous thing that Christ directs us to make this request, for He Himself said that His Kingdom was "at hand." It means that He has made us collaborators in a grand work that has already begun. We are the seen builders in an unseen project. We ought to remember that the Kingdom's coming is achieved by the Holy Spirit's work in spreading the gospel. "If I cast out demons by the Spirit of God, surely the kingdom of God has come upon you" (Matt. 12:28). And from the perspective of our human life, we ask God to hasten His coming due to the burden of our temporal existence. It is essentially a request for mercy and aid. It is as though God has handed us a copy of His blueprint for the world and has asked us to remind Him daily of its contents. It is not a reminder for God, however, but a reminder for us of what He intends to do; and that comforts us.

Your will be done on earth as it is in heaven.

It is interesting that Christ bids us to utter this petition, considering it reflects the pivotal moment of His agony in Gethsemane. The Son's submission to the Father's will is the point at which Jesus passes from a state of fierce distress to one of calm resignation. "O My Father, if this cup cannot pass away from Me unless I drink it,

Your will be done" (Matt. 26:42). This was the supreme instance of God's will being done on earth as in heaven; it ought to wake us up from our indifference to seek God's will for the world—which is its redemption. It is our right to make an hourly request that God's will be done, remembering that at the base of that stands the Cross.

Give us this day our daily bread
The bread we seek is the sustenance for that life approved by God, not by man; for the life that is deemed worthy by God is far superior to the paltry existence we tend to seek. Jesus points mystically to this life by calling it "daily bread." What we need daily is not the bread produced from wheat and cooked in ovens, but the bread that will sustain us through the troubles of this life, the bread that will open our eyes and quicken the beating of our hearts, the bread that will induce us to proclaim resurrection and salvation. Christ gives us the right to ask for bread that will transform our mortal days into the eternal days of the Son of Man. Can this really be? Yes. In the Lord's Prayer, Jesus has given us the mystical keys to transform our whole existence.

And forgive us our debts, as we forgive our debtors.
Christ has given us an immense privilege in saying these words: He allows us to enter the sacred realm of God's forgiveness! But the request is contingent on our action. We say, in effect, "We forgive; so forgive us too." Our act of forgiving our neighbor is performed in time; but then we take the act and fly with it to the eternal realm, where it becomes our plea for the right to live with God. The person who is able to forgive all the sins of every person committed against him—those transgressions that injure his name, or reputation, or career, or finances, or family, or estate—the person who can forgive all these wrongs has truly become crucified to the world. How can his own sins be held against him? This is the single petition that

requires the believer to make himself worthy of it—not by any special form of knowledge or asceticism or piety—but only by lifting his head and stretching his arms toward heaven, and entreating for the forgiveness of everyone's sins, for the sake of God's name.

And do not lead us into temptation, but deliver us from the evil one.
All the foregoing petitions make the faithful swell with the feeling that they are destined for the Kingdom, and as a result, they are currently pilgrims in a strange land. This strange land is moreover teeming with enemies and engrossed in evil. The accuser makes here an easy approach and submits his request to sift them as wheat, that the weaker of them might fall away. The believers, having the simplicity of children, are no match for one who is so well practiced in the art of deception. Jesus therefore bequeaths to them a "mayday cry," one that may be instantly used at the moment of temptation. This cry for help conceals God's mystery of deliverance; it invests the believer with power the moment it is utilized. It can, moreover, fortify the believer before the trial ever arises.

Finally, the Lord ends this great summary of ideal prayer with a doxology:

For Yours is the kingdom and the power and the glory forever. Amen.

Parables of the Lost Sheep, the Lost Coin, and the Lost Son

"THEN ALL THE TAX COLLECTORS and the sinners drew near to Him to hear Him. And the Pharisees and scribes complained, saying, 'This Man receives sinners and eats with them'" (Luke 15:1–3). It is evident from the wording that Christ took the initiative in drawing sinners to Himself. They who felt lost in life came into His presence and felt found. They came with troubled conscience, and in Him they found peace of mind. They loved Him because He first loved them. These sinners felt that the secret to their happiness lay in Him, and they believed that He alone had the key to their new selves. They had eyes to see, ears to hear, and hearts to feel. This was in contrast to the Pharisees, who were so blind and numb that they felt righteous enough before God and in no way needed Christ's help. Jesus therefore began telling them parables to elucidate the sinner's role as a lost sheep, a lost coin, and a lost son.

He begins with the story of the lost sheep, whose central theme is the abounding joy of the shepherd in recovering it. The shepherd leaves the other ninety-nine sheep to roam through fields and pastures, shouting the sheep's name at the top of his lungs, until he begins to lose his voice. When the stray sheep is finally discovered, the shepherd's joy is boundless; and so, says Christ, is God's immeasurable joy when a sinner returns. "When he has found *it*, he lays *it* on his shoulders, rejoicing. . . . I say to you that likewise there will be more joy in heaven over one sinner who repents than over ninety-nine just persons who need no repentance" (Luke 15:5, 7).

It is clear that some of the listeners present were shepherds, and the picture Jesus paints for them is a lively one. Before a shepherd brought his flock out to pasture, he would enter the barn and place his staff horizontally over the door, in order to let the sheep pass under it one by one. This way, the shepherd could take an exact count of his flock as well as see which sheep were diseased or injured. God says to ancient Israel, "I will make you pass under the rod, and I will bring you into the bond of the covenant" (Ezek. 20:37)—meaning not a rod of chastisement but a rod of pastoral love. And so in the story, as the light of day grew dim, the shepherd realized that a sheep was missing, and he immediately went out to recover it. The parable's sense relays a message of encouragement but also of rebuke. Do the pastors of today's faithful pay such close attention to who is safely inside and who is not? The Church's agenda should reflect that of

Christ, who spent at least ninety percent of His time conversing and dining with sinners.

Jesus then tells a corollary parable. A woman loses a valuable coin and searches frantically for it. Whereas the parable of the lost sheep highlights God's joy in finding the lost soul, this parable highlights God's sorrow in seeing a straying soul. This woman is poor, and so the loss of even a single coin makes her distraught. In the estimation of most people, the loss of a single coin might seem insignificant. But not to this woman—this one coin is of immense value. And such is the value of even a single soul in God's eyes. Likewise, the woman's celebration with her friends and neighbors over the recovery might seem venial and excessive to us; but to God, the recovery of the smallest soul warrants such rejoicing.

And finally, we come to the last of this trilogy of parables: the lost [or prodigal] son. The focus of this parable is on God's joy in the voluntary turning back of a sinner. It is a direct response to Jesus' pharisaical critics for upbraiding Him for His special relationship with sinners. He felt special pleasure in the company of tax collectors, prostitutes, and sinners because they were turning from their ways and believing in Him. The clearest evidence of His joy in them was that He *dined* with them; for in the breaking of bread, Jesus is revealed, and the participants are filled with grace and strength.

In the parable, a son demands his portion of the inheritance from his father. The father acquiesces in the son's request and gives him all. In doing so, the father is officially loosed from his legal obligations to the son—which is why, when the son returns, he says, "Make me like one of your hired servants" (Luke 15:19). The son "gathered all together"—an ill-mannered suggestion that his father was now dead—and left for a far country. There he wasted all his sustenance in a wild, abandoned lifestyle. After losing all, he becomes *hungry*—a beautiful indication of the inner state of a lost soul that has come to the end of its rope and begins to long for peace and restoration.

A conflict arises within this young man's conscience. He begins to compare the healthy and blessed lifestyle he once had as a son to the squalor and misery he is now subjected to through his desertion. He is feeding pigs, which are, of course, a curse and an abomination to the Jews. He once lived, back in the day, in a state of bliss in his father's house. Man had likewise spurned his sonship to God and had become a day laborer in the fields of sin.

"And he arose and came to his father" (v. 20). Here is the crux of the story. Theologically, this required that Jesus die on the Cross in order to *rise and go to the Father* bearing all of humanity.[45] Spiritually, this is the most vital point in all of Christian teaching—how a sinner may repent of his way and return to God. Surprisingly, Christ never says that the father pursued the son or asked about his condition. The father apparently sat quietly outside his door, waiting for the son's return. Preachers and counselors and theologians are all certainly important, but they vanish from the story. The entire theme turns on the fact that the *sinner himself* wakes up and realizes his desperate state. The spotlight is on the *sinner's* decision to repent.

The penitent son approaches his father and begins to stammer out the apology he has been contemplating along the road, but the father does not even hear him. He is engrossed in plans to throw a celebratory supper for his son and orders that he be adorned with a robe and a ring. "For this my son was dead and is alive again" (v. 24). It is possible that the younger son's decision to leave home had resulted from a dispute with his father; hence the father's remark, "My son was dead." He was dead both in character and in spirit—so had humanity suffered from the discord with its heavenly Father and

---

45 This is not meant to suggest that Jesus is a sinner like the prodigal son, but that He bears all of humanity's sin.

had squandered its inheritance. Hence, the father's rapturous delight in seeing the son return.

The elder son approaches the house and hears the sound of music and dancing. He is incensed that such festivities are being held in honor of a disreputable son. The reader perceives in this elder son the representative of the scribes and Pharisees, who are offended by Christ's merry dining with tax collectors and harlots. Should not the elder son have happily shared the news of his younger brother's return with his father? Should not the scribes and Pharisees be pleased with Jesus' ministry to sinners? The story's meaning was clear, and the Pharisees gnashed their teeth in furious spite while hearing it.

"And he said to him, 'Son, you are always with me, and all that I have is yours. It was right that we should make merry and be glad, for your brother was dead and is alive again, and was lost and is found'" (Luke 15:31, 32). The father reminds the son of a fact he has forgotten about in his anger, which is that he is the firstborn, and so the greatest portion of the father's possessions will one day be his. But despite this legal preference for the elder son, the fact remains that the younger son was dead and is alive again. Does this not justify celebration? And the one question that remains for us is, did the elder son ever enter the house?

The Raising of Lazarus

"NOW A CERTAIN MAN WAS sick, Lazarus of Bethany, the town of Mary and her sister Martha" (John 11:1). Jesus is called back to Bethany, the beloved town that sat approximately two miles away from Jerusalem, on the eastern slope of the Mount of Olives. The distraught sisters send a message to Jesus with the words, "Lord, behold, he whom You love is sick." The Lord did love him indeed, as well as his sisters; there is the possibility even of a familial link between the three siblings and Christ. The word used here in the Gospel for *love* is the Greek *phileis*, a term expressing profound mutual affection—the same word, in fact, used by John's Gospel to express the love shared between the Father and the Son and between Jesus and the disciples.

Jesus' immediate response is that "this sickness is not unto death, but for the glory of God, that the Son of God may be glorified through it"—the same response given to the disciples regarding the man born blind. And it is God's perennial answer to every loss, every need, every pain, and every trial we suffer. God's intention was there in Lazarus's death, and it did not occur by chance. "Call upon Me in the day of trouble; / I will deliver you, and you shall glorify Me" (Ps. 50:15). This answer enriches our faith, reassures our hope, and confirms our love. The power contained in this response is stronger than any news we might receive that triggers our tears and despair. We do not see as He sees, and our assumptions do not constitute His reality. So, if we abandon our thoughts and rely on His thoughts, we will find the results vastly different from what we had expected.

Notwithstanding the desperation Lazarus's family found themselves in, Jesus lingers for two days after receiving the news. The delay threw the disciples into a state of confusion and vexation, similar to when Jesus lay sleeping in the hull of their ship, apparently heedless of peril, as they nearly drowned in a storm. But the inexplicability of His actions rose from the fact that He dealt with them both as man and as God—and this they could not grasp. They could scarcely comprehend Jesus' remark, "Lazarus is dead. And I am glad for your sakes that I was not there, that you may believe" (John 11:14, 15). And we also hear Martha's sullen complaint, "Lord, if You had been here, my brother would not have died" (v. 21).

When Jesus finally arrived in Bethany, Lazarus's body had lain in the tomb four days. The Gospel particularly relates the *four days* to indicate that decomposition of the body had already begun. There was also a Jewish belief current at the time that the dead person's spirit hovered near the body for three days following death. Once decay had set in and the spirit saw that there was no hope for recovery, it would depart and join the other spirits in the realm of the dead.

Lazarus's sisters react to Jesus' arrival in characteristic form. Martha, ever the active and vocal leader, goes to Jesus and begins to speak, while Mary, being the quiet and reclusive woman, sits near the tomb and mourns in silence. Martha throws her despair onto Christ in the shape of hope: "I know that whatever You ask of God, God will give You." We can rely on hope when time has left us hopeless. We have faith, not just in what we can do through God, but in what Christ can do in God, because His requests are immediately heard by God. This was the upshot of Martha's faith: "I know . . . God will give You." Her burning love lit up the dark and ignorant corners of her heart.

"Jesus said to her, 'Your brother will rise again'" (John 11:23). Jesus announces to Martha that death shall not reign over life. He announces it as a truth before she sees it in fact. Martha responds that she believes Lazarus will rise again at the general resurrection; she states belief, that is, in a general theme but not in a concrete occurrence about to take place. She receives His words as a type of comfort, a nice expression used to show one's condolences. She thinks His words are an incidental confirmation of that doctrine preached by the Pharisees and denied by the Sadducees. Jesus then responds with the pivotal statement of the whole affair: "I am the Resurrection and the Life." The statement differs fundamentally from all the other "I am" pronouncements, in which He was formulating analogies to explain His ministry to mankind. But "I am the

Resurrection and the Life" points not to something *done* by Him but to *who He is*. It is a reflection of His very nature.

Martha then hurries off to tell Mary, "The Teacher has come and is calling for you." Of course, Martha's use of the appellation "teacher" is indicative of the fact that the sisters were followers and disciples of the Lord. Mary rises quickly to go meet the Lord where Martha had met Him—a place outside the city, because Jesus did not want to enter openly. Mary's sudden flight arouses the notice of the Jews who sit mourning at her house; and, assuming she is going to Lazarus's tomb to give vent to her grief, they follow in her tracks. When she find Jesus, she casts herself in reverent homage at His feet and declares with throbbing emotion, "Lord, if You had been here, my brother would not have died." Although hope had forsaken her, her words still express a kind of plea. For love believes all things, and hopes all things, and never fails—even when the mind finds itself frozen and speechless.

When Jesus saw Mary and the Jews who came with her weeping, He "groaned in the spirit and was troubled." The Greek word for "troubled" is the same word used by the Gospels to describe Christ's inner state on the occasions of healing lepers (Mark 1) and the blind (Matt. 9:30), which gives us an idea of the physical and spiritual strain put on Christ in performing these miracles. The deep psychological turmoil experienced by Jesus in such instances was considered by Him part and parcel of the salvation of man. He bore not only our sins, but also our troubles, our pains, and our groanings, all so eloquently expressed by the prophet Isaiah: "Surely He has borne our griefs / And carried our sorrows; / Yet we esteemed Him stricken, / Smitten by God, and afflicted" (Is. 53:4).

Jesus requests to see the place where Lazarus is buried. The Jews take Him there, and what follows is the shortest verse in the Gospels, but one full of singular power: "Jesus wept." The Greek word (*edakrusen*) and Latin word (*lacrimatusest*) for *wept* here indicate the falling of tears. Nothing more is meant here than that tears rolled down His cheeks. The Gospel of Luke employs a different Greek word (*eklausen*) to tell of Jesus' audible and dramatic crying over the future fate of Jerusalem (Luke 19:41). Jesus here weeps for mankind and over mankind. How could He who accepted the sting of death for our sakes fail to weep when facing that very death? Theologians are fond of saying that Jesus' tears are the completest proof of His humanity. But we would add that these tears are also the completest proof of the emotions of God's heart. And just as Christ has trampled down death by His death, so by His tears does He wipe away the tears from our eyes!

"Then Jesus, again groaning in Himself, came to the tomb. It was a cave, and a stone lay against it. Jesus said, 'Take away the stone'" (v. 38). This order was given as an opportunity for the onlookers to have a hands-on role in the impending wonder. His later command, "Loose him and let him go," served the same purpose. It is one thing to witness something with one's eyes; it is another thing to witness it by the touch of the hands. Martha objected that the stench of death would emerge from the cave if the stone were removed; hence, the strength of the witness would be augmented by the sense of smell. Saint John included all these little details into his narrative in order to demonstrate the authenticity of the account. In terms of spiritual symbolism, the lifting of the stone represents the efforts that must be expended by the Church—in service and teaching—to prepare the world for the entrance of God's power, which will bring dead souls back to life.

Jesus then calmly lifts His eyes to heaven and prays, "Father, I thank You that You have heard Me" (v. 41). It was essential that Christ speak to the Father, as He did from the Cross, before performing the wonder. Firstly, it was essential that the audience understand that this miracle was performed through Christ by the Father's power and not by any magical or diabolical power. Secondly, He desired not to hoard the glory of such a work for Himself but to reflect it back to God. And thirdly, the prayer was spoken on our behalf. As St. Athanasius says, every prayer uttered by Jesus was uttered by our human nature.[46]

"Now when He had said these things, He cried with a loud voice, 'Lazarus, come forth!'" (v. 43). It is clear that the Lord is dealing here with a powerful foe. A vehement command is required to achieve the work; Hades heard and convulsed when it found its powers challenged. It was a deep "sleep" in which Lazarus reposed—because, as Jesus said, He went to "wake" him. The Gospels often refer to death casually as "sleep," as if it were a mere trifle when in the presence of the Lord of Life. We may be surprised to read of the Lord using such vocal force, for this is the One of whom it was written, "He will not quarrel nor cry out, / Nor will anyone hear His voice in the streets" (Matt. 12:19). But Jesus' solemn exclamation tells us that an immense measure of vital energy was expended in effecting Lazarus's resurrection. Here was something more than a work of creation; it was the revivification of a creature who had been held by the unbreakable cords of corruption and Hades.

The image of Lazarus emerging from the tomb must have struck terror into the hearts of the onlookers such as we can scarcely imagine today. The idea of resurrection might sound nice to the ear, but its physical reality creates fear. Hence, we read of the dread and alarm the disciples experienced on first seeing the risen Lord. Moreover, seeing a man walk out of a tomb still wrapped in his burial cloths is a sight to terrorize a spectator even more. The Jews of the day embalmed their dead using a method borrowed from the ancient Egyptians, in which each limb was separately wrapped. Lazarus

---

46 Commentary on Psalm 68.

appeared as a walking mummy. Christ's order to "loose him and let him go" was a chance given to the onlookers to recollect their wits and approach the startling image.

This was the final sign given by the evangelist St. John in his Gospel before the commencement of Holy Week. It is a marvelous thing to consider that many, many more signs besides this one were performed by Christ, the number of which would fill too many books to be housed by all the libraries of the world. It is also a marvelous thing to consider that Lazarus's resurrection was a prototype of our own. For we look forward to the day on which Jesus will call to us, "Come forth!"

Zacchaeus the Chief Tax Collector

"THEN JESUS ENTERED AND PASSED through Jericho. Now behold, *there was* a man named Zacchaeus who was a chief tax collector, and he was rich" (Luke 19:1, 2). We have here in this story, given to us only by St. Luke, the last event recorded during Jesus' long journey from Galilee to Jerusalem. It appears to occupy an important place in Luke's account, because it is a sterling example of Christ's pursuit of sinners, told in a Gospel which itself highlights the redemption of sinners. Jesus repeatedly surprises people by the immensity of His compassion for them; He makes Himself a genuine friend of tax collectors by entering their homes and dining with them. And if Jesus be the true personification of God, it staggers the mind to think that God would give so much regard to sinners. Would God really stoop so dramatically to befriend a sinner? Could God so leisurely and with so little hindrance sit and dine with sinners when such an act would revolt the ritually clean?

Zacchaeus was a wealthy man, and his riches had been amassed by employing underhanded and devious methods of tax gathering.

But, in the buoyancy of his joy at Jesus' offer to dine with him, he immediately disavows his scheming past and promises to recompense anyone he had wronged fourfold. Thus, Zacchaeus becomes for us a shining example of how a rich man may enter the Kingdom of God. He had heard that this Jesus was a friend of tax collectors; and so, desiring to see His form and hear His words, he climbs up a sycamore to compensate for his short stature. We may assume that he was unhappy with his shifting and wayward life and wished to make a new beginning.

"And when Jesus came to the place, He looked up and saw him, and said to him, 'Zacchaeus, make haste and come down, for today I must stay at your house'" (Luke 19:5). It was not by chance that Zacchaeus climbed that tree that day, and it was not by chance that Jesus passed by it to look up. Zacchaeus's name was already written into Christ's agenda as the final person to be saved now that His public ministry was coming to a close. Zacchaeus feels a special honor in Jesus' invitation and hurriedly scrambles down the tree to welcome Him into his home.

The people immediately begin to grumble about the incident, because they all know that Zacchaeus is an unscrupulous man, and they interpret Jesus' dining with him as a tacit acceptance of his notorious life. But Jesus indeed meant this in part, for His coming to Jerusalem was for such people as Zacchaeus. He intended to bear our sins on the wood of the Cross. Unfortunately, however, man does not like to have mercy on his brother or to see someone else have mercy on him. Zacchaeus quickly defends himself against the murmurings of his critics. He promises to lead a new and honest life, partly to return the honor Christ showed him by the visitation, and partly to shield Christ from the reproaches He had to endure on Zacchaeus's behalf.

The official rule of the rabbis in cases of embezzlement was that the offender had to return the full amount of money to the defendant plus twenty percent. In severe cases, the ruling could be to return four times the amount extorted, just as King David had ruled against himself (2 Sam. 12:5, 6), and as the Law itself demanded (Ex. 22:1).

"And Jesus said to him, 'Today salvation has come to this house, because he also is a son of Abraham; for the Son of Man has come to seek and to save that which was lost'" (Luke 19:9). How marvelous is our Lord! His never-ending mercies flow from the sinner to the sinner's entire house! God's generosity surpasses anything we can imagine, for His ways are above our ways as the heavens are above the earth (Is. 55:9). The people sneered at Christ's presence in Zacchaeus's house, but He entered the house to remove the sin therein and to place it on the Cross. Was He not the Good Shepherd who said that He gives up His life for the sheep? Zacchaeus was a lost sheep, and Christ found him. Zacchaeus had been rich in money; Jesus made him rich in giving.

Mary Washes the Feet of Jesus

"THEN, SIX DAYS BEFORE THE Passover, Jesus came to Bethany.... Then Mary took a pound of very costly oil of spikenard, anointed the feet of Jesus, and wiped His feet with her hair. And the house was filled with the fragrance of the oil" (John 12:1, 3). The Passover fell on the fourteenth of the Jewish month of Nisan; Jesus, who had lingered temporarily in a city called Ephraim, arrived in Bethany on the eighth of Nisan, which was a Friday. A meal was traditionally prepared Friday evening before sunset in anticipation of the Sabbath, and Martha was busily toiling to finish before sundown, after which work was forbidden in honor of the Sabbath.

Again, we have here in Martha's incessant activity and Mary's quiet reflection a picture of the Church's relative philosophy of service and contemplation. *The Paradise of the Holy Fathers*, for example, relates the Church's ancient distinction between contemplatives and active ministers. As the Church teaches, both Mary and Martha are to be praised.

Mary then approaches Jesus with a Roman pound's worth of a fragrant oil, anoints Jesus' feet with it, and wipes off the oil with her hair. This was an oil extracted from the roots of spikenard, a plant that flourishes in the northern mountains of India. The cost of a Roman pound of this oil equaled about three hundred denarii, where a denarius equaled the salary for a full day's work. When we combine the story as it is told in Matthew 26, Mark 14, and John 12, we learn that Mary broke the vessel holding the oil over Jesus' head, then proceeded to anoint His feet, and completed the reverent act by drying the oil with her hair.

In Moses' Law we read this: "*He who is* the high priest among his brethren, on whose head the anointing oil was poured . . . the consecration of the anointing oil of his God *is* upon him: I *am* the LORD" (Lev. 21:10, 12). And Philo of Alexandria once wrote that the head of the Logos, who is eternal High Priest, would be anointed with oil. What Philo foresaw as a philosophical truth, we now see as Jesus being anointed by the hand of a woman whose heart had been filled with faith and love.

The sweet odor of the oil filled the entire house—a detail long retained in Saint John's memory and recorded in his Gospel. The powerful essence of the odor moved Jesus as well, who declared that all succeeding ages of the Church would remember the generous act of love performed by this woman. This passage opens the Holy Week readings of the Church; and as such, it serves as a model of love for Christ, given to us to emulate during the days of Christ's Passion.

Unfortunately, in this heavenly atmosphere of love and grace, in the midst of Christ's own presence, we hear of grumblings that display the meanest and most foolish insolence. "Why was this fragrant oil not sold for three hundred denarii and given to the poor?" (John 12:5). The humble and glowing face of this blessed sister, who had given her all to Jesus in a moment of gratitude, was quickly overshadowed by a dark and sinister face, one that was enraged to see such wasteful love. Judas, in his sneering mood, suggested that the oil should have been *sold*. Everything in Judas's life was eligible for the selling. He who stole God's money would very easily sell Christ too.

"But Jesus said, 'Let her alone; she has kept this for the day of My burial'" (John 12:7). This is a covert allusion to the activity of the traitor, whose machinations would end in Jesus' death; it is also a mystical allusion to Mary's act, whose oil and hair served as the first supplies for the Lord's burial. She had donated the first pound of those burial spices of which Joseph and Nicodemus would later donate the remaining ninety-nine. But she offered it while Jesus was yet alive, so she received the thankful praise of Jesus' own lips. Joseph and Nicodemus offered it after His death and so have received the praises of the history books.

CHAPTER NINE

Holy Week

Hosanna Sunday (Palm Sunday)

After partaking of the Sabbath meal that evening and passing the night in Bethany, Jesus rises on the morning of the following day, a Sunday, and sends out two of his disciples to "the opposite town"—Bethphage—to make request of a donkey for His use. Since many followers of Jesus lived in the vicinity, the donkey was immediately procured, and they brought it to Jesus. One reason for needing the donkey was to make the passage from Bethany, which sat east of the Mount of Olives, to Jerusalem, which sat to its west. The climb over the mountain would be an arduous one, given that it rose to approximately 2600 feet at its peak. Jerusalem itself sat on a hill, and the temple at its center rose to a point only 250 feet below Mount Olivet's peak, when compared to sea level. The depression between Jerusalem and the Mount of Olives was called the Kidron Valley.

This was a donkey on which no one had ever sat, meaning it had not yet been trained to bear a rider; but it inexplicably consented to bearing this first rider. He who—as we say in Orthodox hymnology—"sits upon the cherubim" condescends to sit on an animal that has received the universal disdain of man. He rides into the city indeed as the Messiah—though His messiahship was sorely misunderstood—to find and redeem the poor, maimed, and lost sheep of Israel.

The incident recalled the words of Zechariah the Prophet to the evangelists' minds, and they record it in their Gospels: "Tell the daughter of Zion, / 'Behold, your King is coming to you, / Lowly, and sitting on a donkey, / A colt, the foal of a donkey'" (Matt. 21:5). It is an amazing thing that Zechariah saw this great procession 550 years beforehand. He also writes:

Rejoice greatly, O daughter of Zion!
Shout, O daughter of Jerusalem!
Behold, your King is coming to you;
He is just and having salvation,
Lowly and riding on a donkey,
A colt, the foal of a donkey. (Zech. 9:9)

The throng accompanying Jesus' movements divided itself into two parties—one preceding and one following the Lord—and began to shout their excited praises in an alternating fashion:

The preceding choir: *Hosanna to the Son of David!*
The trailing choir: *Blessed is He who comes in the name of the* Lord!
The preceding choir: *Hosanna in the highest!*

These words are taken from the Hallel Psalms, which stretch from Psalm 113 to 118 and were typically chanted during Passover. They were considered to be messianic psalms.

The word *hosanna* ("save us") itself had strong messianic overtones to Jewish ears. During the Feast of Tabernacles, which commemorated their escape from Egypt, the Jews would cut down palm branches for the adornment of their tents. The palm branch carried redemptive significance to the Jewish mind. With the same spirit, the people cut down palm branches to hail Christ's approach to Jerusalem. Tree branches and palms became a universal symbol of obedience and joy for a coming king.

As they were still going over Mount Olivet, "some of the Pharisees called to Him from the crowd, 'Teacher, rebuke Your disciples'" (Luke 19:39). These were Pharisees who had mingled with the throng traveling from Bethany to Jerusalem, and they were alarmed by the cries of "Son of David," fearing that it would draw the attention of the Romans. This would be the last appearance of the Pharisees in the Gospel history. Once at Jerusalem, Jesus would be accosted by the scribes and chief priests; and it was the chief priests and Sadducees who would be the key players in all the succeeding events of Holy Week, including the arrest, the trials, and the Crucifixion. "But He answered and said to them, 'I tell you that if these should keep silent, the stones would immediately cry out'" (Luke 19:40). Should not the stones cry out if the chief cornerstone be rejected?

There is a certain point along the descent of Mount Olivet at which the entirety of Jerusalem comes into view. The procession reaches this point, and Jesus, looking on the city in all its grandeur, bursts into tears and utters a lament. "If you had known, even you, especially in this your day, the things *that make* for your peace! But now they are hidden from your eyes" (Luke 19:42). What He saw was different from what everyone else saw, for He was looking deep into the city's past. He saw its former times of peace and prosperity, its glory days under Solomon, the happiness of so many generations that had lived there. He also saw its priests donning corruption rather than righteousness, its kings ruling by injustice and bribery, and its prophets stoned to death.

Jesus then looks upon the city's future and sees the woe and destruction that would come upon it, and concludes by saying, "they will not leave in you one stone upon another, because you did not know the time of your visitation" (Luke 19:44). And indeed, a few short years afterwards, the Roman armies would besiege the city, build an embankment around it, starve the city to the point of utter desperation, then proceed to raze it to the very ground.

"And when He had come into Jerusalem, all the city was moved, saying, 'Who is this?'" (Matt. 21:10). The scene the people of Jerusalem witnessed—the grand procession, the shouting, the singing, the palm branches—was entirely new to their minds. They had never before seen Jesus riding an animal, and the Jewish leaders were particularly galled at the display of ecstatic and unbridled joy. The Greek word for *moved* means "earthquake," showing the social upheaval generated by the event. When some asked who this man was, the answer was readily available, for He had taught recently at the major feasts in Jerusalem. Thus was Christ received into the holy city—as Son of David and Israel's Deliverer—on His final day of ministry on earth. From this moment on, He was to enter into His sufferings.

The Temple Is Cleansed

"THEN JESUS WENT INTO THE temple of God and drove out all those who bought and sold in the temple, and overturned the tables of the money changers and the seats of those who sold doves" (Matt. 21:12). Jesus enters the temple through the Court of the Gentiles and is met by a disconcerting scene: men yelling, boisterous haggling, and animals of sacrifice bleating everywhere. It is a veritable market; but the noise of the merchants and the foul smell of animal droppings made it worse than a market. The animal sellers themselves could not sell their products until they first paid an admission fee to the priests. It was as though the people purchased these animals of sacrifice from the priests' consciences. The revenue generated from this business went into the pockets of Annas, the high priest—who himself paid a fee to sacrifice Christ, in the amount of thirty pieces of silver.

The people purchasing the animals needed to go to the moneychangers in order to exchange their foreign monies for temple money, because foreign coinage was deemed profane and unacceptable. The money would have to be changed (at a fee) whether one was buying an animal for sacrifice or making a donation to the temple. A pair of doves might sell for a nickel outside the temple; but the same pair approved by the priests for sacrifice inside the temple would sell for four pounds. Everyone entering the temple was in fact required to pay a temple tax in the amount of a half-shekel. Any services of cleansing or purification performed within the temple also required payment. The money thus extorted from the people—which amounted annually to thousands upon thousands of silver coins— was equally distributed among the temple clerics. A den of thieves! It was an exploitation of animals, as well as an exploitation of religion.

The expulsion of these marauders and the clean-up of such a scandalous scene would have required at least fifty soldiers to accomplish. But Christ shows Himself to be the true Lord of the house when He hurls at them the thunderous rebuke, "It is written, 'My house shall be called a house of prayer,' but you have made it a 'den of thieves'!" and they are stunned into silence. Whenever Christ rose to display His authority, it was a chilling experience for the religious leaders. They indeed stood guilty and powerless before Him, especially when they found themselves exposed as in the parable of the wicked vinedressers.

When Jesus had entered the temple and "looked around," as Mark so vividly tells us, the entire history of Israel was recalled to His mind, with its long train of patriarchs and prophets, the last of which was Himself, who had come to seal and finish the relationship that heretofore had been exclusively between Yahweh and the chosen people. He had come seeking fruit from the fig tree planted by God's right hand, but what He found was a flourishing green foliage, hanging fruitlessly from the trunk.

His soul is provoked; and so He plaits some cords into a whip, drives out the buyers and sellers and the sheep and oxen, whose sacrifice was soon to prove obsolete in the shadow of that greater Sacrifice. He scatters the drachmas from the moneychangers' tables, which had desecrated God's house more wickedly than any pagan money could do. And He turns over the seats of those who sold doves and orders them to leave, not willing to hurt the caged birds by overturning their tables—for not a single one of them could fall apart from God's will.

Confrontation with the Temple Authorities

THE CHIEF PRIESTS, SCRIBES, AND elders are pushed to the extremity of exasperation by the events that have just transpired, and they demand to know by what authority He went about doing all these things. "But He answered and said to them, 'I also will ask you one thing, and answer Me: The baptism of John—was it from heaven or from men?'" (Luke 20:3, 4). Christ questions His interrogators on a point regarding which the people unanimously agreed: the status of John the Baptist. The teachers of Israel had despised the Baptist's message and stiffly resisted his position as a prophet. But the people received him as a prophet, and in this they proved to be more enlightened than their teachers. What was worse, the leaders of Israel made themselves a stumbling block to the people by slowing the progress of the Baptist's ministry—which bore testimony to Jesus as the Messiah.

Christ's question refers to John's entire mission and message. It was widely known that Jesus had received baptism at John's hands and that John had testified that the Christ was "before him." And now, Jesus requires to hear from their own lips whether John's baptism was from heaven or from men.

The answer to this question would clearly indicate by what authority He was doing these things, for an approval of John's baptism "from heaven" would be an approval of Jesus' messiahship. Jesus here puts them in a logical entanglement from which they could not easily free themselves. Despite their venomous antipathy to the Baptist and to Christ, they were not willing to openly admit their denial of John's baptism, so they confessed ignorance on this point. The fear of public opinion seized their hearts.

Christ proceeds to press His point further by offering a parable in the hearing of the people and religious leaders. A man owns a vineyard, He says, which he leaves to vinedressers for a season while he is away on a distant journey. At vintage-time, he sends several servants to receive the fruit due him, but they are treated viciously at the hands of the wicked vinedressers. The man then sends his own son to receive the fruit, but he is murdered. The owner of the vineyard then comes, destroys the vinedressers, and gives the vineyard to others more worthy.

The first strike of the parable is to assign the rulers of Israel the status of hirelings or wage earners who are meant to present the harvest at vintage time. This they receive as an affront, for they considered themselves owners of the temple and of the religion, and therefore beneath nobody. The second strike is to accuse them of beating the servants (prophets) sent to them by the vineyard's owner (God) and sending them away empty-handed. The owner's journey to a distant country represents God's long-suffering with Israel through the ages, in the expectation that fruit would be presented in due time.

The third strike comes in the identity of the owner's son. They could not have mistaken whom He meant. Jesus' own tears over the city were clear evidence of how earnestly He had sought fruit from the nation, but it was found wanting. The Father had sent the Son to gather fruit from the vinedressers, but they were about to murder Him. The fourth and final strike comes in the threat that the vineyard would be taken from the nation and given to others. They cry "Certainly not!" in horror at the thought, but indeed, it would certainly be so. God sent Jesus to sign a new covenant—with a signature of His blood—not with hirelings, but with the cloud of saints and household of God around the world.

"The chief priests and the scribes that very hour sought to lay hands on Him, but they feared the people—for they knew He had spoken this parable against them" (Luke 20:19).

The Question Regarding the Roman Tax

"THEN THEY SENT TO HIM some of the Pharisees and the Herodians, to catch Him in *His* words. When they had come, they said to Him, 'Teacher, we know that You are true, and care about no one; for You do not regard the person of men, but teach the way of God in truth. Is it lawful to pay taxes to Caesar, or not? Shall we pay, or shall we not pay?'" (Mark 12:13, 14).

This question posed by the adversaries of Christ was a piece of craft designed to openly pit Him against Caesar. We get a sense of the deep peril concealed beneath the question by the catastrophic results of the Jewish rebellion against Rome that would take place forty years later. They nursed a raging hatred for Rome in their breasts, and they were eager to see a rebellion sparked by a single unguarded word dropping from Jesus' lips. The very wording of the question reveals a diabolical delicacy of expression. They pretend to flatter Jesus for His honesty and fearlessness in expressing His true opinions, regardless of the social position of the person He is addressing. They are hoping for a clear and unequivocal answer to their question, so they offer only two options (with no third): "pay" or "not pay."

"But He, knowing their hypocrisy, said to them, 'Why do you test Me? Bring Me a denarius that I may see *it*.' So they brought *it*. And He said to them, 'Whose image and inscription *is* this?' They said to Him, 'Caesar's'" (Mark 12:15, 16).

The reigning Caesar that year was Tiberius, and the coin that was brought to Christ likely had written on it, *Tiberius Caesar Divi Augusti Filius Augustus*—"Tiberius Caesar the Son of Augustus the Divine Augustus." On the flip side of the coin was an image of Caesar's mother sitting on a throne, holding a scepter in her right hand and an olive branch in her left. The imagery was an indication of the coin's authorized status for the remittance of debts owed to the government. But one of the greatest dilemmas faced by a free Jew of the day was how to pay a captive's tax to a power that had seized his freedom. Did the Law sanction the paying of taxes to heathen Rome? It was the dilemma of every member of Jewish society, from the priest to the poor man. The tax was called the *capitularium*,[47] because its payment was exacted on every head.

In extracting the response "Caesar's" from their lips, Jesus makes them openly confess that they must indeed pay the tax to Rome. They might have despised the tax as a galling reminder of their subjugation; but, after all, the Jews would never allow a coin with Caesar's image to be deposited into the temple treasury. The moneychangers saw to it that all Roman coinage was converted to Jewish coinage before it entered the sacred precincts. Caesar's coins, therefore, could ultimately end up nowhere but in Caesar's own coffers.

---

47   From *caput*, Latin for "head."

"And Jesus answered and said to them, 'Render to Caesar the things that are Caesar's, and to God the things that are Gods.' And they marveled at Him" (Mark 12:17).

There are a couple of ways to understand our Lord's saying. Some theologians interpret it to mean that we ought to pay *money* to Caesar and give our *selves* to God. This is predicated on the idea that man bears the image of God, and therefore, man's very being and existence must be remitted to God. Another interpretation of the saying comes from the origin of the money. Since Caesar coined his money using his own production machinery, he naturally had a right to its repayment. And since, according to Jewish tradition, God wrote the Law by His own finger, He had a natural right to demand obedience to it. In short, the civil governor must be obeyed in his proper domain, while in matters of worship and piety and holiness, God alone must be obeyed.

Our Lord's eloquent rule thenceforth became the guiding principle of the Church in dealing with the state. Caesar possesses certain rights; God possesses certain rights; and both should be recognized, but never confused.

"And the scribes and chief priests heard it and sought how they might destroy Him; for they feared Him, because all the people were astonished at His teaching" (Mark 11:18).

The Withered Fig Tree

"NOW IN THE MORNING, AS He returned to the city, He was hungry. And seeing a fig tree by the road, He came to it and found nothing on it but leaves, and said to it, 'Let no fruit grow on you ever again.' Immediately the fig tree withered away" (Matt. 21:18, 19). In St. Mark's Gospel, this story occurs over the course of two days: on Sunday the tree is cursed, and on Monday the disciples find it atrophied. In St. Matthew's Gospel, it is a single event that occurs on Tuesday. And in St. Luke's Gospel, it is related not as an event but as a parable, told by Jesus somewhere in the middle of the book.

On the face of it, the story appears to present Jesus as a typical human being who has grown hungry and so hopes to find some food on a fig tree. The phrase "He was hungry" is one of the evangelists' subtle but common devices in revealing Jesus as truly the Son of Man. The whole story turns, in fact, on Christ's hunger. Jesus is drawn to this particular tree because of its broad green leaves, for they were a sign that one could expect to find fruit hanging from it. The road from Bethany to Jerusalem along which Jesus traveled was ideal for the growth of fig trees; it ran along the eastern slope of Mount Olivet and so received the blessings of the sun's rays and warmth, which contributed to the early leafing of fruit trees.

As is usually the case, this Gospel narrative is a mystical commentary on Christ's whole life and mission. After so long a period of ministry among the Israelites, Jesus desired to eat of the fruit of His labor. But He finds that this fig tree—symbolic of the nation of Israel—is adorned with a fruitless green foliage. The green leaves indicate that Israel possessed the appearance of religion and an external ceremonialism, but no inward fruit of the Spirit to show for it.

And so Jesus utters the only curse ever to fall from His lips in the Gospels. It was an expression of the judgment under which those would fall who willfully rejected the Son of Man. It should not be construed as a harsh or brazen pronouncement; its severity is directed toward those among the nation who stubbornly and violently opposed Christ's redemptive work. Christ's words are also a judgment on those within the Church who are entrusted with a ministry but who have no fruit to show for it.

It is instructive as well to read the record in St. Luke:

He also spoke this parable: "A certain *man* had a fig tree planted in his vineyard, and he came seeking fruit on it and found none. Then he said to the keeper of his vineyard, 'Look for three years I have come seeking fruit on this fig tree and find none. Cut it down; why does it use up the ground?' But he answered and said to him, 'Sir, let it alone this year also, until I dig around it and fertilize *it*. And if it bears fruit, *well*. But if not, after that you can cut it down.'" (Luke 13:6–9)

This is probably the same tradition as recorded by Matthew and Mark but in parabolic form. It includes the additional detail that the owner of the vineyard had waited *for three years* to see fruit on his fig tree, but in vain—an allusion to Christ's three years of ministry in Israel.

The Parable of the Wedding Banquet

AS JESUS' MINISTRY DRAWS TO a close in this final week, He delivers several parables to censure the nation for their treatment of His person and His message. The religious rulers of the nation had implacably resisted His invitation to redemption, so the Lord delivers this parable of the wedding banquet to illustrate the tragedy of this refused invitation. The invitation, in fact, was extended in three different ways, each symbolizing a stage in Jesus' ministry.

"And Jesus answered and spoke to them again by parables and said: 'The kingdom of heaven is like a certain king who arranged a marriage for his son, and sent out his servants to call those who were invited to the wedding; and they were not willing to come'" (Matt. 22:1–3). This first invitation or call was sent out by Jesus personally with the aid of His disciples. The "king" here is God the Father, the Great Shepherd who loves His flock so dearly that He arranges for an exquisite feast to be laid for it and lovingly invites the human stewards and keepers of the flock to come and celebrate.

The son represents the Messiah, and the bride is God's people. Jesus and His disciples had spent three and a half years raising the cry about the Kingdom, bidding all people to come and see, and desiring the fulfillment of that sacred betrothal that had its roots in the Old Testament. But this invitation was largely refused; and the consummation of this divine marriage, which took place on the Cross, happened in the absence of Israel's leaders.

The doors of the Kingdom, however, are never permanently closed. After Christ's physical absence from the world, His power is felt again in the agency of the Holy Spirit, who works mightily through the disciples and believers; and it is these believers who extend the invitation to the chosen people for acceptance once again. This second invitation, moreover, has the Spirit's unction upon it and has reached every corner of the earth: "Again, he sent out other servants, saying, 'Tell those who are invited, "See, I have prepared my dinner; my oxen and fatted cattle *are* killed, and all things *are* ready. Come to the wedding"'" (Matt. 22:4).

The mention of oxen and cattle being killed is a subtle allusion to the fact that the Father offered the ultimate sacrifice in order to prepare for the great banquet. Thus, the invitation is not a merely verbal one; it was an invitation written before all ages, at the preordained cost of the Son of God's precious blood—a price not all the angels of heaven and men of the earth together could have paid.

The refusal of the second invitation comes in two forms. The first group disdain it as worthless and go on with their daily business. The second group—in the spirit of their forefathers who killed the prophets—seize the inviters, abuse them, and murder them. Stephen and James the brother of John were the first of a long line of martyrs who bore witness to this fact. When the Lord's adversaries persecuted the primitive Church in Jerusalem and extinguished its hope in the calling, those sent to issue the invitation return to their Lord with a tearful report. The king in the parable is seized with fury and sends his armies to destroy the adversary's city—a prophetic allusion to the fall of Jerusalem in AD 70.

"Then he said to his servants. . . . 'Therefore go into the highways, and as many as you find, invite to the wedding.' So those servants went out into the highways and gathered together all whom they found, both bad and good. And the wedding *hall* was filled with guests" (Matt. 22:8–10). This third invitation is radically different from the first two. The first and second were sent to a select few; when the third is sent out, all distinctions between persons are dropped, and everyone without exception is invited. The inviters are not even to differentiate between the good and the bad. But all are to be brought into the wedding hall, and the king alone will have the prerogative of making any distinctions.

The king then exercises His prerogative in the following verse: "But when the king came in to see the guests, he saw a man there who did not have on a wedding garment. So he said to him, 'Friend, how did you come in here without a wedding garment?' And he was speechless" (Matt. 22:11, 12). The parable here emphasizes the exacting investigation the king makes personally into each individual's life. He examines this man's clothes and finds them wanting, so the king's servants bind him and cast him out into the darkness.

The question naturally arises: What are these wedding garments that are so essential to making one worthy to stand in the banquet hall? The answer is this: "For as many of you as were baptized into Christ have *put on Christ*" (Gal. 3:27, emphasis added). We have been united to Christ. We have been clothed with His righteousness. We were dressed in our wedding garments on the day of our baptism. The garments were not given to us as a prize for our good deeds but freely bestowed by the Father on all who would believe in His Son. The King made these garments by His own hands, and so all who don them are brought into the wedding hall without distinction.

Woes Pronounced on the Scribes and Pharisees

"THEN JESUS SPOKE TO THE multitudes and to His disciples, saying: 'The scribes and the Pharisees sit in Moses' seat. Therefore whatever they tell you to observe, *that* observe and do, but do not do according to their works; for they say, and do not do'" (Matt. 23:1–3). Saint Matthew presents Christ at the beginning of his Gospel as the teacher of truth and gladness; but now, toward the Gospel's end, Jesus takes up the role of judge. He had begun by blessing the people with the Beatitudes; now He warns the scribes and Pharisees with the eightfold woes.

Jesus begins by emphasizing a vital point. These scribes and Pharisees sit in Moses' seat indeed, but not by God's choosing. These religious rulers had *seated themselves* on Moses' seat; but that was the extent and limit of their authority. Their authority came not from God's election but from their assumed positions. True authority derives from the sanctity and righteousness commanded by the Law. But since the scribes and Pharisees failed to live out the Law, the need arose to distinguish between what these rulers *said* and what they *did*.

Jesus then embarks on a blistering catalog of their sins. They laid heavy burdens on men's *shoulders* but would not help to carry them by moving so much as a *finger*. They broadened their phylacteries—the small leather boxes tied about the head and arm, which contained strips of paper with scriptural verses scribbled on them—in order to display their piety before men. They broadened the borders of their robes, and desired the best places at feasts, and received the hails of the people in the marketplaces—all in order to make themselves more conspicuous to the public eye. When one realizes that these scathing critiques were leveled against the scribes and Pharisees in the presence of the people, with those very leaders standing right before Him, Christ's extraordinary power and boldness become very apparent.

When Jesus began setting forth the principles of the Kingdom at the start of His ministry, He made a telling comment to the disciples: "I say to you, that unless your righteousness exceeds *the righteousness* of the scribes and Pharisees, you will by no means enter the kingdom of heaven" (Matt. 5:20). The spiritual failings of Israel's rulers elicited this rule from our Lord's lips, and it was their rigidity and callousness that caused Him to adopt such a hard-edged tone when addressing them on this day. We must always remember, however, that the harshness apparent in our Lord's rebukes was tempered by the tears He shed over Jerusalem and its blindness. The righteous anger that stirred in His breast was mingled with the sorrow of knowing that the Cross stood at the end of the road. The silent tears He shed over these unworthy scribes and Pharisees were the same as the tears that fell in Gethsemane.

"But woe to you, scribes and Pharisees, hypocrites!" (Matt. 23:13). The Lord affixes this searing label to them as a group because they taught without doing and spoke without acting. Their teaching was worse than useless, because it distanced the people from Christ and stole from them the blessings of discipleship and eternal life. These rulers cared only about their own position and authority; as a result, they could not enter the Kingdom, and they prevented others from entering. They approached poor widows to offer help; but, since they were thieves clothed in religion, they stole what they could, assuming nobody saw and nobody knew. They crossed land and sea to win a single proselyte; but once he was converted, they initiated him into their hypocritical ways. And instead of making him into a son of Abraham, they would turn him into a son of Gehenna.

"Woe to you, blind guides, who say, 'Whoever swears by the temple, it is nothing; but whoever swears by the gold of the temple, he is obliged *to perform it.*' Fools and blind!" (Matt. 23:16, 17). Christ had previously repudiated the practice of swearing as having no part in the Kingdom of God, for it was enough for the believer to be led by the Spirit and for his speech to be always honest and consistent. But the pharisaical rules regarding swearing had reached a new level of hypocrisy. It was known that one swore by what was greatest in value; and if the scribes and Pharisees held one more responsible for swearing by the gold of the temple or by the gifts on the altar than by the temple and the altar themselves, then how much covetousness, impiety, and irreverence did this reveal in their hearts!

"Woe to you . . . for you cleanse the outside of the cup and dish, but inside they are full of extortion and self-indulgence. . . . For you are like whitewashed tombs which indeed appear beautiful outwardly, but inside are full of dead *men's* bones and all uncleanness" (Matt. 23:25, 27). The statement alludes to the Levitical law (Lev. 11:33), which said that a sacred vessel inwardly unclean was not usable; the Pharisees, however, were scrubbing the outside of the vessel with special vigor. The sanctified cup was a symbol of the sanctified life. And Jesus, in exposing the depravity of their secret lives, is declaring that they had desecrated God's house and its reputation. And if this image is not strong enough to prick their consciences, He uses one more calculated to make a decent person shudder. The scribes and Pharisees were like tombs meticulously groomed from the outside; but were a person to enter and see the putrefaction within the tomb, it would cause him to tremble in revulsion.

After completing His rebuke of Israel's leaders, Jesus bursts into a lament over the city: "O Jerusalem, Jerusalem, the one who kills the prophets and stones those who are sent to her! How often I wanted to gather your children together, as a hen gathers her chicks under *her* wings, but you were not willing!" (Luke 23:37). The double cry, "Jerusalem, Jerusalem," reminds us of similar calls, as in "Martha, Martha," "Saul, Saul," and Yahweh's ancient call to the patriarch, "Abraham, Abraham!" The cordial ring latent in these callings is always a sign that God is near and that the chance of a new life is at hand. But Jesus grieved over Jerusalem because it missed its most glorious opportunity—to be the mother of all the earth and the door to heaven's Kingdom.

Discourse on the End Times

THE GREAT DENUNCIATION JESUS CAST on the scribes and Pharisees sparked within His breast broodings about the future downfall of the temple. Christ made some remarks regarding a widow who gave her last two mites to the temple, which were to become the last piece of teaching He gave during His earthly ministry. He left the temple with the disciples to make His way back to Bethany. As they made their ascent up the Mount of Olives, the sun began its westerly course over the mountain as sunset drew near; and, as the solar rays gleamed on the great stone and marble edifice, they bathed the temple in a surreal glory.

As the group turned to behold the scene, one of them broke out in praise of how beautiful were its stones and adornments. This was likely a simple Galilean whose eyes were unaccustomed to such pompous architecture. A typical stone out of which the temple was constructed was forty cubits long by twenty cubits wide—an immense block of rock. When the man lauded the adornments of the structure, he was likely seeing the golden vine that was hung above the front gate of the temple—a symbol of the vine God pulled out of Egypt and planted in the Promised Land.

The comment prompted a lengthy discourse by Jesus regarding the fate of the temple and of Jerusalem, and regarding the end times. It is a single prophecy that mingles foretellings of all three—temple, Jerusalem, and world—and this fact has been a cause of perplexity to many commentators. But prophecy often transcends the limitations of time, as the spirit transcends the limitations of the mind. The prophecy speaks of things soon to happen, as well of events far in the distant future of the world, and this fact would have baffled the listeners of the day. But from our vantage point in time, it is easier to distinguish the events soon to happen from those still in the distant future.

Jesus first speaks of the coming destruction of Jerusalem and the temple; and the sign by which the people would know the beginning of their woes would be that the city would be surrounded by Rome's armies and warhorses. The melancholy details of this war are recorded for us by Josephus. The Roman legions besieged the city in AD 70 and cut off all supplies of food and water to the inhabitants. Fear and panic spread among the people, and in a state of utter desperation and starvation, they began to eat their own children to survive. Jesus pauses in the middle of the prophecy to give an urgent warning: all who are in the city must escape if possible, and even those in the northern parts of Judea should flee to the mountains.

We must remember that Christ consecrated the new temple of His body before the physical temple was to meet its fate: "For their sakes I sanctify myself" (John 17:19). And in place of the golden vine that adorned the temple's facade, He sprouted a new vine of believers and grafted us as branches into its life. The destruction of the temple would not only bring an end to the old priesthood, but it would also prevent the new ministry from confusing itself with the old. The very first believers in Jerusalem, in fact, under the leadership of James, the

Lord's brother, continued to offer sacrifice in the temple and to follow all other forms of ancient Jewish custom. As a consequence, they were viewed as merely a heretical Jewish sect. But once the Church was freed to live its own life, it began speaking fondly of a *heavenly* temple and a *heavenly* Jerusalem.

The Lord proceeds to point out the signs of the end. Many imposters will come in Jesus' name, boasting of a special knowledge of His teachings, but all such claims are hollow and spurious. Peace will be taken from the earth. Sin will proliferate at such an alarming rate, especially among the earth's kings and rulers, that wars and distress will plague the earth. The warring will in turn result in famine and disease. These in turn will lead to the manipulation of world economies and the control of entire populations. Satan's hand will be detectable in the general hatred and division that will afflict mankind. Nature herself will participate in the general unrest; the sun, moon, seas, and stars will all display ominous signs. At last, the Son of Man will be seen coming in glory—when the world's redemption has finally come.

But the upshot of all these prophecies is that believers must *watch*. There is a strong tradition in early Christian history of keeping vigil and being ready by day and by night for the Lord's coming. The parable of the ten virgins had a central place in the eschatology of the early Church, and the monastic movement was an outgrowth of this mindset. The true saint was the person who stood at all times ready to meet the Lord face to face, whose hands held a lamp, burning brightly and full of oil.

Certain Greeks Desire to See Jesus

"NOW THERE WERE CERTAIN GREEKS among those who came up to worship at the feast. Then they came to Philip, who was from

Bethsaida of Galilee, and asked him, saying, 'Sir, we wish to see Jesus'" (John 12:20, 21). During the days of Passover, Jerusalem was naturally thronged with pilgrims coming to celebrate the feast, and among these were a number of Gentile proselytes who had become obedient to the Jewish faith. A small company of these Gentile pilgrims were Greek. Having heard of Jesus' ministry, they desired a personal interview with Him. So they apply to Philip—since he was one of the disciples and carried a Greek name—to carry the request to Jesus on their behalf. Philip passes on the request to Andrew, who delivers it to Jesus.

These Greeks are the counterparts of the Magi. The Magi were Gentiles who came from the East to worship the new king, while these Greeks are Gentiles who came from the West to worship at the feast. These two bands together opened a new era of faith for the Gentile world. The request of these Greeks may have seemed small and nearly drowned out by the clatter and din of the crowds in Jerusalem; but it has since swelled to a roaring sea among the lands of the West.

"Jesus answered them, saying, 'The hour has come that the Son of Man should be glorified. Most assuredly, I say to you, unless a grain of wheat falls into the ground and dies, it remains alone; but if it dies, it produces much grain'" (John 12:23, 24). The visible, public ministry Jesus had carried on for over three years had finally come to a close. Now what remained was the invisible ministry—the redemptive work that must be carried out before the Father in the spiritual Holy of Holies. This is now His time, as the great High Priest, to sprinkle the sacrificial blood on the world while suspended from the Cross. The time of teaching is now past; what remains is the lonely road of suffering. As Isaiah had written, "I have trodden the winepress alone, / And from the peoples no one *was* with Me" (Is. 63:3).

But Christ delivers the message in the image of a grain of wheat.

A grain falls into the ground and, to all appearances, dies—but its death leads to an abundant harvest. The grain is furthermore a single grain, pointing to the solitude of His impending suffering. It was a loneliness that moved Him to the core: "Now My soul is troubled" (John 12:27). And "My soul is exceedingly sorrowful, even to death" (Matt. 26:38). Notwithstanding, He perpetually had the sense of the Father's presence to buoy His soul: "Yet I am not alone, because the Father is with Me" (John 16:32). He was really understood by no one. He came unto His own, but His own did not receive Him. His brethren had not believed in Him. The high priest tore his robes on hearing Him speak. His disciples abandoned Him. Their leader denied Him. One of them sold Him for silver coins. But just as a single grain of wheat leads to a multitude of harvest, so did the death and burial of Christ lead to the life of the world.

Transferring this image over to ourselves, the call is for us to reach for the higher things in spiritual life. The grain of wheat speaks of a principle in Christian life: that every ascent to a higher plane involves the death or loss of what is lower. Saint Paul describes it thus: "But what things were gain to me, these I have counted loss for Christ. Yet indeed I also count all things loss for the excellence of the knowledge of Christ Jesus my Lord, for whom I have suffered the loss of all things, and count them as rubbish, that I may gain Christ" (Phil. 3:7, 8). The renouncing of what is less, no matter how appealing and coveted it may be, always opens the way for the attainment of what is greater—for the soul of man and for his salvation.

The sacrifice of the ego's demands in the interest of the spirit's demands always brings with it a marvelous compensation that far exceeds the sacrifice—Christ Himself. Jesus restores and exceeds what was lost by the ego. The greedy person who seeks to acquire and accumulate and store up the pleasures of this world loses his ego (or self) in the end. His self, that is, is emptied of anything that is meaningful to spiritual life. The person who renounces the conceits of this world, on the other hand, transforms his ego into an ascending staircase that leads to heaven.

In answering the request of these Greeks, Jesus clarifies how exactly one may come and "see" Him. For to truly see Jesus was not as easy as these Greeks supposed, nor as simple as the hordes of pilgrims thought it would be to "see God" in Jerusalem or in the temple. As Jesus once told the Samaritan woman, "Woman, believe Me, the hour is coming when you will neither on this mountain, nor in Jerusalem, worship the Father. . . . But the hour is coming, and now is, when the true worshipers will worship the Father in spirit and truth" (John 4:21, 23). In order to worship God *in spirit*, it is necessary to die to the world. The grain of wheat is thus a fitting symbol of the soul—which dies to itself by falling to the ground and sprouting a rich harvest of eternal life in due time.

CHAPTER TEN

The Betrayal, Arrest, and Trial

The Plot to Destroy Jesus

Now it came to pass, when Jesus had finished all these sayings, *that* He said to His disciples, 'You know that after two days is the Passover, and the Son of Man will be delivered up to be crucified'" (Matt. 26:1, 2). This is the verse used by St. Matthew to end the "gospel of teaching," which comprised the majority of his book, and to begin the "gospel of redemption"—the swift drama comprising the voluntary death and Resurrection of the Lord. Jesus had urged His followers to receive the gospel of teaching by discipleship to Him, but they were to receive the gospel of redemption by taking up the cross. Any person who wishes to follow Christ must first remember His sayings and obey them, and second, must carry his cross. It is impossible to follow His teachings if one is unwilling to take up the cross.

We know from John's Gospel that Jesus celebrated the Last Supper on Thursday at sundown. Since the fourteenth of Nisan (Passover) of that year landed on a Friday, and a Jewish day was reckoned from the previous evening, the Last Supper was the Passover meal; it follows that Christ's "delivering up" occurred on Passover.[48] Passover

---

48   Scholars differ on the question of whether the Passover meal was celebrated

was the feast by which the Jews celebrated their deliverance from slavery in Egypt. As Jesus had said, "I lay down My life for the sheep" (John 10:15)—His arrest and death were acts carried out with His full pre-knowledge and will. What is recorded next in the Gospels is the failed plan by the chief priests to execute Jesus. They had planned to execute Him after the feast, but God overrode their scheme and insisted that the Lamb of God be sacrificed *during* the Passover. The divine intention was for Christ's sacrifice to be the eternal replacement for the earthly and temporal Passover sacrifices that had been performed since early Old Testament times.

> "Remember the former things of old,
> For I am God, and there is no other;
> I am God, and there is none like Me,
> Declaring the end from the beginning,
> And from ancient times things that are not yet done,
> Saying, 'My counsel shall stand,
> And I will do all My pleasure.'"
> (Is. 46:9, 10)

"Then the chief priests, the scribes, and the elders of the people assembled at the palace of the high priest, who was called Caiaphas, and plotted to take Jesus by trickery and kill *Him*" (Matt. 26:3, 4). The final plot begins to take shape. It is to be noted that the Pharisees are absent from the list of conspirators, and their absence continues throughout the trials and Crucifixion of Jesus. They did not

---

on the evening of Thursday or Friday. The synoptic Gospels say that the meal was eaten Thursday evening (Matt. 26:17; Mark 14:12; Luke 22:7–8), while the Gospel of John implies that it was observed on the day of the Crucifixion (John 18:28; 19:14). In the case of the Johannine dating, the 14th of Nisan would have landed on Friday, and the Last Supper would have been a precelebratory meal.

have a direct hand in these final proceedings, which leads to the inference that they did not agree with the violent turn events were taking. Caiaphas, as high priest, was the official leader of the plot; but his father-in-law, Annas, was the de facto high priest and operative mastermind of the plotters' machinations.

"Then one of the twelve, called Judas Iscariot, went to the chief priests and said, 'What are you willing to give me if I deliver Him to you?'" (Matt. 26:14, 15). It is a fact of the deepest shame and regret that it was one of the twelve disciples who was to turn traitor and give Jesus up to His enemies. The evangelists, however, record this appalling truth with complete honesty and do not scruple to hide their companion's crime. It was always Jesus' habit to allow a free and unfettered interchange of speech among His band of disciples. It was furthermore the very disciple who was the most privileged of the group—he sat at Jesus' right hand at every meal because he was the oldest—who eventually went out, without anyone knowing, to confer with the chief priests and elders.

There was a pair of eyes that followed the traitor's footsteps to the high priest's dwelling. We cannot say for sure who it was who knew about Judas's whereabouts, but there is a likely conjecture that it was St. Mark—he was an inhabitant of Jerusalem and had free access to the homes of the religious leaders. Mark is the only one of the disciples who knew the Latin tongue, and so it is widely agreed that his account of the final collision between Jesus and the Romans is the most detailed and accurate. The other evangelists, in fact, used Mark's Gospel as a guide when writing their own. He gives us this particular regarding the chief priests: "And when they heard *it,* they were glad, and promised to give him money" (Mark 14:11). The circumstantial detail, "they were glad," is the report of an eyewitness.

The chief priests see their chance and decide to act swiftly. They immediately weigh out thirty pieces of silver—the price of a slave—and hand them over to Judas. Once Judas receives the payment, he is obligated to set the process of betrayal in motion at once. He starts to look for a ripe opportunity to hand over his Lord to the enemy.

The Last Supper

WE NOW ARRIVE AT THURSDAY, the fourteenth day of the Hebrew month Nisan, according to the reckoning of the synoptic Gospels (the Gospel of John placing Nisan 14 on Friday). The Passover must be prepared; and so Jesus sends Peter and John to find "a certain man" carrying a pitcher of water. They were to follow this man to his home and request of the head of the household a furnished room in which Jesus might celebrate the Passover with His disciples. Church tradition identifies the master of the house with St. Mark, who modestly omits his own name from the account in his Gospel. Jesus purposely conceals the name and the location from the disciples. He wants neither Judas nor Satan to tamper with their plans before the appointed time.

"When the hour had come, He sat down, and the twelve apostles with Him. Then He said to them, 'With *fervent* desire I have desired to eat this Passover with you before I suffer; for I say to you, I will no longer eat of it until it is fulfilled in the kingdom of God'" (Luke 22:14–16). The scene that occurred in the Upper Room, with the disciples reclining on the ground, encircling a low-set table with Jesus in their midst, is the first picture of the Church gathered together on earth. This was the only thing for which Jesus ever said He felt "fervent desire," and it is an indication that this was the most sacred evening He ever spent with His disciples.

Saint Mark's Gospel, being the first of the four Gospels to be written, furnishes us with the oldest record we have of this solemn meal. The particulars related by Mark's Gospel are closely preserved in the other Gospels, as well as in St. Paul's First Epistle to the Corinthians; this meticulous preservation of the words spoken and acts performed by Jesus indicate that this supper was a "liturgy" in the full sense of the term.

However, St. Mark's intention could never have been to record every detail of that first Christian liturgy, but only to relay the points that were seminal to faith and worship. The format of the narrative leaves open the possibility of prayerful additions to be made by the future Church, which indeed occurred for centuries; and the Palestinian tone in which the story is cast is also left open to adaptation by different cultures and peoples for their own particular celebrations of the Eucharist. Matthew and Luke themselves made certain additions to Mark's narrative. In the Gospel of Matthew, for example, written thirty years after Mark, Jesus adds the words "for the remission of sins" to the cup's blessing.

"Now as they were eating, He said, 'Assuredly, I say to you, one of you will betray Me.' And they were exceedingly sorrowful, and each of them began to say to Him, 'Lord, is it I?'" (Matt. 26:21, 22). For the first time the Lord openly reveals that He will be betrayed to His enemies. The announcement fills the disciples with a piercing grief, and each strives to clear his conscience with the plea, "Lord, is it I?" Since the proceedings of such a traditional meal were governed by strict convention, the question is posed by each disciple, one by one, going round the whole table; and each time the question is asked, Christ delivers His answer. It was a work of expiation that needed to be done before they could partake of the sacred meal. In the same spirit, believers are called on to "greet one another with a holy and apostolic kiss" during the Divine Liturgy.

The disciples also toss the question of the identity of the traitor among themselves. Whisperings and furtive glances are exchanged among them as the issue causes a general disturbance in the gathering. A subtle communication begins between Peter and John. John, being the youngest, took his seat to the left of Jesus, whereas Judas, being the oldest, took his seat to His right. Peter is seated immediately after Judas, and so does not have the convenience of the direct communication with Jesus that John enjoyed. He therefore uses a slight tilting of the head and a flickering of the eyes in order to hint to John to ask Christ who would be the traitor.

"Jesus answered, 'It is he to whom I shall give a piece of bread when I have dipped it.' And having dipped the bread, He gave it to Judas Iscariot" (John 13:26). The rules governing the Passover meal indicated that the master of the house should commence the meal by dipping a morsel of bread into a bowl of spiced vinegar and handing it to the oldest guest seated to his right. It is a tribute to Christ's compassionate humanity that He points out the traitor, not by an act of anger, but using a solemn rite intended for the most honorable guest at the table. But Christ expresses how deeply hurt He was by Judas's betrayal in the following words: "The Son of Man indeed goes just as it is written of Him, but woe to that man by whom the Son of Man is betrayed! It would have been good for that man if he had not been born" (Matt. 26:24).

Jesus Washes the Disciples' Feet

AT SOME POINT DURING THE course of the meal, a new point of controversy disturbs the peace of the gathering. "There was also a dispute among them, as to which of them should be considered the greatest" (Luke 22:24). The issue of who should take which place around the supper table evidently triggered a sharp dispute among the disciples regarding who held the chief position. It was a central question in every Jewish meal. The father sat at the head, while the eldest son, who served as the father's deputy when he was absent, sat at his right hand. The youngest child, being closest to the father's heart and toward whom the father typically acted the most tenderly, sat at his left hand. When the disciples came to sit at table, an altercation commenced between Judas, who was the oldest, and Peter, who always asserted his primacy over the rest.

Jesus responds with a powerful lesson:

> And He said to them, "The kings of the Gentiles exercise lordship over them, and those who exercise authority over them are called 'benefactors.' But not so *among* you; on the contrary, he who is greatest among you, let him be as the younger, and he who governs as he who serves." (Luke 22:25, 26)

The rules governing primacy in the Church, Jesus says, are the opposite of those governing social or political institutions. A king rules *over* his people, and certain nobles, wishing to gain power over the people, heap favors and benefits on them in order to win their approval. It is the purchasing of honor with money. But in the new spirit of Christianity, a leader offers the people only love, humility, and sacrifice. In the Orthodox tradition of Egypt, whenever a patriarch was needed, the elders of the people would search the land high and low for a man in whom God's Spirit lived, who breathed the fragrance of humility; and once found, they would take him by force and ordain him patriarch. It was a literal application of Christ's words.

"And supper being ended . . . [Jesus] rose from supper and laid aside His garments, took a towel and girded Himself. After that, He poured water into a basin and began to wash the disciples' feet, and to wipe *them* with the towel with which He was girded" (John 13:2–5). Jesus here drives home the lesson of humility in an exceptionally dramatic way. The hands that held heaven and earth were now employed in the washing of the disciples' feet! This foot washing did not occur before or after supper but during. It was not, that is, a preparation for the Eucharist but part and parcel of it. It follows that the foot washing is itself a mystery: the mystery of humility, or the mystery of the greater kneeling before the lesser. The outward appearance of the Eucharist was bread and wine, while the inner essence was Christ's Body and Blood. The outward appearance here is a washing of the feet, while the inner essence is a partaking of Jesus' divine humility.

The "garments" Jesus lays aside here would typically have consisted of a lavish outfit Jews donned to celebrate important meals. The importance of these garments is apparent in the parable of the wedding banquet, in which the king is surprised to find a guest not wearing a wedding garment, and so casts him out (Matt. 22:11–13). The fact that the Greek word for *garments* comes in the plural indicates that Jesus likely removed not only the outer cloak that was open in the front, but also the tunic underneath. Stripping down in this way would have been considered unseemly in a social gathering. Only a slave would have been expected to appear half naked, prostrate on the ground, washing others' feet. Jesus could have washed the disciples' feet with His clothes still on; but He intentionally took "the form of a bondservant" (Phil. 2:7), and not only that, but He also took up the chore of a slave.

The scene is really beyond description. The Son of God, who has come down from immeasurable glory, stoops with heartbreaking humility to the level of men's feet. And He is occupied in cleaning them. But this was really the only way to illustrate the full significance of that self-emptying He underwent for the sake of His mission to the world. Jesus is communicating to us the extent of God's love for man. It is a love so full that it even reaches the point of washing his very feet! Is this not the meaning of John's expression, "He loved them to the end" (John 13:1)? What more could express the sincerity of His love? It is difficult for a man to wash another man's feet. A man's ego will not allow it. But not so is God.

When Jesus comes to wash Peter's feet, Peter vehemently refuses. He thinks he is to receive *merely* a foot washing, and that Jesus' act is *merely* an act of humility. But little did He understand that, were he to permanently refuse the washing, he would lose his very inheritance in Christ. This foot washing was not just for show but was an integral part of the salvation Jesus was bringing to man from the Father. The placement of the Lord's hands on their feet consecrated the paths they would take for the dissemination of the Gospel. Saint Paul urges us to shoe our feet with "the preparation of the gospel of peace" (Eph. 6:15). He also writes, "As often as you eat this bread and drink this cup, you proclaim the Lord's death till He comes" (1 Cor. 11:26)—hence, the real connection between foot washing and the Eucharist.

The foremost disciple responds hastily, "Lord, not my feet only, but also *my* hands and *my* head!" (John 13:9). Peter is thinking here in the conventional terms of Jewish ritual cleansing. But this is not a cleansing; they had all received that form of Jewish cleansing many times over, which is why Jesus replies, "He who is bathed needs only to wash *his* feet" (v. 10). But how can those feet be consecrated that would soon run off to betray and sell the Lord? "You are not all clean" (v. 11). Judas was washed like the other disciples but did not receive the higher consecration. He lost his chance to ministry, and he lost his place in Christ. This is proof that rituals do not change the heart but reveal what is in it.

"Do you know what I have done to you?" (John 13:12). Jesus finishes the work of humility and immediately proceeds to explain its import for their lives. The impetus behind their new calling would take the form of love and a stooping service to the lowly and meek. For Christ, who was their Lord and Master, stooped to wash their feet with all the meticulous care of a true servant; and they, when they became leaders, must do the same. Jesus shows how the master must be considered the servant and the servant be considered master—thus inverting the normal patterns of this life. A minister of the Church—whether he be priest, bishop, or apostle—can never be a domineering figure over others; for he is, at the end of the day, a *servant.*

The tradition of foot washing has been preserved as one of the Orthodox Church's most essential rites down to the present day. It enshrines the principle of humility and memorializes the priest's role as servant of the people. It is observed on Covenant Thursday (Holy Thursday), as well as on the Feast of the Apostles.[49] It is in connection with these two feasts that the Orthodox Church declares the essential link between the rite of foot washing and the ministry of preaching and apostleship.

The Eucharist

THE FORMAT OF THE LAST supper celebrated by Jesus with His disciples included all the ritualistic details typically performed during a Passover meal. Following studies conducted by the most accomplished biblical scholars, an outline of a typical Passover meal would appear as follows.

The meal begins with the drinking of the first cup of wine: the cup is shared by all, starting with the head of the family and ending with the youngest member. Before the family's head drinks, he recites a memorized prayer of thanksgiving to God. He also recites a formal "blessing" to God ("to Him who brings forth fruit from the earth"). Next, a lump of bitter herbs is taken—a reminder of the bitter life their ancestors endured in Egypt—dipped in a fruit paste and eaten.

---

49 This is the practice in the Coptic Church. In the Eastern Orthodox Church, the practice is observed only on Holy Thursday.

This *charoset*—a reddish paste made of dates and figs—was symbolic of the reddish bricks and mortar used by the Israelite slaves for their labor. Each family member imitates the action after its completion by the father. The Passover lamb is consumed at this time.

The father then takes a second cup of wine and mixes it with water, then proceeds to explain the meaning represented by each item on the table. The leftover items are distributed among the members present, and they eat a second course to finish whatever is remaining. Everyone around the table chants the first part of the Hallel psalms, comprising Psalms 113 and 114. The father recites a second blessing, and a second cup is drunk. He washes his hands at this point, takes up the unleavened bread, breaks it, and distributes it to everyone around the table. He continues the breaking of the bread while reciting another prayer of blessing ("to God who brings forth wheat from the earth"), then dips a morsel into the fruit paste and eats. Another prayer of thanksgiving is recited, and the remainder of the Passover lamb is completely consumed.

The father washes his hands again, and a third cup of wine goes around the table. The second part of the Hallel psalms (Ps. 115—118) is chanted. A fourth and final cup is drunk by all, while the third and final part of the Hallel psalms (Ps. 120—136) is sung. The feast would be considered completed only when this last step was accomplished. Throughout the duration of the supper, no one is allowed to speak on any topic save that which relates to Passover.

"And as they were eating, Jesus took bread, blessed and broke *it*, and gave *it* to the disciples and said, 'Take, eat; this is My body'" (Matt. 26:26). Here Christ transforms a conventional Passover ritual into a divine work of redemption; in an instant, we pass from Old Testament tradition to New Testament grace. We must remember that the animal sacrifices of the Old Testament served as a *covering* for sin; whereas, in the time of grace, Christ's sacrifice is the *defeat* of sin and of death. The sacrifices of the Old Covenant qualified a person to enter the temple and worship with his fellow pilgrims. The great sacrifice of the New Covenant justifies a person to enter heaven itself and converse with God.

So Christ *blessed*, *broke*, and *gave*—the three cardinal acts of consecration during the eucharistic service. When we connect that which is broken ("My body") with the one whose hands are breaking (Jesus), we arrive at the conclusion that this act is a mystical foreshadowing of the Cross. And when Jesus commands us to "take and eat" His broken body, He is in a sense giving us an active role in the Cross. The term *the breaking of bread* comes to be, liturgically speaking, the most lofty title ever given to the Lord's self-sacrifice. It is offered to us by His own hands, and so it is the deepest and holiest form of consecration ever granted to humanity.

"Then He took the cup, and gave thanks, and gave *it* to them, saying, 'Drink from it, all of you. For this is My blood of the new covenant, which is shed for many for the remission of sins'" (Matt. 26:27, 28). This was the fourth cup drunk by the Passover celebrants while they sang the last part of the Hallel psalms. Nothing could be consumed after this cup; the final blessing is uttered by Christ when the wine is finished, and the feast is officially completed.

And here again, the blood shed by Christ on the Cross permanently replaces the bloodshed of the animals sacrificed in the Old Testament. Jesus preserves, however, the redemptive meaning that was attached to those old sacrifices and translates them in a new way. As St. Paul writes, "For indeed Christ, our Passover, was sacrificed for us" (1 Cor. 5:7). Every student of theology knows that the blood shed from the lambs and bulls of the Old Covenant was a symbol of that greater Blood that would be shed in the fullness of time. Jeremiah wrote of old, "Behold, the days are coming, says the LORD, when I will make a new covenant with the house of Israel and with the house of Judah—not according to the covenant that I made with their fathers in the day *that* I took them by the hand to lead them out of the land of Egypt" (Jer. 31:31, 32). Since the New Covenant was formally proclaimed and inaugurated at the Last Supper, it follows that the Eucharist is itself the driving force of the New Covenant.

Jesus adds these words: "Do this in remembrance of Me" (Luke 22:19). It is an affirmation of Jesus' presence among the believers when they celebrate the breaking of bread. The ritual is not a mere memorial of a good man who once died. It is the remembering of an eternal living presence among us—the substitution for a physical presence that once was. The Lord stands in every liturgy, feeding us the broken bread and the shed blood with His own hands. Our partaking of the Eucharist is our living testimony to the atonement of sin accomplished on the Cross. So writes St. Paul: "For as often as you eat this bread and drink this cup, you proclaim the Lord's death till He comes" (1 Cor. 11:26). The very ideas of redemption and atonement cannot be proclaimed in a comprehensible way without Jesus' living presence among us.

When the Lord had finished reciting the last of the Hallel psalms with His disciples, and the formal proceedings of the Passover feast were reaching their conclusion, dark forebodings of what was about to take place on that somber night began to weigh on Jesus' mind. Although He knew all that would transpire in the coming hours, the burden that proved heaviest on His soul was the unbecoming conduct of His disciples. Judas was out scheming with the adversary, and the other disciples sat at table engrossed in their petty arguments. And now, He tells them plainly, "Indeed the hour is coming, yes, has now come, that you will be scattered, each to his own, and will leave Me alone" (John 16:32). The painful prophecy from Zechariah instantly came into His mind: "Strike the Shepherd, / And the sheep will be scattered" (Zech. 13:7). Despite the grief which the disciples' desertion would cause to His heart, the Lord did not press their failure on them too strongly, but included a hopeful future: "But after I have been raised, I will go before you to Galilee" (Matt. 26:32).

Peter, always hasty and headstrong in his speech, does not apologize to Jesus or ask for further clarification, but rather at once repudiates His words: "Even if all are made to stumble because of You, I will never be made to stumble" (Matt. 26:33). He had once before attempted to rebuke Christ for prophesying His own death, receiving a sharp censure from Him in return. And now, Peter once again tries to defend his ego against an accusation that his human courage would eventually fail to withstand. We need not, however, count Peter's mistakes but our own. We all carry Peter's shortcomings, and we are all less than the disciples; and we will all similarly fail when not supported by the Lord's grace.

"Jesus said to him, 'Assuredly, I say to you that this night, before the rooster crows, you will deny Me three times.' Peter said to Him, 'Even if I have to die with You, I will not deny You!'" And so said all the disciples" (Matt. 26:34, 35). When we consider Peter's denial of Christ in light of this bold assertion, we realize how truly exposed our inner selves are before the searching eye of God. The evangelists have recorded this event as a reminder never to rely too much on one's ego or on one's human abilities. We can feel the pain in Jesus' words. And if it were not for Jesus' following statement to him, "I have prayed for you, that your faith should not fail" (Luke 22:32), his end might have been the same as that of Judas. It should be noted that Jesus did not shield Peter from the trial, but He instead prayed that he should not ultimately fail. It ought also to be noted that from Peter's fall in the trial, from that state of cowardice, and from those bitter tears emerged the greatest defender of the Christian Faith. God allows His children to pass through grievous trials in order to produce from them giants of the Faith.

Gethsemane

WE NOW COME TO ONE of the most difficult and trying stages of
our Lord's life. Jesus walked into the Garden of Gethsemane as the
first stepping-stone on the final path to the Cross. The story of what
occurred in the garden is one of the liveliest and richest in detail of
all the scenes recorded during Holy Week. Jesus is preparing for crucifixion and for the final standoff with the unseen powers of darkness. It was a grievous thing to surrender Himself to the powers of
evil. But this was the Father's will, and it was for this that the Son
took flesh and came to earth. And it was the consciousness that His
self-surrender was not ultimately to the satanic powers, but to the
Father's will, that made the ordeal bearable to the soul of Jesus. The
acceptance of this "cup" meant bearing the sins of mankind—being
arraigned as a murderer, thief, adulterer, and everything else—but
the sorest trial would be the sense of estrangement from God. This
would culminate in that agonizing cry, "My God, My God, why have
You forsaken Me?" (Matt. 27:46).

"Then Jesus came with them to a place called Gethsemane, and
said to the disciples, 'Sit here while I go and pray over there'" (Matt.
26:36). The Upper Room in which Jesus celebrated Passover with the
disciples belonged to the family of St. Mark; and it is most likely that
he also owned the small garden in this story that sat on the western
slope of the Mount of Olives. The Hebrew original of the name, *gat
shemanim*, means "winepress." Scholars surmise that Mark's family
came originally from Cyrene in Libya; and, having amassed considerable wealth in that country, they emigrated to Jerusalem, purchased
the spacious house with its adjoining garden, and built a winepress
for use as their family business.

It is also likely that Mark's family erected a guesthouse in this garden in which visitors could pass the night, and it was here that Jesus
often resorted for prayer and seclusion. Saint John provides us with

this telling detail: "Judas, who betrayed Him, also knew the place; for *Jesus often met there with His disciples*" (John 18:2, emphasis added).

Jesus departs from St. Mark's house by the eastern door facing the Mount of Olives, crosses the Valley Kidron, and enters the garden. He takes along three elect disciples to accompany Him during His agony. Once surrounded by the dark olive trees of Gethsemane, He kneels to pray, enters a state of deep perplexity, and becomes sorely troubled in His soul. It was a state that exceeded man's capability of mental endurance. His soul was righteous and holy to an absolute degree; but now, it had to face all that was ugliest and most vile in man's sinful state. Saint Paul strives in Romans to express the appalling nature of human sin. But not even all the descriptions of that apostle come close to expressing for us how sin truly appears to the mind of God as when Christ, facing sin in its naked horror, says, "My soul is exceedingly sorrowful, even to death." The Enemy proceeds with his greatest weapon against mortal man, the weapon called *death*; and Jesus knows that He is to feel its edge.

"He went a little farther and fell on His face, and prayed, saying, 'O My Father, if it is possible, let this cup pass from Me; nevertheless, not as I will, but as You *will*'" (Matt. 26:39). It is difficult to explain such a prayer—one that has baffled the minds of commentators and defied the attempts of scholars to understand. What could this be that seemed to be a hindrance to the Son's perfect obedience to the Father; that elicited such desperate words from Jesus' lips; that made mere kneeling insufficient, but threw Jesus onto the ground, to make His face mingle with the dust? It is a frightening scene for humanity. What could have caused such turbulence in the Son's relation to the Father? It was surely something that touched humanity's future, because Jesus allowed it to happen before the disciples' very eyes. But did not Jesus predict the Cross and these sufferings? Did He not progressively reveal to His disciples the grisly details of His fate during those last days? So is it possible that now, as the sufferings were closing in upon Him, His mind was changing? Could it be that there was something about the pain of crucifixion that He had not calculated beforehand? No—impossible!

We stand before a great and imponderable mystery. This cup which proved so unbearable to Jesus' soul, which threw Him into such a posture of humiliation, was not His. It was humanity's cup. And it was full of the most foul and unspeakable depths of mankind's shame. But the hour had come. *He* had to drink it, because He embodied humanity. He had to empty its contents completely into His body, then have His body "hung upon a tree"—in the words of St. Peter. The thought caused His soul to tremble and His body to shrink from the sentence. He who knew no sin, in whose mouth was never found deceit, must feel the sting of man's sin. How *could* His will easily accept it? And again we ask—how? His heart could not accept it, and His mind could not endure it.

So, Jesus requests to be spared the cup. It was humanity's natural request; but He puts a condition on it: *nevertheless, not as I will, but as You will.* Saint Paul writes inspired words on this issue: "For He made Him who knew no sin *to be* sin for us, that we might become the righteousness of God in Him" (2 Cor. 5:21). He also writes, "The sting of death *is* sin, and the strength of sin *is* the law" (1 Cor. 15:55). So, by His death He abolished the curse of the law, which abolished sin, which abolished death, which abolished Hades.

The night was growing long among the moonlit shadows of Gethsemane, and in those small hours of the night, exhaustion began to settle in on the disciples. Jesus had ordered them to watch and pray because He wanted them prepared for the great trial that was about to break on them. But He was disappointed to find them—including Peter, who had sworn he would die for Jesus—not able to keep awake a single hour. "He came and found them sleeping, and said to Peter, 'Simon, are you sleeping? Could you not watch one hour? Watch and pray, lest you enter into temptation'" (Mark 14:37, 38). "Watch and pray," Jesus orders, for temptation is ever liable to overtake a man while he is asleep. It is also a warning to the Church to be ever watchful in spirit. For drowsiness might overtake the body, but it can never conquer the watchful soul. This is expressed in the continuation of the verse: "The spirit indeed *is* willing, but the flesh *is* weak." Watchfulness of spirit provides the strength to defeat temptation before it even arrives.

It is with a heavy heart that Jesus turns from His sleeping disciples to return to His place of prayer. He had hoped they would be a support to lean on, but their sleep was preparing them instead for escape. Jesus will not be found in a church that does not pray together, nor among a family that does not pray together. It is incredible that Peter did not heed Jesus' thrice-repeated plea to watch and pray; but that is why the temptation found him ill-prepared and resulted in a triple denial of the Lord.

Jesus repeats the prayer to the Father two more times, with each supplication solidifying the harmony between His will and the Father's. He at last accepts the cup and intends to empty it to the very dregs. That cup terrified Him, but He knew and accepted the Father's will—that its contents should soon course through all His veins. He returned to find the disciples still in deep slumber. It was no matter now. He no longer needed their support, for the spiritual contest had been won. But now they must rise; His betrayer was fast approaching with a host of guards. His hour had come.

The Arrest

"WHILE HE WAS STILL SPEAKING, behold, Judas, one of the twelve, with a great multitude with swords and clubs, came from the chief priests and elders of the people" (Matt. 26:47). At the very moment when Jesus was prostrate in the dust of Gethsemane, with the sweat trickling down His skin like drops of blood, the chief priests and leaders of the people had been collecting their troops to apprehend Him.

The forces of darkness from three distinct classes now joined to seize Christ. The first was Judas, one of the twelve; the second was the chief priests and leaders of Israel; the third was a company of soldiers from the Roman power. The Roman force included a "captain." (Gr. *chiliarchos*), a high-ranking official who oversaw one thousand soldiers. This great display of force, carrying torches and weapons, reveals just how nervous the Jewish authorities were regarding this arrest. They were not afraid of any resistance from the people, as they were in the habit of saying. They were afraid of Christ.

Judas now approaches and kisses Jesus on the cheek, a signal prearranged with the conspirators. The kiss immediately draws a quiet rebuke from the Lord's lips: "Judas, are you betraying the Son of Man with a kiss?" (Luke 22:48). We could never evaluate Judas's character or his conduct in this scene more thoroughly than when Jesus Himself said that it would have been better if his traitor had never been born (Mark 14:21). And the clearest judgment on Judas came when he hanged himself by his own hands.

The moment Judas kisses the Lord, the troops and officers lay their hands on Jesus to take Him. The sight throws Peter into a passion, and he immediately pulls his sword and strikes the high priest's servant on the ear. Jesus stretches out His hand and heals the servant's ear. To Peter He says, "Put your sword into the sheath. Shall I not drink the cup which My Father has given Me?" (John 18:11).

Jesus teaches Peter that acceptance of the cup, acceptance of the cross, rules out the sword. One cannot carry the cross and use violent self-defense at the same time. Peter was attempting to use his sword to protect Jesus from the Cross. But this was the same error he made earlier when he rebuked Jesus for predicting His death. Jesus continues, "For all who take the sword will perish by the sword" (Matt. 26:52). The day you take up the sword, you write on its blade your own sentence to death. But Christ abolished the concept of the enemy when He bade us to love our enemies; for love itself is the one true sword that will defeat every enemy in life.

> In that hour Jesus said to the multitudes, "Have you come out, as against a robber, with swords and clubs to take Me? I sat daily with you, teaching in the temple, and you did not seize Me. But all this was done that the Scriptures of the prophets might be fulfilled." Then all the disciples forsook Him and fled. (Matt. 26:55, 56)

Had they not just a few hours previously been sitting near Him and listening to Him teach in the temple? Jesus exposes the deceit of Satan in exploiting the position and authority of the Jewish leaders to arrange His death. "Then the detachment *of troops* and the captain and the officers of the Jews arrested Jesus and bound Him. And they led Him away to Annas first, for he was the father-in-law of Caiaphas who was high priest that year" (John 18:12, 13).

The Religious Trial

JESUS' TRIALS CAN BE STUDIED under two major divisions: the religious trial and the civil trial. The religious trial in turn comprises three stages:

1. Before Annas, who heard introductory remarks from Jesus (John 18:12–23).

2. At night before the Sanhedrin, including Caiaphas, the scribes, and the elders of the people (Matt. 26:57–68).
3. Before the Sanhedrin again, in the morning (Luke 22:66–71).

The civil trial is also divisible into three stages:

1. Before Pilate.
2. Before Herod.
3. Before Pilate again.

The biblical scholar Wescott[50] has compiled for us a list of the procedural rules that governed the religious trial system of ancient Judaism, using primarily the tractate entitled *Sanhedrin* in the Mishnah. The list illuminates for us much of the legal protocol—along with the irregularities—that occurred during Jesus' trials. The list runs as follows:

1. Capital cases must be tried by at least twenty-three members of the Sanhedrin.
2. Trials involving charges of false prophecy must be tried by all seventy-one members.
3. Witnesses must be individually and thoroughly investigated before giving testimony. When the testimony of two or more witnesses agrees, it is deemed to be true.
4. In capital cases, the seconds who accompany the main witnesses are thoroughly questioned; and they are advised to carefully consider the truthfulness of their words, as the life and soul of the defendant is at stake.
5. The court must sit in a semicircle, with the court's president sitting in the center, in order that he may clearly see the face of each judge.
6. In capital cases, the defendant must be given the benefit of every

---

50 Wescott, *The Pulpit Commentary*, 262–3.

doubt regarding his guilt. The votes for "innocent" must always be taken before those for "guilty."

7. In civil cases, the trial may be held at night, and the verdict may be delayed to another day.

8. In capital cases, the trial must be held during the day. A verdict of innocence may be given on the same day of the trial, but a verdict of guilt can only be given on a later day. It is also prohibited for a capital trial to be held on the eve of a Sabbath or a feast day.

9. In the case of a guilty verdict, the defendant must be given four to five opportunities, according to the demands of the case, to present fresh reasons for a reconsideration of the verdict.

10. Blasphemers are to be stoned. Their bodies are to be hanged until dusk, at which point they are removed and placed in a public burial plot.

"And those who had laid hold of Jesus led *Him* away to Caiaphas the high priest, where the scribes and the elders were assembled" (Matt. 26:57). And so the religious trial is held in Caiaphas's own residence. The residence, in fact, originally belonged to Annas, but when Caiaphas married Annas's daughter, they moved into Annas's home. Caiaphas served as the official high priest that year, but Annas was the de facto ruler of the Sanhedrin behind the scenes. The two lived in opposite wings of the palace; a large chamber that separated these two wings served as a meeting room for the Sanhedrin—an arrangement made by necessity since the buildings that were erected for the Sanhedrin's work had been closed by the Roman authorities. The synoptic Gospels provide us with a somewhat detailed account of Jesus' trials by Caiaphas and the council, but it is from the Gospel of John alone that we learn that He was taken first to Annas. Annas poses certain preliminary questions to Jesus regarding His disciples and His doctrine, then sends Him bound to Caiaphas for a formal hearing.

Peter and John follow the company to see the results of the case. Peter sits outside with the high priest's servants and waits, while John, since he is personally known to Caiaphas, is granted entrance to the courtyard (John 18:15). John provides us with a unique eye-witness account of the events of that night. It is also surmised by some that Mark gained access to the Sanhedrin's chamber by virtue of the connections his family enjoyed in Jerusalem.

> Now the chief priests, the elders, and all the council sought false testimony against Jesus to put Him to death, but found none. Even though many false witnesses came forward, they found none. But at last two false witnesses came forward and said, "This *fellow* said, 'I am able to destroy the temple of God and to build it in three days.'" (Matt. 26:59–61)

A fraudulent trial and a false court! A false charge is brought, false witnesses are called, and unworthy judges sit to decide. The sentence of death is agreed on before the case is even heard. The claim that He threatened to destroy the temple thus becomes the first charge leveled against Jesus during the trial. John's Gospel gives us the true substance of the Lord's words (John 2:13–21). When the Jews had asked Him for a sign that authorized Him to cleanse the temple, Jesus responded, "Destroy this temple, and in three days I will raise it up" (John 13:19). Saint John explains that He was speaking symbolically about the temple of His body. The cheat in their testimony is found, however, in the exact wording: He did not say, "I am able to destroy the temple," but, "Destroy[51] this temple . . ." The false accusation was again hurled at Jesus by His enemies while He was on the Cross: "And those who passed by blasphemed Him, wagging their heads and

---

51 The tense of the verb is second person plural imperative. It is directed, in other words, to the audience, not to Himself. *They* will destroy the temple.

saying, 'Aha! *You* who destroy the temple and build *it* in three days, save Yourself, and come down from the cross!'" (Mark 15:29, 30).

The second charge that is brought against Jesus is His claim to be Israel's Messiah. And this too became a sneering gloat uttered by Jesus' enemies during the Crucifixion: "He saved others; Himself He cannot save. Let the Christ, the King of Israel, descend now from the cross, that we may see and believe" (Mark 15:31). The first charge, therefore, was construed to be a challenge to God's authority. The second charge was construed as a challenge to Caesar's authority.

The high priest rises from his chair at this point and demands that Jesus speak to His accusers: "'Do You answer nothing? What *is it* these men testify against You?' But Jesus kept silent" (Matt. 26:62, 63). He could have offered a complete defense of Himself and a thorough justification of His words. But instead He chooses not to break His silence. He is fulfilling the promise made with the Father in Gethsemane, that He would drink the cup to the very lees, if it be the Father's will. And now, as He stands before the council, all of mankind stands with Him to be judged. He answers not, because humanity is indeed guilty.

"The high priest answered and said to Him, 'I put You under oath by the living God: Tell us if You are the Christ, the Son of God!'" (Matt. 26:63). The statement compels Jesus to break His silence. Caiaphas puts Him under oath to reply, and so reply He must; but Caiaphas's own conscience is clouded. He had already told the council, long before they seized Jesus, that it was better for one man to die than for the entire nation to perish (John 11:50). The judicial oath, then, which should be uttered in whispered reverence, was spoken with lying lips in order to extort a confession that would lead to the defendant's death. But this does not discourage Jesus. He makes the good confession, regardless of the results: "It *is as* you said." Jesus often drew His reply from the questioner's own lips.

Caiaphas is thrown into a rage by Christ's boldness; he rends in half the robe he is wearing and bellows, "He has spoken blasphemy! What further need do we have of witnesses? Look, now you have heard His blasphemy! What do you think?" (Matt. 26:65, 66). It was the answer He expected of Jesus, and he had prepared this theatrical display in advance. But, we may ask, in what way would the high priest distinguish Jesus' life from that of any other claimed Messiah? What of the miracles, the healings, the changed lives of thousands of people? After all that, does the high priest still require a confession from Jesus? But Caiaphas turns the hope of the ancient patriarchs and prophets into blasphemy; and, according to the Sanhedrin's code, the tearing of the high priest's clothes constituted a formal verdict of blasphemy. The council, of course, agreed in condemning Jesus. There was one dissenting voice, however: "Now behold, *there was* a man named Joseph, a council member, a good and just man. He had not consented to their decision and deed" (Luke 23:50, 51). Joseph would later express his dissent again by removing the dead body of Jesus from the Cross and burying it in his private tomb.

"Now the men who held Jesus mocked Him and beat Him. And having blindfolded Him, they struck Him on the face and asked Him, saying, 'Prophesy! Who is the one who struck You?'" (Luke 22:63, 64). He who showed the splendor of the Father on His face and possessed God's very nature was struck in the face and shouted at with derisive words. It is a wonder that He allowed the image of the Father to be so insulted by man as all of heaven's host looked down in amazement. But the prophets had foretold this strange event: "I did not hide My face from shame and spitting" (Is. 50:6).

Peter's Denial

"BUT PETER STOOD AT THE door outside. Then the other disciple, who was known to the high priest, went out and spoke to her who kept the door, and brought Peter in" (John 18:16). John, descending from a priestly family, was given the privilege of entering the high priest's residence. He speaks to the servant girl who keeps the door, and she allows Peter to enter too. Peter immediately finds a group of servants warming themselves by the fire, and he quietly blends in with the group so as not to attract attention. His facial features and clothes and accent, however, betray his Galilean origins, so the servant girl quietly questions him: "You also were with Jesus of Galilee." Peter gives the curt reply that he does not know what she is talking about—hoping to quickly cut off any further questions that could lead to trouble. He feared being recognized as the man who raised his sword against Malchus; and possibly what he feared more was the prospect of being tried as a follower of Jesus.

The scenario is presented as a warning to us all, because the Gospels are not primarily concerned with storytelling but with teaching us how to live a life of faith. The two errors that led to Peter's downfall were his pride and his self-sufficiency. If he had humbled himself and requested strength from Christ to avoid falling into temptation, he might have prevailed. But he follows behind Jesus now, not as one bearing his cross, but as a distant spectator. His intention was merely to wait outside in the courtyard the whole time; but when John brought him inside, he pretended not to have any ties with Jesus' circle, and not even to know Jesus personally. We will all one day be questioned regarding our connection to Christ. And so we should be ready to give a reason for the hope that is in us (1 Pet. 3:15). If our minds and tongues are not practiced in giving testimony to Christ, we will deny Him—like Peter—when the question is unexpectedly raised. But when we begin to offer a courageous testimony to Christ, power from on high will immediately fill us, and words of grace and wisdom will flow from our lips.

Peter is asked again if he is one of Jesus' disciples, and this time he swears with an oath, "I do not know the Man!" At that moment, it was true, Peter surely did not know Jesus. And when he is asked a third time about his allegiance to Christ, he begins to curse and swear. Grace had completely abandoned Peter, because Peter denied grace. Judas sold Jesus for thirty pieces of silver, and now Peter sells him for nothing at all. The rooster suddenly crows, and its sound brings Peter to the realization of what he has just done. It is at this point that they are transferring Jesus from Caiaphas's chamber to the Sanhedrin's hall; and as He is walking, He turns momentarily to see Peter, and their eyes meet. It is one of the most poignant moments in the Gospels, fraught with the mingled emotions of compassion and pain. The Lord's prophetic words are recalled to Peter's mind, and he goes out and weeps tears of heart-rending grief.

"As soon as it was day, the elders of the people, both chief priests and scribes, came together and led Him into their council" (Luke 22:66). Jesus' enemies now assemble in the morning to form an official council, with the aim of condemning Him by law and finding a pretext to deliver Him to Pilate. The law required seventy-one members of the Sanhedrin to be present for capital cases, and such cases were to be tried inside the temple. However, given that the Pharisees were absent from the proceedings (and so the quota was not reached), and given that the judges were gathered inside Annas's residence (not in the temple), this was clearly an illegal proceeding.

Nevertheless, they begin the trial with their most pressing interrogation: "If you are the Christ, tell us." The people of Israel tended to favor this conclusion, as evidenced by their fervent outbursts during Jesus' entry into Jerusalem; but the idea was anathema to His enemies, for they were not prepared to accept Him. They desired, therefore, to dispense with this question at once and to confirm His condemnation. "But He said to them, 'If I tell you, you will by no means believe'" (Luke 22:67). They ask their second question, "Are You then the Son of God?" Jesus answers in the affirmative, extracting the reply from the question itself as He had done with Caiaphas; and their reaction is much the same as that of the high priest. Having therefore secured, as they thought, grounds for declaring Him guilty of blasphemy, as well as grounds for delivering Him to the Roman authorities for treason, they bring the dramatic spectacle to a close and lead Him away to the Roman governor.

The Civil Trial: Pilate Encounters Jesus

"THEN THEY LED JESUS FROM Caiaphas to the Praetorium, and it was early morning. But they themselves did not go into the Praetorium, lest they should be defiled, but that they might eat the Passover" (John 18:28). The official residence for the governor of Judea was in the city of Caesarea, but during festal days, Pilate would stay in a temporary residence in Jerusalem, a fortress called Antonia. Passover could bring in up to three million Jewish pilgrims from every quarter of the earth, and so Pilate's presence in Jerusalem was necessary to keep the peace.

The Jewish courts were powerless to put a capital sentence into execution without the consent of the Roman authorities, so the chief priests and elders of the people take Jesus to Pilate's headquarters for the ratification of their verdict. This is, of course, in direction violation of the Jewish statute that prohibited condemning a defendant to death on the same day as the trial; but these judges, in their haste and desperation to bring Jesus to a quick end, trample on established law with the assumption that no greater power will hold them accountable. The entire world, however, along with every generation since then, bears witness and holds them accountable for their deed.

"Pilate then went out to them and said, 'What accusation do you bring against this Man?'" (John 18:29). Pilate's agreement to speak to them so early in the morning is another odd irregularity, because Roman law set down that cases were to be tried after sundown. It appears, however, that Pilate had a prearranged appointment with the Jewish leaders, and he is also likely the one who authorized the cohort of soldiers to accompany them to Jesus' arrest. Annas—the wealthiest man in Jerusalem—had formed intimate ties with the governor's circle, and he could orchestrate events to his liking using rich bribes. Pilate was always thrown into tension, therefore, in straddling between Roman law and Jewish law. Pilate knows indeed why they have brought Jesus, but he persists in urging the question on them as though he were ignorant.

We have this interesting detail from St. Matthew's Gospel: "While he was sitting on the judgment seat, his wife sent to him, saying, 'Have nothing to do with that just Man, for I have suffered many things today in a dream because of Him'" (Matt. 27:19). It seems then that Pilate's wife, and possibly Pilate's whole family, had gained knowledge of the plot that was being hatched in the dark. They knew that Jesus was "just," and that a miscarriage of justice was about to take place. So Pilate's question is intended to goad the Jewish leaders; it is an indication that Pilate does not consent to their deed. Pilate then tells them to judge the victim by their own law, but the comment further inflames the wrath of Jesus' enemies. They reply that they are legally prohibited from handing down a death sentence—thus indicating the verdict before Pilate has even questioned the defendant—a statement that serves as a high-pressure demand for Pilate's cooperation.

All this was foreknown to the mind of God. Both the Jews and the Gentiles of the world are represented here in the two quarreling

parties—quarreling, but at the same time, working together in preparing the Lamb of God for His sacrifice for the life of the world.

At this point, Pilate enters his residence and faces Jesus for the
first time with the question, "Are You the King of the Jews?" All four
Gospels record the question, because it is the most critical one for
Pilate. To claim to be "King of the Jews" carried with it certain political implications and was fraught with danger for the claimant. Jesus
questions him in return: "Are you speaking for yourself about this, or
did others tell you this concerning Me?" Is your conscience, O Pilate,
seeking the truth, or are you merely repeating an accusation voiced
by My enemies? Do you mean to give me the title in its lofty spiritual
sense, which does not conflict with your political aspirations, or do
you mean to attach to me a label that amounts to political treason?
Pilate offers the elusive reply that he is not a Jew and cannot know
why Jesus' own nation delivered Him up. Jesus then goes to the heart
of the matter: "My Kingdom is not of this world." Had the Jews and
Romans grasped this pivotal truth, they could have avoided the turbulence that was now shaking the country.

"For this cause I was born, and for this cause I have come into
the world, that I should bear witness to the truth. Everyone who is
of the truth hears My voice" (John 18:37). Everyone who rests his
or her thoughts on truth, everyone who acts by truth, and everyone
who lives by the truth—these will surely hear Christ's voice. Jesus
here is touching Pilate's conscience, as well as the conscience of every
human being who reads. Pilate offers only a curt reply: "What is
truth?" In the Greek, Pilate does not ask the question with the defi-
nite article (*the truth*) but without it (*truth*), thus indicating his hope-
lessness in discovering any general idea of truth. It is the question of
a man who does not know the truth, does not want to know it, and
half-sneers at the idea of ever knowing it. He might have attempted
to find some truth in the shifting facts of the material world or in the

unpredictable events of life; but things that are always changing and passing away cannot reveal truth.

Jesus once said, "I am the way, the truth, and the life" (John 14:6); and "You shall know the truth, and the truth shall make you free" (John 8:32). Truth breeds freedom. And when truth liberates, it also sanctifies. Truth, freedom, holiness, eternal life—these are all synergistic terms. Moreover, truth cannot be divided up or parceled out. It is one, whole, and complete. Any "truth," therefore, that defeats itself is a lie. Any light that darkens with time is no light, because true light is enduring. Any joy that flips suddenly to sadness is untrue, because true joy cannot be taken away. Any peace that gives way to worry is untrue, because true peace is everlasting.

The Civil Trial: Pilate Strives to Release Jesus

PILATE'S INTERVIEW WITH JESUS CONVINCES him that He is an innocent Man, and so he goes back outside to where the Jews are waiting for him. He announces, "I find no fault in Him at all." The unexpected utterance by Pilate inflames their anger even more, and they shout, "He stirs up the people, teaching throughout all Judea, beginning from Galilee to this place" (Luke 23:5). Once Pilate learns that Jesus is from Galilee, he sees a potential way out of the trial. He had already spoken his verdict, but the pressure exerted by the Jewish leaders stripped it of its finality. So Pilate transfers the case, as it were, to a higher court. It was not a higher court in any legal sense, but Pilate treated it as such in order to escape the peril in which he found himself trapped.

The Gospels have already acquainted us with this Herod. He was the one who so eagerly desired to hear John the Baptist; but he is also the one who, at the behest of a sinful and adulterous woman, ordered John's execution. It is the same Herod of whom the

Pharisees told Jesus, "Herod wants to kill you" (Luke 13:31). Herod now has the chance to meet with Jesus face to face. The chief priests and scribes furiously demand that Herod deliver a verdict of condemnation against Jesus; but after posing a multitude of questions, and receiving nothing but silence from Jesus, he finds himself unable to write a single word regarding a judgment. And so, after allowing his soldiers to insult Jesus with wanton acts of abuse and contempt, Herod sends Him back to Pilate.

> Then Pilate, when he had called together the chief priests, the rulers, and the people, said to them, "You have brought this Man to me, as one who misleads the people. And indeed, having examined *Him* in your presence, I have found no fault in this Man concerning those things of which you accuse Him; no, neither did Herod, for I sent you back to him; and indeed nothing deserving of death has been done by Him. I will therefore chastise Him and release *Him*." (Luke 23:13–16)

"I have found no fault in this Man"—the second proclamation of Christ's innocence from Pilate's own mouth! Neither Pilate nor Herod could find a shred of evidence to prove the accusations presented by the chief priests and rulers. Nevertheless, in his desperation to calm the nerves of Jesus' enemies, he devises what he considers a workable compromise: he declares that he will "chastise" Him and release Him. But far from calming their nerves, the offer merely opens the door for more demands, because Jesus' enemies perceive that the compromise signals a clear mental weakness on Pilate's part. And it is a small step to push from chastisement to crucifixion.

Pilate then searches for another loophole to escape his impossible dilemma.

Now at the feast the governor was accustomed to releasing to the multitude one prisoner whom they wished. And at that time they had a notorious prisoner called Barabbas. Therefore, when they had gathered together, Pilate said to them, "Whom do you want me to release to you? Barabbas, or Jesus who is called Christ?" (Matt. 27:15–17)

The chief priests and elders understand the ploy, and they incite the crowd to demand the release of Barabbas. Barabbas was the ring-leader of a revolt that had spread throughout Jerusalem and resulted in a multitude of deaths; he was being held in prison at this time awaiting sentence. *Bar-Abbas* is not, in fact, a name, but a title: "son of the father." Origen refers in his commentaries to early man-uscripts of the Gospels which state that this man's full name was Jesus Bar-abbas. The people, therefore, had to make their choice between one Jesus who was a quasi-messianic character and mur-derous zealot, and another Jesus, the true Son of the Father and the Christ. Since the Sanhedrin doubtless approved of Barabbas's agi-tations against the Roman authorities and disapproved of Christ's claims, they demanded the release of Barabbas and the crucifixion of Jesus.

"So then Pilate took Jesus and scourged *Him*. And the soldiers twisted a crown of thorns and put *it* on His head, and they put on Him a purple robe. Then they said, 'Hail, King of the Jews!' And they struck Him with their hands" (John 19:1). Pilate still has hopes that he may be able to release Jesus. He allows Jesus to be subjected to the most brutal inhumanities, unknowingly fulfilling the require-ments of our salvation.

For Jesus took upon His head and His back the punishments humanity deserved. Pilate's intent was to strip Jesus of all kingly pretensions in the hopes of placating the Jewish leaders. So Pilate's soldiers array His naked body with a purple robe, the color of royalty. They place a crown of thorns on His head, a mock replacement for the leafy wreath that was placed on the heads of victorious kings. They place a reed in his right hand, a mock scepter to satirize His royal authority. They kneel scornfully before Him and shout "Hail!" to ridicule the King of the Jews. Then they finally take the reed out of His hand, strike the crown of thorns sitting on His head, spit on Him, and return Him to Pilate.

"Pilate then went out again, and said to them, 'Behold, I am bringing Him out to you, that you may know that I find no fault in Him.' Then Jesus came out, wearing the crown of thorns and the purple robe. And *Pilate* said to them, 'Behold the Man!'" (John 19:4, 5). For the third time, Pilate announces Jesus' innocence. His Roman instinct for justice insisted that he declare the truth of the case, but his human weakness kept him stuck in a mortal struggle with the will of the Jewish leaders. "Behold the Man!" Pilate presents Jesus' mutilated form to the crowd in order to stir their feelings of human sympathy toward Him, as well as to show that Pilate has reduced Jesus' status from that of a king to a mere "man." For us, it is also a reminder that the Word took flesh and became Man; the Son emptied Himself to become mortal; and the incarnate Word humbled Himself to take on the image of a slave. Although Pilate desired to hear a word of mercy from the people, he instead heard the incessant cry, "Crucify Him!"

Pilate finds himself at his wits' end and goes back into the Praetorium to question Jesus again. When he finds his victim speechless, he yells out in frustration, "Are You not speaking to me? Do You not know that I have power to crucify You, and power to release You?" (John 19:10). Pilate does not threaten Jesus with these words but only supplicates His attention. He wants Jesus to understand that, with just a single word, Pilate can have Jesus set free and let the curtains fall on this whole drama. Jesus answers, but only to clarify for Pilate the true facts of the matter: "You could have no power at all against Me unless it had been given you from above" (John 19:11). With a single phrase, Jesus subjects all worldly power and might to a higher authority. He means to tell Pilate, your power does not simply flow from the emperor, but you and the emperor both will one day give account to a higher power.

Pilate might have spoken a verdict of innocence three times, but he ultimately succumbed to his fear of the people. He had not the moral strength to stand by his word. In his calculation, it was either Jesus or Pilate who must perish. Herein lies the curse of worldly politics: that the truth must be sacrificed for personal gain. And the integrity of law is impaired so that one may keep up one's political position.

"From then on Pilate sought to release Him, but the Jews cried out, saying, 'If you let this Man go, you are not Caesar's friend'" (John 19:12). May Caesar live, and may Jesus die! This is the point to which Caiaphas's and his minions' uncontrollable wrath has pushed them. So intent are they on shedding Christ's blood that they forget their accountability toward God and throw themselves at the feet of Caesar. Caiaphas thus plays his final card. The game is up, and Pilate knows it. The fear of being associated with a political rebellion in Jerusalem seizes Pilate, and he loses his last shred of nerve. "When Pilate saw that he could not prevail at all, but rather *that* a tumult was rising, he took water and washed *his* hands before the multitude, saying, 'I am innocent of the blood of this just Person. You see *to it*'" (Matt. 27:24). And finally, Pilate orders Jesus to be delivered up to be crucified.

CHAPTER ELEVEN

The Crucifixion and Resurrection

The Crucifixion

In an instant, the scene changes at Pilate's word. The tortures and humiliations cease as Pilate's special officers deliver Jesus over to the centurion who will take charge of the work of crucifying the prisoners. It was deemed forbidden by Jewish law for any person to be crucified inside the holy city. And so Jesus is made to carry His Cross and to walk from the governor's headquarters based inside Fortress Antonia, through the winding paths of the city, till they reach the western gate of the city, in order to be crucified outside the city walls. While He is walking, the women who have followed Him till now encounter the procession and let out a great wail of grief at a sight at which, if no human eye had been present to weep, the stones of the city would have shed tears. He is followed by a large concourse of onlookers: friends, family, the women who were His followers, along with the scribes and chief priests who had insisted on His death. The time is about nine in the morning.

He bore His Cross. The day Jesus bore His Cross was the day it ceased to be simply a symbol of torture and death; it has now become an emblem of faith, of redemption, of grace, of sacrifice, of love, and of glory:

» Children bear the cross to receive joy.

» Youth bear the cross to mold a triumphant character.

» Women bear the cross to receive grace and strength.

» Men bear the cross to receive wisdom and integrity.

» Monks bear the cross as armor on the breast and on the back.

» The elderly bear the cross to overcome the world.

The cross is lifted as a symbol of armistice in wars, a symbol of charity and medicine to the poor and sick, and a symbol of mercy to the world. There is a reason it has become the focus of so much art and imagination—because the cross has come to represent the loftiest thoughts and sentiments of humankind.

Jesus, fatigued by the punishments He has endured, stumbles repeatedly under the weight of the Cross.

He has experienced a significant loss of blood; the thorns from the crown on His head sink deep into His scalp; He has had no food or sleep since the supper of the previous night; the gashes on His back are open and swollen; His face is in pain from the repeated beatings from the soldiers' fists; and His soul is downcast from the derisive insults of His captors. "From the sole of the foot even to the head, / *There is* no soundness in it, / *But* wounds and bruises and putrefying sores; / They have not been closed or bound up, / Or soothed with ointment" (Is. 1:6). The soldiers in charge realize that He is no longer able to lift the wooden beam. They meet a certain Simon, from the city of Cyrene in Africa, walking into the city just as they are walking out. Saint Mark is the only evangelist to mention the names of this Simon's two sons (Alexander and Rufus), thus indicating that Simon was likely a relative or close friend of St. Mark, who was possibly staying with him in Jerusalem during the feast. The soldiers order Simon to carry the Cross on Jesus' behalf. Simon immediately complies and walks with the procession along the remaining distance.

Jesus was nearly crushed by the wood of the Cross, but the glory of God supported Him. His body quivered under the weight of man's transgressions, but His will persevered to complete the mission of redemption. The women who followed Him could hardly endure the inhumane spectacle of their Lord passing through so much suffering, "Yet it pleased the LORD to bruise Him; / He has put *Him* to grief" (Is. 53:10). But as for us, we revere the image of One who carried the Cross. We worship the broken body and the shed blood, and we kiss the wounds by which we were healed. His weakness became our strength. His prostration became our ability to stand upright. His collapse beneath the Cross became our resurrection. His footsteps toward Golgotha created a path for us to walk from sadness to joy. If we weep, we are to weep over our sins, which placed the Cross on His back; but our tears will quickly turn into the laughter and joy of salvation.

They finally reach a rocky mound or hill outside the city gate, called Calvary for its skull-like appearance, and here they prepare the Cross. The condemned person was customarily offered wine mingled with myrrh to drink—a potent tranquilizing mixture that served to dull the victim's senses—in order to reduce the severity of his sufferings. Christ tasted the contents of the cup, then refused to drink— that He might drink from the cup of suffering to the lees. The Lord was stretched out on the Cross, and His hands and feet were secured to it by a swift hammering of the nails. Each wrist received a nail across the wooden beam, and the two feet were secured together by a single large nail run through the ankles.[52]

The crowd might have considered it a lamentable fact that He was crucified between two common malefactors; but it was Jesus who said, "I say to you that this which is written must still be accomplished in Me: 'And He was numbered with the transgressors'" (Luke 22:37). Christ's mission in coming to the world finds practical

---

52   Recent archeological evidence suggests that each foot was nailed separately.

expression in the presence of the two criminals beside Him, because it was for sinners that He came. He was counted a sinner during His life and in His death also; and though this signaled defeat to the enemies of Jesus, it signaled victory to Jesus Himself. The first thief heard the taunts of the chief priests and mingled his voice with theirs in reviling Christ. But the second thief, the blessed thief, had an open heart. He rebukes the first thief for his obstinacy and defends Jesus' innocence. Then he utters the plea that has become the beloved watchword of the Church ever since: "Lord, remember me when You come into Your kingdom" (Luke 23:42). How is it that Peter, who heard the promises and the voice from heaven, denied the Lord, while this thief believed and confessed Christ while suspended over the hill of Calvary? But he who stole on earth was now stealing into paradise; the "prince of penitents" would soon follow the Prince of Peace into eternal life.

Pilate posted the accusation brought against Jesus on a placard hung over His head. Written in Greek, Latin, and Hebrew was the title: THIS IS THE KING OF THE JEWS. The place of crucifixion was only minutes away from the city walls, on a busy highway that led to Damascus. Tens of thousands of travelers must have read the sign as they walked to and from the city, especially since it was the time of the feast and Jerusalem was teeming with pilgrims who had come from all over the surrounding country. Each of these read in his or her own language the proclamation that the King of the Jews was being crucified, and they doubtless carried the strange tidings back to their homelands.

Thus, in Hebrew, Latin, and Greek—the languages of religion, government, and society—was published the message of salvation to the inhabitants of the known world. The chief priests balk at the writing and demand that it read, "He said . . ." But Pilate, with deep feelings of antagonism toward these religious leaders and with that cold haughtiness that characterized imperial Rome, dismisses their complaint: "What I have written, I have written" (John 19:22).

After the soldiers had finished raising their victims onto the crosses, they sat down to divide the victims' clothing among themselves, according to Roman tradition. The weather was likely cold those days, and Jesus was in the habit of wearing at least four pieces of clothing to keep warm: a cloth over his head, one about the shoulders, a tunic for the torso, and some form of undergarment. Around this clothing He wrapped one large, finely woven robe that was made without seam. As there were four soldiers keeping watch, the Lord's clothes were easy to divide among them. But when they found that His outer robe was woven seamlessly of a single fine material, they decided to cast lots for it, in order that one soldier might win the whole rather than each receive a torn fragment.

"And those who passed by blasphemed Him, wagging their heads and saying, 'You who destroy the temple and build *it* in three days, save Yourself! If You are the Son of God, come down from the cross'" (Matt. 27:39, 40). Although Jesus' enemies know that the accusations against Him came from false witnesses, yet they persist in taunting Him with the same words. They sneer at Him who would "destroy the temple and build it in three days"; but He would soon accomplish through His rising from the dead the erection of the temple of God's people. As St. Paul writes, "You are the temple of the living God. As God has said: 'I will dwell in them and walk among *them*'" (2 Cor. 6:16). They scoff that "He saved others; Himself He cannot save," not understanding that through these very sufferings, He was saving generations of people for all time. They said, "If He is the King of Israel, let Him now come down from the cross," not knowing that He who voluntarily endures a Cross is a true King over all righteous people. They scornfully declaimed, "He trusted in God; let Him deliver Him now if He will have Him; for He said, 'I am the Son of

God'"; but when He would rise only three days thence, He would prove that He is indeed the Son of God and that God is pleased with Him. Thus, the cruel words of these scoffers fulfilled the prophecy of Isaiah:

> He is despised and rejected by men,
> A Man of sorrows and acquainted with grief.
> And we hid, as it were, our faces from Him;
> He was despised, and we did not esteem Him.
> (Is. 53:3)

The Death of Christ

"NOW WHEN THE SIXTH HOUR had come, there was darkness over the whole land until the ninth hour" (Mark 15:33). The four evangelists make a point of telling us that darkness covered the earth from the sixth to the ninth hour. The message implied in this event is significant: the Father's countenance was turned away from the Son. For three hours, the earth's light failed, and all was dark. And if Jesus, the Light of the world, entered into darkness, from where could the earth find any other light? If the Father's face is turned away, then the darkness that results is thick indeed! From this very passage one can develop an entire theology of light and darkness. The sun derives its luminescence from the original creative source of light; but if that source were to be veiled from us, then we would be hopelessly lost in darkness. While we have the light, let us walk in the light! During the three hours of darkness, Jesus enters into a final struggle with the prince of this world.

The Father's turning away from the Cross evokes a great cry from Jesus: "'Eloi, Eloi, lama sabachthani?' which is translated, 'My God, My God, why have You forsaken Me?'" (Mark 15:33). This is an utterance whose meaning is not easy to grasp. How can Christ say that God had *forsaken* Him? On the face of it, it is an incomprehensible, even an insufferable idea. But Jesus' righteousness is far greater than the curse of sin; and so, while accepting the curse in His body on our behalf, His righteousness remained intact. By finally accepting death on our behalf, Christ finished the work of redemption; and by His Resurrection He finally triumphed over both the curse and death.

We have mentioned the chief priests and rulers present at the scene of the Crucifixion, as well as the Roman soldiers. There was another class of people (whom we have not yet mentioned) who were present from the very beginning and remained till the very end. These were the women who loved the Lord. The chief priests hurried away at the ninth hour in order to carry out the religious tasks appointed to them in the temple, such as preparing the Passover lambs and reciting prayers; and when Jesus' enemies dispersed, His friends drew near. These were Mary the Lord's mother, and Salome her sister, as well as Mary the wife of Clopas, Mary Magdalene, and John the disciple.

Here the Lord's mother comes to the foot of the Cross, and in the darkness and gloom that enshrouded the land, she looks up in sorrow at her crucified Son. The sword foretold long ago by Simeon the Elder, while Jesus was yet a baby in her arms, was now thrust into her soul. The Scriptures do not tell us that she wailed or shrieked. But He was her own flesh and blood, and so the pain He felt on the Cross she surely felt in her own body. She struggles in silence. Of all those who have had a fellowship in the sufferings of Christ, none has experienced it more deeply or more truly than the Lord's mother. The tears she sheds for Him are shed on behalf of all mankind.

But the Lord, in the throes of His agony, does not forget His mother. "When Jesus therefore saw His mother, and the disciple whom He loved standing by, He said to His mother, 'Woman, behold your son!' Then He said to the disciple, 'Behold your mother!'" (John 19:26, 27). If we call to mind the fact that St. Mary came down through the line of Jesse, of the tribe of Judah, we realize that her body was the historical link to the divine promises spoken to the patriarchs and prophets of old. And so, in making her the mother of John, Christ transfers all the sure and enduring promises of the Old Testament to John himself—that is, to the Church. John immediately obeys the Lord's command and takes Mary to his home.

Now Jesus, knowing that the work of the Cross is approaching its end, cries out, "I thirst!" A sponge soaked in sour wine is brought up to His mouth, and He drinks. At the beginning of the Crucifixion He had refused such a palliative; but now, with all things nearing completion, He accepts the small bit of mercy: "For my thirst they gave me vinegar to drink" (Ps. 69:21). The moisture from the sponge enables Him to articulate His last words: "It is finished!" This declaration will continue to baffle the attempts of even the cleverest commentators to explain. The evangelist John himself does not even try to explain the words, but writes them as they are and leaves the world to witness. We may at least say this: that Jesus has now finished the work given to Him by the Father. He finished the work to its smallest details—those we know of, and those of which we know nothing. Why He came from the Father's bosom, and divested Himself of divine light in order to be wrapped in human flesh, and took on the appearance of a slave—this impossible task was now completed! "And when Jesus had cried out with a loud voice, He said, 'Father, into Your hands I commit My spirit.' Having said this, He breathed His last" (Luke 23:46).

There is a clause in the Law of Moses which the members of the Sanhedrin were very scrupulous to observe: "If a man has committed a sin deserving of death, and he is put to death, and you hang him on a tree, his body shall not remain overnight on the tree, but you shall surely bury him that day, so that you do not defile the land which the LORD your God is giving you *as* an inheritance; for he who is hanged *is* accursed of God" (Deut. 21:22, 23). Therefore, in order to prevent the desecration of the high Sabbath that was fast approaching—as well as to ensure a speedy death for their enemy—they go to Pilate and request the *crurifragium* to be used on the victims. This was a heavy wooden beam that was used to forcibly crush the legs of crucified criminals, thus turning what would have been days of hanging on the cross into mere hours. The soldiers wield the *crurifragium* and break the legs of both the penitent thief and the scoffing thief—a patent illustration of how the world cannot distinguish between the righteous and the wicked. But when they come to Jesus, His death is so evident already that they see no need to break His legs—a fact that caused Pilate to "marvel" (Mark 15:44).

There is one soldier present who has a lingering doubt about Jesus' death. He therefore takes his Roman spear—an instrument so sharp and lethal that it could run effortlessly through a human body—and drives it, according to Roman custom, from the right side of the body to the left. If there was a trace of life left in a crucified criminal, this procedure would extinguish it in a matter of minutes. Saint John informs us in his Gospel that blood and water flowed out of the wound produced by the spear, and he lays significant stress on the fact that he was an eyewitness to these things. We have here, on the one hand, a *dead sacrifice*, in the earthly sense of the term, certified by soldiers who were experts in the business of death. On the other hand, we have a *living sacrifice*: free-flowing blood defies the natural laws of decomposition and coagulation that immediately take effect once a body has died. The blood and water are signs of life emerging from a body that had all the signs of death. In the eyes of the Roman guards, Jesus' body was a lifeless corpse; but to the eyes of faith, that body was the provision of life for the world. When Jesus gave the disciples the cup and said, "this is My blood of the new covenant, which is shed for many for the remission of sins" (Matt. 26:28), that was the hidden and mystical Eucharist. But now, on the Cross, the blood and water that flowed were the open and visible Eucharist.

The Burial

"AFTER THIS, JOSEPH OF ARIMATHEA, being a disciple of Jesus, but secretly, for fear of the Jews, asked Pilate that he might take away the body of Jesus; and Pilate gave *him* permission" (John 19:38). Jesus had died at about three o'clock in the afternoon; and as sunset was fast approaching, and with it a high Sabbath, the Jews were anxious to remove the bodies from the crosses as quickly as possible. As six o'clock was the official demarcation for sundown, three short hours remained for the work to be done. But who was to render this service? The disciples had all fled except John, and John himself was now busied with the care of Jesus' mother. It was God's will that there should be present this Joseph who plucked up the courage to request the care of Jesus' body.

We learn from the Gospels that this Joseph was a "rich man" (Matt. 27:57); a "council member" (Mark 15:31); a "good and just man" (Luke 23:50); one who was "waiting for the kingdom of God" (Luke 23:51); and secretly a "disciple of Jesus" (John 19:38). It is likely that Joseph of Arimathea provided a constant supply of information to Jesus and the disciples regarding the discussions held by the Sanhedrin and the plots that were hatched by them behind closed doors. Pilate had already granted the Jewish leaders permission to remove the bodies the same day (John 19:31), but Joseph now goes to request personal custody of Christ's body. Doubtless all the honorable descriptors used by the evangelists regarding Joseph were qualities that prepared him for this single great moment in his life.

He owned a plot of land just outside the city walls; he had hewn a tomb for his personal use; the tomb had never before been used. God had clearly equipped Joseph for this act of service; maybe it was for this hour that he was born.

"And Nicodemus, who at first came to Jesus by night, also came, bringing a mixture of myrrh and aloes, about a hundred pounds" (John 19:39). Nicodemus was a co-member with Joseph of the Sanhedrin council, and they had agreed in their refusal to consent to the council's decision against Jesus. He once spoke in Christ's defense—"Does our law judge a man before it hears him and knows what he is doing?" (John 7:51)—but the glares and sneers of the chief priests silenced him. Both Nicodemus and Joseph were constrained to keep their discipleship to Christ a secret due to their fear of the chief rulers. But it is clear that an understanding existed between them, because when they saw Jesus hung on the Cross, they divided the duties of tending to the body between themselves. Joseph goes to Pilate while Nicodemus prepares the burial spices, and they meet again at the foot of the Cross. Now all fear leaves them, and they publicly administer the last rites to their deceased Lord.

The body is detached from the wood and lowered from the Cross in a mood of solemn reverence. Nicodemus presents his hundred pounds of myrrh and aloes—a mixture borrowed from the burial practices of the ancient Egyptians. When Asa the king of Israel died, he was laid in "the bed which was filled with spices and various ingredients prepared in a mixture of ointments" (2 Chr. 16:14). The great amount of spices brought by Nicodemus, therefore, was not only necessary to anoint the multitude of burial cloths in which Jesus would be wrapped, but also served as a symbolic gesture that, to the mind of Nicodemus, Jesus deserved a royal burial. The Church has availed itself of this immense treasure of spices that lingered with the burial cloths. By mixing them with oil, it has produced its *myron*,[53] which is used to chrismate new believers as they emerge from the baptismal font.

They bore Jesus' body in their arms and carried it down the mound of Calvary, a short distance to a garden owned by Joseph of Arimathea, in which he had prepared a new tomb for himself. When he was laying the foundations of the tomb, little did he realize that he was preparing what would become the holiest spot on earth—a patch of land to which all the nations of the earth would one day come to visit and to which the kings and leaders of the earth would come to bend the knee. Joseph had meant it to be a grave for the dead—but it has become a witness to resurrection and to life! Jesus' sufferings in the garden of Gethsemane and in the garden of Calvary recall to our minds Adam's transgression in the garden of Eden—but these were precursors to the risen Jesus' victory in the garden of the Resurrection.

If the Holy One Himself lay in a grave, then the grave has lost its meaning. If the Rock of Ages was enclosed in lifeless rock, then that rock has partaken of eternity. Hail to the Tomb in which Joseph stored the world's greatest treasure! Hail to the Tomb in which the powers of darkness were shaken, and out of which emerged a light to reveal the everlasting way! Hail to the Tomb upon whose surfaces dripped the precious ointments from which the Church draws its fragrant life!

The Resurrection

"NOW ON THE FIRST DAY of the week, very early in the morning, they, and certain *other women* with them, came to the tomb bringing the spices which they had prepared" (Luke 24:1). The women

---

53   Greek, "ointment."

who followed Jesus had observed where His body was laid, then they "rested on the Sabbath according to the commandment." That was the last Sabbath of the Old Testament. It was the last day in which the grave could claim victory over its dead. With the dawning of the first day of the week, a new era had begun. And so, early in the morning on that Resurrection Day, the women gather their spices and set out before the rising of the sun to finish the burial rites for their Lord. They proceed to the western gate of the city in darkness; but since the gate was opened daily only after sunrise, they were obliged to wait for the opening of the doors before they could set out to the Tomb.

We learn from the various Gospel accounts the identities of the women: Mary Magdalene, Mary the mother of James and Joses, Joanna, and Salome. They are induced to visit the Tomb, not by any remembrance of Jesus' words about rising from the dead, but simply by the fervor of their love for Him. Where is Peter, and where is the rest of the band? Alas, they are driven by neither remembrance nor fervor, but recent events put a freeze on the disciples' movements. Yet the spirits of the women remained warm. They ventured out into the dark, hazarded the dangers of the city, in order to reach a cold and rocky tomb outside the city gates. What boldness! And so, just as it is granted to woman to be the first witness to life that emerges from the womb, so it was granted to these women to be the joyful heralds of the life that had emerged from the Tomb.

As they walk along the path leading to the Tomb, they discuss with some anxiety the problem of the massive stone they had seen Joseph and Nicodemus roll against the face of the cave. Who would move it for them? But an angel of the Lord appears whose face and raiment shine with a heavenly luster, and he performs the service for them. The guards shake with fear at the sight of the unexpected visitor. The women enter the Tomb to find angels sitting near the stone where the body had lain. Saint Mark tells us it was a young man sitting in a white robe. Saint Matthew says it was one angel, whereas St. Luke and St. John say there were two angels. The disparities in detail need not disturb the reader. When we speak about Christ's Resurrection from the dead, we are speaking about an event that cannot be reduced to the usual laws of nature. What appears or does not appear, what is seen or is not seen, depends greatly on what God desires to show, as well as on the receptivity of the seer. The risen Lord Himself could be seen and recognized only by certain people and under certain circumstances, as the case of the disciples at Emmaus proves. Moreover, writers differ in their modes of description. One writer is extensive, the other is brief; one author says one, another says two.

The women bow their faces to the earth in the presence of the celestial beings, and they hear the marvelous words, "Why do you seek the living among the dead? He is not here, but is risen! Remember how He spoke to you when He was still in Galilee, saying, 'The Son of Man must be delivered into the hands of sinful men, and be crucified, and the third day rise again'" (Luke 24:5–7). The women run out in a state of astonishment and perplexity to deliver the news to the apostles.

Mary Magdalene is the first of the women to arrive at the Tomb, and seeing that the stone was removed and the body of the Lord is missing, she is the first to run with the news to the disciples. Saint John writes that she fled *to* Peter and *to* John separately, indicating that they were staying at separate locations at this point. "They have taken away the Lord out of the tomb, and we do not know where they have laid Him" (John 20:2). Despite the humiliations He had endured, despite the Crucifixion, death, and burial—He is still *the* Lord. Here is genuine loyalty and love! Her eyes always see what is great and glorious in Christ, regardless of outward circumstances.

Peter and John immediately set out running toward the Tomb.

"So they both ran together, and the other disciple outran Peter and came to the tomb first" (John 20:4). John—here omitting his own name in his Gospel—is possessed of a youthful energy and arrives at the Tomb before the more aged Peter. He looks in but does not enter, leaving that honor first to Peter out of respect for his age. But it was not John's youthful energy alone that brought him so quickly to the Tomb. It was also the profound love that Jesus showed him and which he in turn felt for his Lord. He refers to himself as "the disciple whom Jesus loved" throughout his entire Gospel. And now, that love gives him wings to fly on that most special day and in that most special hour of his life. This quiet hint John gives us of his surpassing love for Christ—that he outran his elder disciple—is also hinted at in Jesus' special charge to John to watch over His mother.

Peter enters the Tomb and looks into the inner chamber where the body was laid to see if and how the body was stolen. He collects all his mental faculties to ponder the evidence before him, and the first inklings of the truth begin to dawn on him when he sees the wrapped burial cloths lying in their original place. *The body was not stolen*—this was the first certain conclusion to be drawn from the empty Tomb. Next, he sees that the handkerchief that had been wrapped around His head is folded in a place by itself, rather than thrown in among the other cloths. This gave the appearance that the cloths and the handkerchief were still lying in the exact positions they had been in when the body was laid to rest, but with the body itself missing. *The body left its burial wrappings without disturbing them*—this was the second conclusion. It was not the hand of man, then, nor the hand of a thief that took the body; but the body divested itself of mortal wrappings in order to be clothed in the vestments of immortality! Intimations of the resurrection from the dead thus begin to suggest themselves to Peter's mind even before the first formal declaration of it is made.

John then enters the Tomb and notices the same things Peter saw. The burial cloths lie undisturbed in their place, and the handkerchief is serenely folded in a place by itself. The scene is calm and natural, without a single sign of tampering by rough hands. He sees Peter standing astonished and speechless, and the wonder transfers to John's mind, forming the beginnings of belief. He does not yet believe in the full resurrection, but only in the thought that something supremely uncommon has happened. The first rays of faith begin to shine in John's heart, but that faith halted before receiving further revelation. Saint John relates to us his honest journey of faith on that day. He does not hasten to tell us his faith was full; he admits it was slow and immature, yet prepared for the truth.

"For as yet they did not know the Scripture, that He must rise again from the dead" (John 20:9). Here St. John records for us another essential truth. The Scriptures, despite their prophecies, were not the primary driver of the disciples' faith in the Resurrection. What moved their minds rather was the chain of events they had witnessed: the lifted stone, the empty Tomb, the women's testimony, and the undisturbed burial cloths. These things opened their minds to what the Scriptures alone could not, and they in turn illuminated the word of Scripture for them. Saint John is honest in his assessment of himself and his fellow disciples: they were slow to believe and slow to understand. This serves as evidence for us of the resurrection story's authenticity. The declaration of Christ's rising from the dead was not premeditated by the disciples; it was not expected; there was no prior bias or inclination to believe it. It took everyone by surprise.

And in saying they knew not the Scriptures, John might have had the Psalms in mind:

Therefore my heart is glad, and my glory rejoices;
My flesh also will rest in hope.

For You will not leave my soul in Sheol,
Nor will You allow Your Holy One to see corruption.
(Ps. 16:9, 10)

Peter also refers to the Psalms during his great sermon in the Book of Acts:

"Men *and* brethren, let *me* speak freely to you of the patriarch David, that he is both dead and buried, and his tomb is with us to this day. Therefore, being a prophet, and knowing that God had sworn with an oath to him that of the fruit of his body, according to the flesh, He would raise up the Christ to sit on his throne, he, foreseeing this, spoke concerning the resurrection of the Christ, that His soul was not left in Hades, nor did His flesh see corruption. This Jesus God has raised up, of which we are all witnesses." (Acts 2:29–32)

Jesus Appears to Mary Magdalene

AFTER MARY MAGDALENE DELIVERS THE news to Peter and John, she returns to the Tomb with them and kneels in waiting. The two disciples leave, each to his own place, contemplating the riddle of the empty Tomb; meanwhile, Mary remains and ruminates, as if beseeching the Tomb itself to solve the riddle for her. Her tears and her hope were a type of plea for the Tomb to utter a response. But as she stands weeping, she gathers the courage to stoop down and look into the Tomb—despite her grief, the light of heaven attracts her gaze from within the Tomb.

"She saw two angels in white sitting, one at the head and the other at the feet, where the body of Jesus had lain" (John 20:12). The image hearkens back to the Old Testament, where the presence of the Lord was represented by the mercy seat:

> Make one cherub at one end, and the other cherub at the other
> end; you shall make the cherubim at the two ends of it *of one
> piece* with the mercy seat. . . . You shall put the mercy seat on
> top of the ark. . . . And there I will meet with you, and I will
> speak with you from above the mercy seat, from between the
> two cherubim which *are* on the ark of the Testimony. (Ex.
> 25:19–22)

Hence, St. John's description of the scene implies the sanctity of the
spot where the Lord's body had lain between the angels. It was the
mercy seat of the New Testament, as the Tomb was the new ark of
the covenant. The two angels do not stand next to the spot, however, but sit—the Lord had risen, and there was no longer any need
to guard the body.

"Then they said to her, 'Woman, why are you weeping?'" (John
20:13). To Mary, this was likely a strange question posed by the two
visitors. Her Lord had been taken away; how could she not weep?
The absence of Jesus made the angels' presence inconsequential to
her. Nothing mattered anymore, and the only thing she could find to
say was, "I do not know where they have laid Him." At that moment,
Jesus appears immediately behind her, and His presence causes the
angels to shift and stand at attention. Mary takes note of the change
in their faces, and she turns to see the cause. She looks at Jesus but
does not recognize Him. Her eyes are blurred by tears and her mind
clouded by grief, but Jesus stands beaming with joy. Mary was reliv-
ing the pain of the past, but the past is always a stranger to the new.
"Old things have passed away; behold, all things have become new"
(2 Cor. 5:17).

"Mary!" Jesus calls her by name as he did with Lazarus and the word awakens new life within her. Her eyes of despair are filled with a hopeful radiance, and the light of the Resurrection enters her heart. The Shepherd called His sheep by her name, and she heard the voice. It was not sufficient that she merely see and hear Him, but she must grasp His feet and worship. She wished not to lose Him again, and so she makes an attempt to apprehend Him physically. "Jesus said to her, 'Do not cling to Me, for I have not yet ascended to My Father; but go to My brethren and say to them, "I am ascending to My Father and your Father, and *to* My God and your God"'"(John 20:17). The old teacher and healer could no longer be clung to; the risen Jesus was a new reality. "I am ascending to open a new way to the Father. I am going to prepare a place for you to dwell with Me. There you will not merely live *with* Me, but will live *in* Me. You shall no longer touch me as a teacher or healer, but shall eat My flesh, that I may abide in you, and you in Me."

Mary immediately goes out and, after being the first person ever to see the risen Lord, becomes the first person ever to announce the Resurrection to the world.

Jesus Appears to the Disciples

"THEN, THE SAME DAY AT evening, being the first *day* of the week, when the doors were shut where the disciples were assembled, for fear of the Jews, Jesus came and stood in the midst, and said to them, 'Peace *be* with you'" (John 20:19). That "day" is an eternal day in the history of mankind. It is the day on which Christ was proclaimed victor over death. It was the day on which a new life began for humanity. It was the day Jesus breathed God's Spirit onto the disciples, in place of the original breath God breathed into Adam epochs prior, but which man had quenched through sin.

Jesus chose Sunday in particular for all this to occur. He met with the disciples on Sunday in order to consecrate it and hallow it for the entire Church. All of His resurrection appearances to His followers—including that to Thomas a week later—were made on a Sunday, not on any other day of the week.[54] Hence, every Sunday is considered by the Church to be a day of resurrection.

Saint John's Gospel informs us that in the evening of that new day, the disciples were assembled together behind closed doors, hoping in fear to escape the notice of the chief priests and Sadducees.

We may assume that a good number of Jesus' sympathizers had congregated in the Upper Room with the disciples. When, for example, the two disciples return from Emmaus to inform the disciples that they had seen the Lord, they find other followers in hiding with the disciples: "they rose up that very hour and returned to Jerusalem, and found the eleven and those *who were* with them gathered together" (Luke 24:33). Their nervous concealment was a sign of lack of faith in the Lord. They had lost all hope. The Gospel says the "doors" were closed—indicating the main door of the house, as well as the door leading up to the Upper Room, and the door of the Upper Room itself; all these were shut and secured with locks. We should remember that St. John's Gospel usually has mystical undertones in its details. It was because He who said "I am the door" was absent that they had to lock up the earthly doors.

About this time two other followers of Jesus—Cleopas and probably Luke—are on their way back to their city of residence once the tumult of the past few days had dwindled. "Now behold, two of them were traveling that same day to a village called Emmaus, which was seven miles from Jerusalem" (Luke 24:13). They are so engrossed in talk about the recent happenings in Jerusalem that they fail to notice that Jesus is walking right behind them. Jesus then addresses them

---

54 Obviously, this does not include the Ascension, which took place exactly forty days after the Resurrection, on a Thursday.

directly: "What kind of conversation *is* this that you have with one another as you walk and are sad?" (Luke 24:17). They fail to recognize Him. Whether or not a person sees Jesus is determined by the person's spiritual preconditioning. Is the heart ready to see? By the same token, Jesus may decide whether or not to reveal Himself to a particular person based on circumstances.

Cleopas expresses surprise that this stranger has not heard of the events that had taken place of late in Jerusalem surrounding "Jesus of Nazareth," a prophet mighty in word and deed. He summarizes the fate that had befallen their Lord, with the forlorn remark, "We were hoping that it was He who was going to redeem Israel." It expressed the pain of dashed hopes and unfulfilled dreams. Christ immediately rebukes their hardness of heart, because the doctrine of the redemption He taught was built on His death and Resurrection—which had already been announced to the women by the angels! Jesus desires to draw them on to a deeper faith, for the evidence of the eyes can never be a prerequisite for faith in the heart.

"O foolish ones, and slow of heart to believe in all that the prophets have spoken! Ought not the Christ to have suffered these things and to enter into His glory?" (Luke 24:25, 26). Jesus is obviously grieved at the slowness of their minds. The numerous times He had spoken of His death and Resurrection had fallen on deaf ears. How is it that not a single verse from the Scriptures had opened their minds? Jesus' words here teach us the significance of Old Testament prophecy and how seriously we ought to attend to it. "And beginning at Moses and all the Prophets, He expounded to them in all the Scriptures the things concerning Himself" (Luke 24:26). He likely spoke to them about the prophetic auguries of the future Messiah in David's psalms; about Isaiah's prophecy of Emmanuel; about the righteous branch in Jeremiah; about the uncut stone that filled the earth in Daniel; about the new Israel in Hosea; about the people's great refuge in Joel; about the blessed future day when the plow-man would overtake the reaper and the grape-treader overtake the sower in Amos; about their redemption from the enemy in Micah; and about the rest of the inspired foretellings of the major and minor prophets. God would have to grant me a second life in order to hear the Lord's voice in everything He told the two disciples on the road to Emmaus!

Jesus' path was about to take Him in a different direction, but the two disciples entreat and compel Him to stay a while where they were residing. Jesus was not one to allow another to compel His actions, but He delighted in their earnestness to learn more, so He submits to their entreaties. They sit at table; Christ blesses bread and gives it to them, thus accomplishing the first Christian Eucharist after the Resurrection. The mystical nature of the supper stirs their hearts, and they recognize Him, but He disappears from sight. They set out immediately to bring word to the disciples.

Jesus Appears to Thomas and to the Disciples by the Sea

LUKE AND CLEOPAS ARRIVE IN the Upper Room where the disciples are hiding and excitedly relay the strange tidings to the eleven. As they are speaking, and without any forewarning, Jesus suddenly appears in their midst. The disciples are terrified at the apparition, but Jesus allays their fears and allows them to touch His hands and feet, proving that it is truly flesh and blood standing before them. It is no longer simply an earthly body; He now possesses a resurrected body! As St. Paul writes, an "earthly body" is one thing, while a "heavenly body" is another.[55] His appearance to the disciples here as an assembled body complements His appearances to select individuals, and it furthermore recognizes the Church's identity as the

---

55   1 Cor. 15:40.

resurrected body of Christ. The Bridegroom meets with His bride and consecrates her, because He gave up His body and blood for her.

Thomas was not present at the gathering. His reaction to the sad events involving the Lord was to return to his hometown, just like the disciples from Emmaus. But when he rejoined his brethren, they had news for him. "The other disciples therefore said to him, 'We have seen the Lord.' So he said to them, 'Unless I see in His hands the print of the nails, and put my finger into the print of the nails, and put my hand into His side, I will not believe'" (John 20:25). The Gospel does not record this exchange in order to display Thomas's personal lack of faith, but rather to demonstrate how difficult it was to believe in the Resurrection. Saint Matthew tells us about their meeting with Jesus in Galilee: "When they saw Him, they worshiped Him; but some doubted" (Matt. 28:17). The Gospels are honest records, and their plain truthfulness increases our confidence in the narrative.

Thomas required to see the prints of the nails for himself, but the prints of the nails were signs of death. He is requesting the evidence of life to be drawn from the tokens of death! It is of course an impossible thing to ask. He desired his finger to be placed into the spear's wound as unbelieving, then to be withdrawn as believing. *I will not believe.* Thomas risked his entire faith on the touch of his hands. He made the possibility of believing subject to the evidence of his eyes. We must note that when Jesus appeared to the other disciples, He provided them with the same evidence: "He showed them *His* hands and His side" (John 20:20). So, after all, Thomas was requesting his right as an apostle; he was insisting on the same proof that had been given to the disciples in his absence.

Nevertheless, Thomas receives the same rebuke from Jesus as the others. After eight days, the disciples are gathered again in Jerusalem, waiting and yearning for another appearance of the Lord, and they have Thomas with them. Jesus appears again while the doors are closed, grants them a benediction of peace, then turns to address Thomas. "Reach your finger here, and look at My hands; and reach your hand *here,* and put *it* into My side. Do not be unbelieving, but believing" (John 20:27). He gently and compassionately submits to Thomas's conditions for belief. Saint John wrote in the beginning of his Gospel, "The Word was God." Thomas immediately feels the force of this truth when he touches the Lord, and he prostrates himself before Him and confesses, "My Lord and my God!"

Thomas was not an unbelieving person. Had he been a complete unbeliever, Jesus would not have appeared to him. When Christ breathed the gift of the Holy Spirit on the apostles, it was a shared gift, not an individual one. The Holy Spirit was breathed into a body, not into a collection of singular persons—and Thomas was part of that body. So when doubt loitered in Thomas's mind, it did not take up a permanent residence. He indeed requested the proof of the eyes and even of the touch; but he was already on the path to faith and simply needed these as aids in his journey. "Lord, I believe; help my unbelief!" (Mark 9:24).

> After these things Jesus showed Himself again to the disciples at the Sea of Tiberias, and in this way He showed *Himself:* Simon Peter, Thomas called the Twin, Nathanael of Cana in Galilee, the *sons* of Zebedee, and two others of His disciples were together. Simon Peter said to them, "I am going fishing." (John 21:1–3)

Although the sons of Zebedee are usually mentioned after Peter's name in the Gospels, here they are given no distinguished place—an incidental reminder that John himself is the writer of the Gospel. Also, Thomas is uncharacteristically placed at the head of the list after Peter. It is probably because these two men needed special attention from the Lord—Peter because of his denials, and Thomas because of slowness of belief.

It is perhaps strange for us to see the disciples returning to their usual occupations after having witnessed the risen Lord and received the breath of the Spirit. It might be because the Lord directed them to tarry in the city until they would be endued with power from on high (Luke 24:49)—that power which placed them in the boat of salvation and launched them out onto the sea of evangelism, far away from the shores of their national borders.

Despite fishing all night, they catch nothing. From a natural standpoint this is an unusual result, because nighttime is ideal for catching fish. But from a mystical standpoint, it makes sense: nighttime refers to the darkness of the soul, when Jesus is not present. Moreover, in early Christian typology, the Greek word for "fish," ΙΧΦΥΣ, was an acronym for "Jesus Christ, Son of God, Savior." They had thrown in their nets many times that night and had pulled them up empty. Both their hands and their hearts were weary with failure. "But when the morning had now come, Jesus stood on the shore" (John 21:4). In John's deep symbolism, this is an image of the Sun of righteousness rising after a dark night. Jesus brings with Him the morning of faith! Saint Paul echoes the same symbolic language in his epistles: "The night is far spent, the day is at hand. Therefore let us cast off the works of darkness, and let us put on the armor of light" (Rom. 13:12).

Jesus tells them to cast their nets over the right side of the boat, which they do, and the net becomes so heavy with fish that they pull it back into the boat with great difficulty. John, who is always quickest to perceive the Lord—because he is "the disciple whom Jesus loved"—recognizes Him and declares it to the others. Peter, who is always quickest to act, plunges into the sea and begins swimming toward Christ. The other disciples bring the boat laden with the large catch of fish up the shore behind Peter. The scene is beautifully symbolic: it is the Church, carrying the souls it has caught from the deep waters of the world to meet Christ on the shore of the eternal world. Jesus tells them, "Bring some of the fish which you have just caught" (John 21:10); but truthfully, it was not they who caught them, but the Lord gathered the fish for them in their nets. Then they sit together to have an agape meal.

"So when they had eaten breakfast, Jesus said to Simon Peter, 'Simon, *son* of Jonah, do you love Me more than these?'" (John 21:15). Jesus turns His attention to Peter; He addresses him not by his new given name (Peter), but by the old (Simon, son of Jonah). It is an allusion to the fact that he is still a natural, untransformed human being. And when Jesus asks Simon if he loves Him more than the rest of the disciples, it is an allusion to his former promise that he would behave better than all his brethren in time of danger: "Even if all are made to stumble because of You, I will never be made to stumble" (Matt. 26:33). But Jesus is establishing a fundamental rule—that the single most important credential for ministry is *love*. When the Church seeks to ordain a bishop, a priest, or any other form of servant, she must ask how true is the candidate's love. Peter responds, "Yes, Lord; You know that I love You." He claims to love Christ indeed, but makes no claim to have more love than his brethren. Peter has learned not to promote himself above others, and he leaves the exact proportion of his love up to Jesus' own knowledge.

Jesus says to him, "Feed my lambs." With this simple phrase, Jesus restores Peter to his apostleship. Saint Augustine points out that Jesus calls them "*My* lambs," indicating that an apostle or a minister has no sheep of his own, but is assigned a watch over the lambs that belong to God alone. If Peter denied Christ three times, Jesus asserts his restoration to the apostleship three times by a triple repetition of the question about love and a triple command to feed His sheep. When Jesus asks the question for the third and last time, Peter is exasperated and grieved, for his love is rightly called into question. All he can do is to remember the cold emptiness of his heart toward Jesus during the trials before the Sanhedrin and the bitter tears that fell from his eyes at the crowing of the rooster. So Peter answer in full surrender to Christ: "Lord, You know all things; You know that I love You" (v. 17). Jesus accepts Peter's confession, and He accepts Peter's love.

The Great Commission and the Ascension

"THEN THE ELEVEN DISCIPLES WENT away into Galilee, to the mountain which Jesus had appointed for them" (Matt. 28:16). The command to meet Him in Galilee was delivered by the women on the day of the Resurrection, so they hurry off to the appointed mountain for a final meeting with their Lord. The critical phases in Jesus' life occurred mostly on mountaintops. It was on a mountain that Jesus defeated Satan and his temptations; Jesus gave His first great sermon on a mountain; He was transfigured on a mountain; He fed the five thousand on a mountain; and it was to a mountain that He frequently resorted for rest and prayer. As the psalmist says, "His foundation *is* in the holy mountains" (Ps. 87:1).

The disciples may have denied and abandoned Him in time of danger, but He had already decided on a place to meet with them again. Even when the Church forgets her first love, Christ is still present and mindful to pull her back close to Him. In obeying the *command* of Christ to climb the mountain and wait, they receive the *vision* of Him. He chooses to meet with them not one by one, but collectively, that the grace bestowed on them that day would be a communal gift. This final meeting with Jesus and the sending out of the apostles was a turning point for the Church. Her three-and-a-half-year period of instruction has finally come to a close, and the period of mission begins.

"When they saw Him, they worshiped Him; but some doubted" (Matt. 28:17). It has been said that the vision and worship of Jesus can sometimes coexist with doubt. This is a natural result of the fact that the unseen things of the Spirit cannot be verified by visible means, and the heart is often slow to believe. This is what evoked the Lord's rebuke to the disciples of Emmaus: "O foolish ones, and slow of heart to believe in all that the prophets have spoken!" (Luke 24:25). But that wise scholar Bengel makes an important observation: "They doubted, so that we need not doubt."[56] The Gospels record their story with the utmost candor, which is why we can be sure that some of the disciples doubted; and their doubt emboldens our faith. For is there any form of certainty that does not begin with a doubt? Can someone verify or certify a particular truth without first allowing for the doubt that it is true? Did the doubting of the few prevent belief in the Resurrection and its preaching in the world? On the contrary, the exception proves the rule. If we consider the phenomenon of doubt objectively, without becoming defensive or disturbed, we will discover that certainty itself cannot be established without it. Let us remember the plea of the anguished father: "Lord, I believe; help my unbelief!" (Mark 9:24).

> And Jesus came and spoke to them, saying, "All authority has been given to Me in heaven and on earth. Go therefore and make disciples of all the nations, baptizing them in the name of the Father and of the Son and of the Holy Spirit, teaching them to observe all things that I have commanded you." (Matt. 28:18–20)

---

56   Bengel, John Albert, *Gnomon of the New Testament* (Edinburgh, 1866), 488.

Jesus delivers to them the Great Commission for all generations. The disciples are here called by a heavenly authority to change the world and to teach mankind to subject itself to the history of salvation. The apostles are given a sacred name in which new believers are to be baptized, under which new disciples are to be trained, and through which all are to be sanctified. The Church shall receive aid from above in order to properly conduct its administration below. She will be given power to enable her to carry out her work, as well as power to preserve her from danger. She will be a stranger in the earth, and yet "fellow citizens with the saints and members of the household of God" (Eph. 2:19).

"And lo, I am with you always, *even* to the end of the age" (Matt. 28:20). This is a promise and a covenant that is worthy of our remembrance every day of our lives. It is a covenant to which He has bound Himself—to watch over the disciples daily, as well as over the disciples' disciples—indeed, over every person who becomes a member in the body of Christ. He promises not to leave us even for a single day. When Jesus makes such a statement, it will surely come to pass; because it is made by Him to whom all previous ages are as yesterday when it is past, and all future ages are as the present moment. In effect, Jesus says this: "I have committed Myself to you forever. And I never change." He will be with us in the good times and in the bad; in days when the sun shines and in days when it is hidden by gray clouds; in times of health and in times of sickness; in days that bring good news and in days of grievous news. In any event, it is enough to know that He is with us!

After uttering His last saying on earth, Jesus lifts His hands over the disciples and bestows on them, as the Church, a final benediction. This is His last earthly ministration as our great High Priest; He would afterward oversee the Church from above. The Church has preserved this final benediction given by Christ and has handed it down to every generation. It is the blessing bestowed by the Church's pastors upon their congregations during liturgies, during morning and evening prayers, and during the sacraments.

The Lord is carried up into heaven while the disciples worship. Here we have the first mention in the Gospels that the disciples "worship" Christ—it is an acknowledgment of His divine lordship. They return to Jerusalem brimming with joy, and they mingle their happy voices with those of worshipers attending the daily prayers and canticles in the temple. This was the holy gladness of which Jesus had promised, "Your joy no one will take from you" (John 16:22).

We hope you have enjoyed and benefited from this book. Your financial support makes it possible to continue our non-profit ministry both in print and online. Because the proceeds from our book sales only partially cover the costs of operating **Ancient Faith Publishing** and **Ancient Faith Radio**, we greatly appreciate the generosity of our readers and listeners. Donations are tax deductible and can be made at **www. ancientfaith.com.**

To view our other publications,
please visit our website: **store.ancientfaith.com**

 **ANCIENT FAITH RADIO**

Bringing you Orthodox Christian music, readings, prayers, teaching, and podcasts 24 hours a day since 2004 at **www.ancientfaith.com**

www.ingramcontent.com/pod-product-compliance
Lightning Source LLC
Chambersburg PA
CBHW021708120626
46545CB00004B/1463